The Life of the Real
Brigadier Gerard
The Imperial
Aide-de-Camp

The Life of the Real
Brigadier Gerard
The Imperial
Aide-de-Camp

Volume 2:
A French Cavalryman of the Napoleonic Wars
at Saragossa, Landshut, Eckmühl, Ratisbon
Aspern-Essling, Wagram, Busaco & Torres Vedras

1807 - 1811

Jean-Baptiste de Marbot

*The Life of the Real Brigadier Gerard: The Imperial Aide-de-Camp
Volume 2:
A French Cavalryman of the Napoleonic Wars at Saragossa, Landshut,
Eckmühl, Ratisbon, Aspern-Essling, Wagram, Busaco & Torres Vedras
1807 - 1811*
by Jean-Baptiste de Marbot

Published by Leonaur Ltd

First Edition

Copyright © 2006 Leonaur Ltd

ISBN (10 digit): 1-84677-052-1 (hardcover)
ISBN (13 digit): 978-1-84677-052-4 (hardcover)

ISBN (10 digit): 1-84677-041-6 (softcover)
ISBN (13 digit): 978-1-84677-041-8 (softcover)

http://www.leonaur.com

Publisher's Notes

In the interests of authenticity, the spellings, grammar and place names used have been retained from the original editions.

The opinions of the authors represent a view of events in which he was a participant related from his own perspective, as such the text is relevant as an historical document.

The views expressed in this book are not necessarily those of the publisher.

Contents

1. The Emperor Turns Towards Iberia	9
2. I Join Murat's Staff	13
3. The Spanish Rise Up Against Us	21
4. Awarded the Legion d'Honneur	31
5. A Close Encounter with Death	41
6. The Pursuit of the English Army	52
7. The Siege of Saragossa	59
8. Landshut and Eckmühl	70
9. Ratisbon	81
10. I Become a Sailor	95
11. Major Marbot at Vienna	106
12. The Battle of Aspern-Essling	112
13. Aspern-Essling (2)	124
14. I Attend to My Wounds	132
15. The Island of Lobau	138
16. The Battle of Wagram	143
17. Wagram (2)	151
18. After the Battle	158
19. My Own Adventures at Wagram	165
20. I Announce the Armistice	173
21. The 'Sheperdess' and the Three Fleeces	184
22. To Spain Again	193
23. I 'Slay a Lion' in a Fever	206
24. Events in the Peninsula	214
25. The Second Invasion of Portugal	221
26. The Road to Busaco	226
27. The Battle of Busaco	235
28. The Lines at Torres Vedras	242
29. Steeplechasers & Deserters	249
30. My Cavalry Duel With the English	257
31. Fuentes d'Onoro	270
32. The Last of Spain	283

Chapter 1
The Emperor Turns Towards Iberia

It has been said with truth, that in 1807 the Emperor was at the height of his power. He had beaten the Austrians, the Prussians, and the Russians, and concluded a peace glorious for France and for himself. But hardly had Napoleon finished the war with the Northern Powers, when his evil genius led him to undertake one far more terrible in the extreme south of Europe.

The country of Portugal, being rich in natural products, and possessing no manufactories, had become a vast field for the commerce and industry of the English. They treated it almost like a colony, and profited by the wealth of the country without having the trouble of governing it. De facto if not de jure the country belonged to them. Napoleon had long awaited an opportunity for driving them out and ruining their commerce. After the Peace of Tilsit he thought the time was come. To complete the continental blockade he ordered Portugal to close her ports to the English. The execution of this measure was difficult, for the Portuguese nation only lived by changing its raw materials against English manufactured goods. You will see in the sequel of these Memoirs that I am far from approving Napoleon's policy throughout, but I am bound to say that from the political point of view this measure was excusable as putting a constraint on England to make her accept the general peace.

The Emperor then collected at Bayonne in September, 1807, an army of 25,000 men destined for the invasion of Portugal. But he committed two serious mistakes. The first was forming the expeditionary force of recently organised regiments; the second, giving the command of it to General Junot.

More than once Napoleon made an error in his choice of persons, because he followed his personal likings rather than the general opinion. In Junot the army saw a very brave man, but not a genuine commander. The first time that I saw him I was struck and disturbed by his haggard eyes. His end justified my apprehensions. The foundation of his fortune is well known. As a mere quartermaster sergeant in the Côte d'Or battalion he earned the regard of Captain Buonaparte of the artillery by a bon-mot in the trenches before Toulon. He followed him to Egypt, commanded in Paris, and became ambassador at Lisbon. His gaiety, his frank soldierly manner, his reputation for valour, his open-handedness, earned for him the friendship of great people and the affection of common people. His popularity in Portugal no doubt decided the Emperor to select him for the command of the Army of Occupation. It would, in fact, have been an advantage if Junot had shown more foresight as a general.

Spain was then in alliance with us, and was bound to supply our troops with food and lodging as they marched through. It was the commander-in-chief's duty to make sure that this promise was executed; but Junot merely entered Spain on October 17, and sent forward his columns along the roads where no preparations had been made to receive them. Our troops slept in the open air and got only half rations of food. Autumn was drawing to an end, the army was traversing the spurs of the Pyrenees, where the climate is severe, and very soon the road was covered with sick men and stragglers. The Spaniards, flocking from all sides to behold the conquerors of Marengo, Austerlitz, and Friedland, saw only wretched recruits hardly able to carry their knapsacks and their arms, and looking when assembled more like a hospital delivery than like an army marching to conquer a kingdom. This sorry spectacle gave the Spaniards a very poor impression of our troops, and produced disastrous results in the following year.

Napoleon underrated the nations of the Peninsula, and thought that he need only show French troops to obtain what he would from them, making therein a great mistake. It must also be said that not having been apprised of the difficulties in the way of their march, the Emperor kept repeating his order to advance promptly. Junot carried out the instructions badly, and his army of boy soldiers soon found itself scattered in little detachments over more than 200 leagues of road between Bayonne and Salamanca. Luckily, the Spaniards were not yet at war with France—nevertheless, to keep their hand in, they assassinated some fifty of our men.

On reaching Ciudad Rodrigo, Junot caused his leading columns to halt for several days; he had left behind more than 15,000 men. As soon as a third of them had rejoined he crossed the mountains of Penha Parda, which separated him from the valley of the Tagus, taking with him only a half ration of bread per man. These mountains, which I have crossed, are uncultivated and inhabited by a poor and barbarous population. The troops passed them with all manner of difficulties and at the cost of extreme fatigue, which compelled them to seize some flocks belonging to the inhabitants, who revenged themselves by assassinating some hundred French travellers. The army at length reached the town of Alcantara, and entered Portugal by the town of Castello Branco. It was only with much effort and after suffering every kind of hardship that they reached Abrantes with five or six thousand men, tired out and mostly barefooted. At Abrantes begins the beautiful part of the Tagus valley. The stragglers and the sick who were still among the mountains, hearing of the comfort which awaited them at Abrantes, made haste to come up, and the army gradually came together.

A general of any foresight would have given it full time to re-assemble, but Junot, under the pretext that the Emperor had ordered him to seize all goods belonging to the English, and that he must reach Lisbon quickly to prevent them from carrying them off, got together 4,000 of the least-fatigued men, and with this feeble column marched upon the capital, leaving to his generals the task of getting the rest of his army together and coming to join him. This daring attempt might have caused the loss of his army, for Lisbon contained a garrison of 12,000 to 15,000 men, and an English fleet was stationed at the mouth of the Tagus. Less than this would have been enough to repulse Junot and his 4,000 men; but so great was the magical effect produced by Napoleon's victories, that the Portuguese Government, acceding to all the Emperor's demands, hastened to declare war against England in the hope of staying Junot's march, but the advanced guard of the French general proceeded onwards and threw the capital into utter confusion. The Regent, not knowing at first what steps to take, ended by deciding to transfer the seat of government to Brazil. The insane Queen, the Regent, the Royal Family, the nobles, nine or ten thousand persons in all, embarking on board a great fleet, and taking immense treasure with them, sailed for Brazil on November 28.

On the same day Junot attacked Santarem, but his small column having had to cross the plain of Golegan through two feet of water, so large a number of the troops were seized with fever that on the morrow not more than 1,500 men were fit to go on. Junot continued his march none the less with this weak force, and boldly made his entry into Lisbon. I must do Junot the justice to admit that, when he had once got his troops together, he provided sedulously for their needs, so that in the course of December he had an effective army of 23,000 men in fairly good condition. Finding the Portuguese troops an embarrassment, Junot gave leave to the native soldiers who wished to remain at home, and formed the others into a division, which he sent to France. It did good service, and went on the Russian campaign.

Chapter 2
I Join Murat's Staff

All this time I was living quietly with my mother at Paris where I passed part of the winter, and took part in the numerous entertainments which were given, the finest being the reception given by the city to the imperial guard on their return. Thus ended the year 1807, in which I had incurred so many dangers and led so chequered a life. I little thought that in the course of the year which was now beginning I should again be face to face with death.

In the course of January, Napoleon at length replied to the King of Spain, but in an evasive fashion, for, without positively refusing to give the hand of one of his nieces to the Prince of the Asturias, he put off the date of the marriage indefinitely. The alarm of the court of Madrid at the receipt of this answer was increased by hearing that more French troops were on the march towards Catalonia and Aragon, which, with the army in Portugal, would raise the Emperor's forces in the Peninsula to 125,000 men. Finally, Napoleon in great part lifted the veil under which his plans had been hidden. Under the pretext of sending troops on board the French fleet stationed at Cadiz, he caused a powerful army corps to advance in February towards Madrid, through which the road from Bayonne to Cadiz passes, and named Prince Murat generalissimo of all the French forces in Spain.

I had now been in Paris more than six months, and although Marshal Augereau, to whom I was still aide-de-camp, was far from anticipating the war which was about to break out in the Peninsula, he thought it neither right nor conducive to my advance in my profession that I should stay at Paris when a large army was assembled beyond the Pyrenees. Being himself still kept in France by the effects of his wound, he took me to Prince Murat to ask him to attach me provisionally to his staff. I have already said that my father, who belonged to the same part of the country as Murat, had done him many kindnesses. Murat, who had always shown himself grateful, consented very readily to take me until such time as Augereau should have a command. I was well satisfied with this decision, although the position of supernumerary officer has its inconveniences, but I was anxious to show zeal, I reckoned on the Emperor's goodwill and, further, I was glad to go back to Spain and witness the great events which were in progress there. Considerable expense was necessary to make a fitting appearance on the staff of Murat, which at that time was the most brilliant in the army, but this was made easy to me by what was left of my splendid travelling allowances during and after the Friedland campaign. So I bought three good horses, with which my servant, Woirland, was to await me at Bayonne, whither I went when I had got my new uniforms.

This was the third time that a change of employment had taken me to Bayonne. Prince Murat and his staff received me most kindly, and I was soon on the best of terms with them all, though I steadily refused, in spite of continual pressure, to take part in their play. These gentlemen had cards or dice in their hands all day, winning or losing thousands of francs with most perfect calm; but besides that I have always detested play, I knew that I must keep what I had in order to renew my outfit in case of accidents, and that it was dishonourable to risk what I perhaps could not pay.

Part of the troops which Murat was to command were, perhaps, already in Castile. He entered Spain on March 10, and in five days we were at Burgos. From this time Murat regulated his march on that of the columns, and passed in succession to Valladolid in Segovia. The Spaniards, always flattering themselves that the French had come to protect the Prince of the Asturias, received our troops very well, though again astonished by their extreme youth and want of robustness, or under some incomprehensible delusion, Napoleon had persisted in sending into the Peninsula none but newly-raised regiments.

We occupied in Spain none but open towns, and two fortified places only, Barcelona and Pampeluna. But as their citadels and forts were still in the hands of the Spanish troops, the Emperor ordered his generals to try to get possession of them. To this end a thoroughly base trick was employed. The Spanish Government, while forbidding its generals to let us occupy the citadels and the forts, had ordered that the French troops should be received as friends, and everything done for their comfort. The commanders of our regiments asked permission to place their sick and their stores in the citadels, which was granted. Then they disguised their grenadiers as sick, and hid arms in the provision sacks of several companies, who, under pretext of going to the store houses for bread, made their way into the place and disarmed the Spaniards. In this way, General Duhesme, with only 5,000 men, got possession of the citadel of Barcelona and of Fort Monjuich. The citadel of Pampeluna and nearly all those in Catalonia shared the same fate.

On the 23rd Murat entered Madrid at the head of Marshal Moncey's corps. The new king had called upon the people to give a good reception to his friend Napoleon's troops. He was punctually obeyed; we saw nothing but friendly faces among the vast and curious crowd. But it was easy to perceive how astonished they were at the sight of our young infantry soldiers. The moral effect was wholly to our disadvantage, and as I compared the broad chests and powerful limbs of the Spaniards who surrounded us with those of our weak and weedy privates, my national pride was humbled. Though I did not foresee the disasters which would arise from the poor opinion of our troops on the part of the Spaniards, I was sorry that the Emperor had not sent into the Peninsula some veteran regiments from the Army of Germany. Still our cavalry, and especially our cuirassiers, an arm unfamiliar to the modern Spaniards, excited their admiration, and the same with the artillery. But a shout of enthusiasm went up when the imperial guard appeared. The sight of the Mamelukes astonished the Spaniards, who could not conceive how the Christian French should have admitted Turks into their ranks. Ever since the Moorish domination, the peoples of the Peninsula have loathed the Mussulmans, though much afraid of having to fight against them. Four Mamelukes would put twenty Castilians to flight, as was proved before very long.

Murat established himself in a palace belonging to the Prince of the Peace, the only one which the mob had spared, under the impression that it still belonged to the Crown. I was lodged hard by with a much respected member of the Council of the Indies. Hardly had I alighted when Prince Murat, hearing that Godoy's enemies were sending him to prison at Madrid, no doubt to have him murdered there, and that the poor wretch was already at the gate of the town, ordered me to set out with a squadron of dragoons, and prevent at any cost the entry of the Prince of the Peace into the capital, letting the officers of his escort know that he, Murat, would hold them responsible for their prisoner's life. Two leagues from the suburbs I came upon Godoy. Although the unhappy man was terribly wounded and covered with blood, the guards who escorted him had been cruel enough to put irons on his hands and feet, and to tie him on a rough, open cart where he was exposed to the scorching rays of the sun, and to thousands of flies attracted by his wounds, which were scarcely covered with coarse linen rags. I was indignant at the sight, and glad to see that it produced the same effect on the French squadron which accompanied me.

The guards escorting the Prince of the Peace, about one hundred in number, were supported by half a battalion of infantry. I explained my object politely to the commanding officer, but he replied with extreme arrogance that he did not take his orders from the commander of the French arms. Adopting the same tone, I said that my business being to execute those orders, I should use every means to prevent the prisoner from being taken any farther. My dragoons were not recruits, but stalwart veterans of Austerlitz; determination could be read in their faces. I placed them in line so as to bar the passage of the cart, and told the officer of the guard that I waited for him to fire the first shot, but that I should then at once charge with my squadron upon him and his men. The officers of my dragoons had already given the order to draw swords, and the ardour of our adversaries appeared to be cooling a little when the commander of the half battalion in the rear came to the head of the column to see what the disturbance was about, and I recognised in him Don Miguel Rafael Cœli, the jolly officer with whom I had travelled from Nantes to Salamanca in 1802. Being a sensible man he understood Murat's reasons for objecting to the Prince of the Peace being brought into Madrid. If he were murdered, as was pretty certain, the French army would incur obloquy for not preventing it, while if it interfered it would provoke a bloody collision. As second in command Don Rafael had the right to give his opinion. He spoke to the officer commanding in the same sense that I had done, and it was agreed that Godoy should be detained for the time in the village of Pinto. The poor wretch had been a silent witness of what took place, and on reaching his prison he expressed his thanks to me in very good French, begging me to convey his gratitude to Prince Murat.

I took the liberty of pointing out to the guards the cruelty and disgrace to the Spanish uniform in putting irons on a prisoner who was guarded by 4,000 men. Don Rafael supported me, and we succeeded in getting the prince set free from his iron collar, handcuffs, and fetters. He was only held by a chain attached to his body, so that, though not free in prison, he could move a little and lie down on a mattress which I made them give him. His wounds, received five days ago, had not yet been dressed; the surgeon of our dragoons attended him, and the officers and even the troopers lent him linen.

Though I could reckon on the honesty of the infantry commander, I had little confidence with regard to the treatment which the Prince of the Peace would receive when I had left him in the hands of his cruel enemies, the guard. I took it on myself, therefore, to quarter the French squadron in the village, and arrange with the captain that a sentry should always be placed inside the prison to keep an eye on the one posted there by the guards. Murat approved what I had done, and for further security sent a battalion to take up its quarters at Pinto with orders to keep a sharp look out on the guards. Finally, Ferdinand VII., passing through the place next day on his way to Madrid, received from the officer of the guards a report of what had happened. Dreading above all things any complications with the French, the new king and his ministers commended him for having avoided a conflict with the dragoons, and ordered Godoy to be left in the prison at Pinto. Some days later they had him moved to the old fortress of Villa Viciosa, at a greater distance from the capital.

On March 24 Ferdinand made his royal entry into Madrid, being received by the people with indescribable joy. An immense crowd greeted him with cheers, women threw flowers in his path, and men spread their cloaks under his horses' feet. Our troops did not appear officially. Murat did not even visit Ferdinand, not knowing, until the Emperor had decided, whether the father or the son was to be recognised as sovereign of the Spains. If Napoleon intended to seize the crown, he would probably prefer to see it restored for the moment to the feeble Charles, rather than have the more difficult task of taking it from the nation's favourite, Ferdinand. Murat, therefore, felt pretty sure that the Emperor would refuse to recognise the new king.

Ferdinand, meanwhile, uneasy as to the view which Napoleon might take of his accession, consulted M. de Beauharnais; who, too upright a man himself to think it possible that Napoleon could take any steps against the liberty of a prince coming to seek him in the character of arbiter, advised Ferdinand to meet the Emperor at Bayonne. The King's friends doubted; but General Savary unexpectedly appeared with a letter from Napoleon, which determined him to the the course suggested. Moreover, he learnt that his father and mother were on their way to lay their version of the case before the Emperor, and it seemed well to anticipate them. The advice given by M. de Beauharnais had in fact been prompted by Murat and Savary. The Emperor had started for Bayonne on April 2, travelling slowly, in order to leave time for events to mature. Ferdinand sent his brother Charles on in advance, and himself left Madrid on April 10, on the faith of Savary's assurances that Napoleon was already at Bayonne. Accompanied by that general, he reached Burgos where he did not, as he had been led to expect, find Napoleon; but did find the roads covered with French columns on the march. His suspicions that some trap was being prepared for him were calmed by Savary's assurances that Napoleon was at Vittoria. On arriving at that town, Ferdinand learnt with some surprise that, so far from having crossed the frontier, the Emperor had not yet arrived at Bayonne. This was more than his Spanish pride could endure; his counsellors pointed out that he had gone as far to meet a foreign sovereign as was consistent with his dignity, and in spite of all that Savary could say, he decided to go no farther. Furious at seeing his prey on the point of escaping him, the general posted off to Bayonne, and found that the Emperor had arrived on the 14th.

By the next day Ferdinand was practically a prisoner. Marshal Bessières had been secretly ordered to arrest him if he attempted to return, and Savary was coming to see that the order was executed. But no step of this kind was necessary, for Ferdinand, hearing that his parents, at the instance of his sister the ex-Queen of Etruria, were already on their way from Madrid to Bayonne, in fear of letting them get the ear of the Emperor before him, insisted on setting out at once, undeterred by the protests of the people and the forebodings of older advisers. On April 20 he crossed the Bidassoa. Not an infantry picket was there to present arms to him, nor a trooper to escort him. When at length some officers of the Emperor's household met him they accosted him as Prince of the Asturias. It was too late to go back; Ferdinand was in France and in Napoleon's power.

The Emperor, who was occupying the château of Marac, where I had been lodged in 1803 with Augereau, called upon Ferdinand, treated him politely, and invited him to dinner, but never gave him the title of king. On the next day he threw off the mask and announced to Ferdinand and his ministers that having been charged by Providence to create a great empire and lower the power of England, and having learnt by experience that he could not count on the assistance of Spain so long as the Bourbon family governed it, he had determined to restore the crown neither to Ferdinand nor to Charles, but to place it on the head of a member of his own family. Ferdinand and his advisers, overwhelmed by this statement, refused at first to accept it, answering with some reason that in any case no member of the French imperial family had any right to the crown of Spain.

Meanwhile the old King and Queen were approaching Bayonne, which they reached of April 20. Napoleon received them with royal honours, and brought them to dine with him at the château of Marac. There they found their beloved Manuel Godoy, whom they had not seen since the outbreak of Aranjuez. Before leaving Madrid, however, they had had an interview with Murat, and implored his intervention on behalf of the Prince of the Peace. The Emperor also had instructed him that Godoy's life was to be saved at all costs. To Murat's overtures, the provisional Junta, under the presidency of Prince Anthony, Ferdinand's uncle, replied that they had not the power to release so important a prisoner. Murat thereupon surrounded the castle of Villa Viciosa with a French brigade, ordering the general to bring away the Prince of the Peace amicably or otherwise. His guards, with the assent of the commandant, the Marquis of Chasteler, a Belgian in the Spanish service, having declared that they would stab him rather than give him up alive, Murat let them know that if they carried their purpose into effect they should be shot without mercy over his corpse. Thereupon the Junta ordered his release. The poor wretch arrived in our camp in a pitiable state; Murat received him kindly, provided for his wants, and sent him off at once with an escort of cavalry to Bayonne. Happening to recognize me as one of those who had saved him at Pinto, he expressed his desire that I should be of his escort. I should have liked it very well, but as I have already said the supernumerary aides-de-camp only get the disagreeable duties. This task was therefore entrusted to one of the regular staff, while I before long had one of extreme danger.

During the interview between Godoy and the elder sovereigns, Ferdinand came to pay his respects to his father. Charles received him with contumely, and had he not been in the Emperor's palace, would have driven him from his presence. On the following day, yielding to the persuasions of the Queen and the Prince of the Peace, who argued that as he would no longer be able to reign over Spain he would do better to accept the position which the Emperor offered him in France, and thus secure at once repose for his declining years and vengeance upon Ferdinand, Charles offered no more resistance to Napoleon's plans.

While great events were maturing at Bayonne, Prince Murat, who had provisionally the control of the Government at Madrid, had caused Charles' protest to be published, and Ferdinand's name to be suppressed on all public documents, much to the discontent of the people and the grandees. When the news from Bayonne arrived, brought by secret emissaries in the disguise of peasants, whom Ferdinand's friends had sent, their agitation increased. The storm was grumbling around us, nor was it long before it broke out at Madrid.

Chapter 3
The Spanish Rise Up Against Us

Charles IV, the Queen, Ferdinand, and his brother, Prince Charles, being all at Bayonne, the only members of the Royal Family remaining in Spain were the ex-Queen of Etruria and her son, the old Prince Anthony, and Charles IV.'s youngest son, Prince Francis, who was then only twelve or thirteen years old. Murat, having received orders to send these members of the house of Bourbon to Bayonne, the Queen of Etruria and Prince Anthony expressed themselves willing to leave Spain, but the young Prince Francis was still a ward of the Junta, and that body, in alarm at seeing all the princes of the royal family carried off one by one, definitely opposed the child's departure. Then public excitement became very great, and in the course of May 1 numerous groups assembled in the principal streets of Madrid, and especially in the large square known as the Puerta del Sol. These were dispersed by some of our cavalry, but on the following day, just as the princes were getting into their carriage, some servants came out of the palace exclaiming that Don Francis was crying bitterly and clinging to the furniture, declaring that he had been born in Spain and would not leave it. It is easy to understand the effect which such generous sentiments, expressed by a child of the royal house, who, in the absence of his two brothers, was the hope of the nation, would produce upon the mind of a proud and free people. In an instant the mob armed itself, and massacred every Frenchman who was caught by himself in the town. Most of our troops being camped outside, it was necessary to warn them, and this it was not easy to do.

On hearing the first shots I wished to go to my post near the marshal, whose hotel was close to my lodging. I leapt on my horse, and was going out, when my host, the venerable member of the Indian Council, stopped me, pointing out that the street was occupied by some thirty armed insurgents, whom it was clear that I could not escape. I remarked to the excellent man that my honour required me to brave all dangers in order to get to my general. He advised me to go out on foot, and leading me to the end of the garden, opened a little gate, and very kindly himself led me by back lanes to the rear of Prince Murat's house, where I found a French sentry. This much respected gentleman, to whom in all probability I owed my life, was, as I shall never forget, called Don Antonio Hernandez.

At head-quarters I found great excitement, for although Murat had with him only two battalions and some squadrons, he was preparing to march resolutely to face the tumult. Everybody but myself was on horseback; I was in despair. Presently, however, General Belliard, chief of the staff, having given orders that some pickets of grenadiers should be sent to drive back the enemy's sharpshooters, who already were occupying the approaches to the palace, I offered to guide one of them through the street in which the house of Don Hernandez stood, and as soon as the gate was cleared I got my horse and joined Prince Murat.

No military duty is more dangerous than that of a staff officer in a country, still more in a city, which is in a state of insurrection. Having to go almost always alone through the midst of the enemy when carrying orders to the troops, he is exposed to the risk of assassination without the power of defending himself. Hardly was Murat out of his palace when he sent off officers to all the officers round Madrid with orders to bring the troops in by all the gates at once. The cavalry of the imperial guard and a division of dragoons were quartered at Buen Retiro. This was one of the nearest camps to head-quarters, but one of the most dangerous to reach, since in order to get there it was necessary to go through the two largest streets of the town, those of Alcalà and San Gronimo, where nearly every window was lined with Spanish sharpshooters. I need not say that, as this was the most difficult mission, the commander-in-chief did not assign it to one of his regular aides-de-camp. It was on me that it devolved, and I started at a smart trot over a pavement which the sun had made very slippery.

I had hardly gone two hundred yards from the staff when I was received by numerous musket-shots, but as the tumult was but just beginning, the fire was endurable, all the more so since the men at the windows were shopkeepers and workmen, without much practice in handling muskets. Still, the horse of one of my dragoons was knocked over by a bullet, and the people came out of the houses to slaughter the poor soldier; but his comrades and I laid about us with our sabres, and when we had stretched a dozen of the rioters on the ground the rest took to their heels. Then the dragoon, taking the hand of one of his comrades, was able to run with us till we reached the outposts of our cavalry camp.

While defending the dismounted dragoon, I had received a blow from a dagger in my jacket sleeve, and two of my troopers had been slightly wounded. My orders were to bring the divisions to the Puerta del Sol, and they started at a gallop. The squadrons of the guard, commanded by the celebrated Daumesmil, marched first, with the Mamelukes leading. The riot had had time to increase; we were fired upon from nearly all the houses, especially the palace of the Duke of Hijar, where every window was lined with good shots. We lost there several men, among others the terrible Mustapha, that Mameluke who went near to catching the Grand Duke Constantine at Austerlitz. His comrades swore to avenge him, but for the moment it was impossible to halt, and the cavalry rode on rapidly under a hail of bullets. In the Puerta del Sol we found Murat engaged with a huge compact crowd of armed men, among whom could be seen some thousands of Spanish soldiers, who had brought guns and were firing on the French with grape. On seeing the dreaded Mamelukes arrive, the Spaniards made some attempt at resistance but the sight of the Turks alarmed the bravest of them too much for their resolution to last long. The Mamelukes, dashing scimitar in hand into the dense mass, sent a hundred heads flying in a trice, and opened a way for the chasseurs and dragoons, who set to furiously with their sabres. The Spaniards, rolled back from the square, tried to escape by the many wide streets which meet there from all parts of the town, but they were stopped by other French columns whom Murat had bidden to rendezvous at that point. There were also partial combats in other quarters, but this was the most important, and decided the victory in our favour. The insurgents had 1,200 or 1,500 men killed and many wounded, and their loss would have been much greater if Murat had not given the order to cease firing.

As a soldier I was bound to fight any who attacked the French army, but I could not help recognising in my inmost conscience that our cause was a bad one, and that the Spaniards were quite right in trying to drive out strangers, who after coming among them in the guise of friends, were wishing to dethrone their sovereign and take forcible possession of the kingdom. This war, therefore, seemed to me wicked, but I was a soldier, and I must march or be charged with cowardice. The greater part of the army thought as I did, and like me, obeyed orders all the same.

Hostilities had now ceased almost everywhere; the town was occupied by our infantry, and the cavalry received orders to return to camp. The insurgents who had fired so briskly from the Duke of Hijar's palace on the imperial guard when they first came by, had had the imprudent boldness to remain at their post, and recommence their fire as our squadrons returned. These, however, indignant at the sight of their comrades' bodies, which the inhabitants had barbarously cut to pieces, dismounted a number of troopers, who, climbing into the windows of the ground floor, penetrated into the palace, and hastened to take terrible revenge. The Mamelukes, who had suffered the heaviest loss, entered the rooms, scimitar and blunderbus in hand, and pitilessly massacred every insurgent that they met, the greater part being the Duke's servants. Not one escaped, and their corpses, thrown over the balconies, mingled their blood with that of the Mamelukes whom they had slaughtered in the morning.

Thus the fight was ended and victory assured. Murat had now to attend to two important matters: to report to the Emperor what had happened at Madrid, and to secure the departure of the Queen of Etruria, the old Prince Anthony, and above all the young Don Francis. The child, frightened by the sound of the firing, now agreed to go with his sister and his uncle, but this party could only travel by short stages, while it was important that Murat's despatches should reach the Emperor by the first possible moment. You will guess what happened. So long as Spain had been tranquil, the Prince had entrusted his frequent reports to members of his regular staff; but now that it was a question of crossing a great part of the kingdom in the midst of a population who, at the news of the fighting at Madrid would be ready to murder French officers, it became a job for a supernumerary aide-de-camp. As I quite expected, although according to the roster for duty it was not my turn to go, this dangerous mission was entrusted to me, and I accepted it without remark.

Murat, who quite misjudged the Castilian character, imagined that they would be frightened by the suppression of the revolt at Madrid, and would make a complete submission without venturing to take up arms. As he flattered himself that Napoleon destined him for the throne of Charles IV. he was beaming, and, as he handed me the despatches, said more than once: 'You may repeat to the Emperor what I say in this letter; my victory over the insurgents in the capital assures us the peaceable possession of Spain.' I did not believe a word of it, but was careful not to say so, and merely asked permission to take advantage as far as Buitrago of the escort which was going with the Spanish princes. I knew that many peasants from the neighbourhood who had taken part in the outbreak were now hiding in the country villages, and would be quite ready to attack me if I left the town. Murat recognised the justice of my remark. I hired a horse, and travelling with the escort reached Buitrago that evening. The princes were to sleep there, so from that point there was no more escort for me, and I had to launch out into the unknown.

Our dragoon officers, seeing me make ready to start at nightfall to cross the Guadarrama Mountains, advised me to wait for daylight. But in the first place I knew that the despatches were urgent, and I did not wish the Emperor and Murat to accuse me of having slackened my pace through fear, and further I knew that the quicker I got away from the neighbourhood of the capital, and outstripped the news of the fighting, the less I should have to fear the exasperation of the people on my road. I found, in fact, that the inhabitants of Buitrago had received their first news of what had happened that morning at Madrid from the muleteers who conducted the princes' carriages, but as the postilion whom I took from Buitrago had probably heard the news from the one who had brought me there, I resolved to get rid of him by a trick. After we had gone about two leagues, I told the man that I had left in the stable of the post a handkerchief containing 20 douros, and that while I considered the money as practically lost, I thought it was still just possible that no one had found it, and that he must therefore go back at once to Buitrago, and that if he brought me the handkerchief and its contents at the next stage, where I would wait for him he should have five douros for himself. Delighted with the prospect of this windfall, the postilion turned back at once, and I went on to the next stage. Nothing had been heard there of the fighting; I was in uniform: but to remove any suspicion which the postmaster and his people might have at seeing me arrive alone, I told them that the horse of the postilion who had been with me having fallen and hurt himself, I had advised the man to walk him back to Buitrago. They gave me at once a fresh horse and another postilion, and I galloped off without any qualms about disappointing the Buitrago postilion. The important thing was, that I was now in sole possession of my secret, and I knew that if I stopped nowhere, I could reach Bayonne before rumour had brought the intelligence of the events at Madrid.

All night I travelled through the mountains—the road is good, and at daybreak I entered L'Herma. Here there was a French garrison, as indeed there was in every town which I had to pass on the way to Bayonne. Everywhere the generals and officers offered me refreshment, asking what news there was; but I kept my mouth shut, fearing lest an accident should compel me to halt somewhere, and so be outstripped by news which I had myself spread, whereby I should be exposed to an attack from the peasants.

From Madrid to Bayonne is the same distance as from Bayonne to Paris; that is to say 225 leagues, a long journey when one has to ride post with one's sword by one's side without a single quarter of an hour's rest, and in a scorching heat. I was tired out and overcome with the need of sleep, but I did not yield to it for a moment, knowing well the necessity for getting on quickly. To keep awake I paid the postillions something extra on condition that as we galloped they should sing to me their Spanish songs. At last I saw the Bidassoa, and entered France.

Maraac is only two stages from Saint-Jean de Luz. I got there on May 5, covered with dust, at the moment when the Emperor was taking an after-dinner walk in the park with the Queen of Spain on his arm and Charles IV. beside him. The Empress Josephine and the Princes Ferdinand and Charles followed them, and the rear was brought up by Marshal Duroc and several ladies. As soon as the Emperor was informed by the aide-de-camp on duty that an officer had arrived with despatches from Prince Murat, he came towards me, followed by the members of the Spanish royal family, and asked aloud: 'What news from Madrid?' The presence of the listeners was embarrassing, and as I thought that Napoleon would no doubt be glad to have the first fruits of my intelligence, I deemed it wise to do nothing but present my despatches to the Emperor and look steadily at him without answering his question. His Majesty understood me, and retired a few paces to read Murat's report. Having finished, he called me and went towards a solitary garden-walk, asking me all the time many questions about the fighting at Madrid. I could easily see that he shared Murat's opinion and considered that the victory of May 2 must put an end to all resistance in Spain. I held the contrary belief, and if Napoleon had asked my view I should have thought it dishonourable to conceal it; but I had to confine myself to answering the Emperor's questions with due respect, and I could only indirectly let him know my presentiments. In narrating the revolution at Madrid I depicted in most vivid terms the despair of the people at hearing that the remaining members of the royal family were to be carried away, the fierce courage which the inhabitants, even the women, had shown during the fighting, the gloomy and threatening demeanour retained by the populace after our victory. I might perhaps have revealed all my thoughts, but Napoleon cut short my thoughts, exclaiming: 'Bah! they will calm down and will bless me as soon as they see their country freed from the discredit and disorder into which it has been thrown by the weakest and most corrupt administration that ever existed.' After this outburst, uttered in a sharp tone, Napoleon sent me back to the end of the garden to request the King and Queen of Spain to come to him, and followed me slowly reading over Murat's despatches. The ex-sovereigns came forward alone to meet the Emperor, and I suppose he informed them of the fighting at Madrid, for Charles came up quickly to his son Ferdinand, and said to him in a loud voice and in a tone of extreme anger: 'Wretch! you may now be satisfied! Madrid has been bathed in the blood of my subjects shed in consequence of your criminal rebellion against your father; may their blood be on your head!' The Queen joined in heaping bitter reproaches on her son, and went so far as to offer to strike him. The ladies and the officers, feeling that this distasteful spectacle was not one for them, withdrew, and Napoleon put a stop to it.

Ferdinand, who had not replied by a single word to the objurgations of his parents, resigned the crown to his father that evening, less through contrition than through fear of being regarded as the author of the conspiracy which had overthrown Charles. Next day the old King, in his ignoble desire for revenge, encouraged by the Queen and the Prince of the Peace, made over to the Emperor all his rights to the throne of Spain on certain conditions, the principal one being that by which he was to have the estate of Compiègne with a pension of seven and a half million francs. Ferdinand was cowardly enough also to renounce his hereditary rights in favour of Napoleon, in return for a pension of a million and the château of Navarre in Normandy. As both these houses required repair, Charles, with his Queen, his daughter, and the Prince of the Peace, went for the present to Fontainebleau, while Ferdinand, his two brothers, and his uncle were sent to Valencay, in Berri, where they were well treated but kept under strict surveillance. Thus was consummated the most iniquitous spoliation which modern history records. In all times a conqueror in a fair and open war has been held to have the right to take possession of the dominions of the conquered, but I can say with sincerity that the conduct of Napoleon in this scandalous affair was unworthy of so great a man. To offer himself as mediator between a father and a son in order to draw them into a trap and then plunder them both—this was an odious atrocity which history has branded, and which Providence did not delay to punish. It was the war in Spain which brought about Napoleon's fall.

Still, to do him justice, with all his lack of political honesty, the Emperor was under no delusion as to the reprehensible nature of his action. I have heard, on the authority of one of his ministers, M. Defermon, that he admitted this at the council board, but he added that in politics one must never forget the great axiom 'Success and necessity justify the means.' Now, rightly or wrongly, the Emperor was firmly convinced that the only way of keeping the north in check was to found in the south of Europe a great empire under the protection of France, which could only be done by taking possession of Spain.

Having now this fine kingdom to dispose of, Napoleon offered it to his eldest brother, Joseph, then King of Naples. He has been blamed for not giving it to his brother-in-law Murat, who, as an experienced soldier, seemed better suited to govern a proud nation than the timid, careless, and luxurious Joseph. Doubtless when Murat first entered Spain everything about him, even to his extraordinary costume, delighted the Castilians, and if they had had then to accept a king from Napoleon's family they would have preferred the chivalrous Murat to the feeble Joseph; but since the fighting at Madrid their admiration for him had been changed to bitter hatred. I have no doubt that the Emperor had originally destined Murat for the Spanish throne, but as soon as he realised the dislike of the nation towards him he gave up the plan as impossible, and sent him to replace Joseph at Naples when he gave the Spanish crown to the latter. It was unfortunate, for in the war which presently broke out Murat would have been most useful, while King Joseph was only a hindrance.

In order to give some colour of legality to his brother's accession, Napoleon called upon all the provinces to select deputies who should come to Bayonne to frame a constitution. Many abstained, but the greater number answered the summons, some through curiosity, others in the patriotic hope that one of their kings would be restored to them. When assembled, they soon perceived that they would have no freedom of deliberation; nevertheless, whether convinced that a brother of the mighty Emperor could alone restore happiness to Spain, or urged by the desire of escaping from the trap in which they found themselves, they all recognised Joseph's sovereignty. Very few, however, remained with him, the greater part returning hurriedly to Spain, where, as soon as they arrived, they protested against the vote, which had been extorted from them.

I had left Bayonne on May 11 to return to Madrid with despatches from the Emperor to Murat. Throughout the provinces which I traversed I found people's minds much disturbed. It was known that Ferdinand, the darling of the people had been forced to abdicate, and they perceived that Napoleon was about to grasp the throne of Spain. An organised insurrection was growing up on either side. I should certainly have been assassinated had not our troops been in occupation of all the towns and villages between France and Madrid. Though I had an escort from one post to another, I was more than once attacked. A trooper was killed by my side in the defile of Pancorvo, and I came across the dead bodies of two of our soldiers in the mountains of Somo Sierra. It was the first taste of what the Spaniards were preparing for us. The despatches which I carried to Murat contained the official announcement of his elevation to the throne of Naples. For several days he was very gloomy, and at last fell so seriously ill that Napoleon had to send General Savary to take the command of the army—a task to which his military talents were unequal, especially in the difficult circumstances which were about to occur. Murat's illness for a time endangered his life. As soon as he was better he made haste to leave Spain. Before his departure he asked me if I would stay at Madrid with General Belliard, who wished to keep me. I had foreseen this question, and as it by no means suited me, after serving under several marshals and a prince, to be lost in the obscure crowd of the officers on the general staff and do postman's work under fire, earning no glory nor hope of promotion, I answered that I was still Marshal Augereau's aide-de-camp, that he had agreed to my doing duty with Prince Murat, but that when Murat left Spain I considered my mission at an end, and asked leave to return to my former chief. So I left Madrid with Murat on June 17. We travelled by easy stages, and reached Bayonne on July 3. There Murat took the title of King of Naples. The officers of his staff going to congratulate him, he proposed to us to follow him into Italy, promising rapid promotion to those who would take service with him. All accepted except Major Lamothe and myself; for I had firmly resolved to wear no uniform but that of the French army. Leaving my horses at Bayonne, I returned to Paris, and passed three happy months with my mother and Marshal Augereau.

Chapter 4
Awarded the Legion d'Honneur

The combat of May 2 and the abduction of the royal family had made the nation furious. Every province rose against Joseph's Government, and though he reached Madrid and was proclaimed on July 23, he had no authority in the country. Madrid, although the habitual residence of the sovereigns of Spain, has no influence on the provinces, each of which was once a separate kingdom, and has preserved the title. Each has its capital, its customs, its own laws, and its own local administration; so that the possession of Madrid by an enemy does not affect its independence. Thus in 1808 each province had its junta, its army, its stores, and its revenues; but the junta of Seville was recognised as the central power.

The French army would thus have been in a critical condition, with the whole of Spain in arms against it, even if it had been under the orders of an able general, and its composition as strong as it actually was weak. We suffered reverses by sea and land; a squadron had to surrender in Cadiz roads just as Marshal Moncey had to retire from the kingdom of Valencia. The junta of Seville declared war against France in the name of Ferdinand VII. General Dupont, whom Savary had imprudently despatched without support into Andalusia, found at the beginning of July that the people were all rising round him, and, learning that 10,000 men from the camp of San Roque were advancing under the orders of General Castaños, resolved to withdraw towards Madrid, and with that view sent Vedel's division to occupy the Sierra Morena and re-open communications. But, instead of following his advanced guard promptly, Dupont, who from an excellent general of division had become a very bad commander of an army corps, resolved to give battle where he stood, and ordered Vedel's division, which was already ten leagues away, to come back. This was the first mistake, and besides this, Dupont scattered the troops that remained with him, and lost precious time at Andujar, on the banks of the Guadalquivir.

The Spaniards, reinforced by several Swiss regiments, took advantage of this delay to send part of their troops over to the bank opposite to that which our army occupied; so that we found ourselves between two fires. Still, so far nothing was lost, if our men had fought courageously and in good order; but Dupont had handled his troops so badly that on arriving before the defile of Baylen the rear of the column was three leagues from the head. Then, instead of bringing his force together, General Dupont sent each regiment and each gun into action as they came up. Our weak young soldiers, exhausted by fifteen hours' marching and eight hours' fighting, were dropping with weariness under the rays of an Andalusian sun. The most part could neither march nor bear arms any longer, and lay down instead of fighting. Then Dupont asked for a truce, which the Spaniards were all the more ready to accept that they feared matters might shortly change to their disadvantage. Vedel's division had, in fact, at that moment come up in rear of the Spanish force and was attacking them successfully. They sent a flag of truce to let the general know that an armistice had been agreed upon with General Dupont. Vedel took no notice of it and fought on vigorously. Two Spanish regiments had laid down their arms; others were in flight; and Vedel was only a short league from Dupont, and would soon have completely relieved him, when an aide-de-camp came from the latter through the enemy's army bringing orders to take no further steps as arrangements were being made for an armistice. Thereupon Vedel, instead of yielding further to the happy inspiration under which he had refused to recognise the authority of a chief who could send orders to his subordinates only by passing them through the hands of the enemy, halted in the middle of his victory and gave the order to cease firing. The Spaniards meanwhile had only eight cartridges per man left; but their supports were coming up and they wished to gain time. General Dupont asked permission from General Reding, a Swiss in the Spanish service, to pass through with his army and return to Madrid. Reding at first agreed, but afterwards declared that he could do nothing without the authority of General Castaños, who was some leagues away. He in his turn wished to refer the matter to the junta, and they raised all sorts of difficulties.

Meanwhile Dupont's young recruits were in a most unfortunate position; he kept giving contradictory orders alternately requiring Vedel to attack and to take back his division to Madrid. Vedel took the latter course, and the next day was at the foot of Sierra Morena, out of reach of attack from Castaños. But unluckily General Dupont had decided to capitulate, and with indescribable weakness had comprehended Vedel's troops in the capitulation, ordering them to return to Baylen. Having the way to Madrid open to them they tumultuously refused; but instead of taking advantage of their enthusiasm, Vedel pointed out that they would expose Dupont's men to reprisals, adding that the terms of capitulation were not severe since it was stipulated that they would be taken back to France, where they would get their arms again. The officers and soldiers declared that in that case they had better retreat, arms and all, to Madrid; but General Vedel preached passive obedience until he succeeded in bringing his division back to Baylen, where it lay down its arms. General Dupont deserves much blame for having included in the capitulation a division which was already out of the enemy's reach; but what must we think of General Vedel, who obeyed the orders of a commander no longer at liberty and handed over to the Spaniards nearly 10,000 efficient men? Dupont pushed his infatuation so far as to include all the troops of his army corps, even those who had not crossed the Sierra Morena. General Castaños required that these detachments should come twenty-five leagues to lay down their arms. One commander only, who deserves to be named, the brave Major de Sainte-Eglise, replied that he would not take orders from a general who was a prisoner of war, and by a rapid march, in spite of the attacks of the insurgent peasants, he succeeded with little loss in reach the outposts of the French camp before Madrid. The Emperor promoted him to the rank of colonel. With the exception of this battalion, the whole of Dupont's army, 20,000 strong, was disarmed. Then the Spaniards, having no more to fear, refused to keep the articles of the capitulation, which stipulated for the return of the French troops to France, and not only declared them prisoners of war, but shamefully ill-treated them and allowed several thousand soldiers to be slaughtered by the peasants.

Dupont, Vedel, and some generals alone obtained leave to return to France. The officers and the soldiers were at first packed on board pontoons in Cadiz roads, but an epidemic fever broke out among them, and the Spanish authorities, fearing that Cadiz might be infected, sent the survivors to the desert island of Cabrera, where there was neither water nor houses. There our poor men, receiving every week some casks of brackish water, some damaged ship biscuit, and a little salt meat, lived almost like savages. Without clothing, linen, or medicine, getting no news of their families, or even from France, they were obliged to shelter themselves in burrows like wild beasts. This lasted six years, until the Peace of 1814, by which time most of the prisoners were dead of misery and grief. M. de Lasalle, who became orderly officer to King Louis Philippe, was among the number, and when he was released he, like most of his comrades, had been almost entirely naked for more than six years. When it was pointed out to the Spaniards that their violation of the Treaty of Baylen was contrary to the law of nations in force among all civilized peoples, they replied that the arrest of their king, Ferdinand VII., had been no less illegal, and that they were merely following the example which Napoleon had set them—a reproach which, it must be admitted, was not without foundation.

When the news of the disaster at Baylen reached the Emperor his rage was fearful. Up to then he had regarded the Spaniards as on a par in courage with the Italians, and supposed that their rising was merely a peasant revolt which would quickly be dispersed by a few French battalions. But his eagles had been humbled, and French troops had lost the prestige of unbroken victory. Deeply must he have regretted that he had allowed his army to be composed of recruits, instead of sending the veterans whom he had left in Germany. His rage against the generals was indescribable. He made the mistake of imprisoning them to avoid the scandal of a trial, which led to their being regarded as the victims of arbitrary power. It was five years before they were brought to trial by court-martial. The capitulation of Baylen, as may be supposed, caused the insurrection to spread widely; nor did the defeat of the army of the Asturias by Bessières do anything to check it. The Spanish contingent, under General La Romana, which had served under Napoleon, and had been left on the coast of the Baltic, was brought back with the help of the English. The fortresses which the Spaniards still held were defended vigorously, and open towns, following the lead of Saragossa, turned themselves into fortresses. The Spanish army of

Andalusia was set free to march on Madrid, and King Joseph with an army corps retreated beyond the Ebro, where the remainder of our troops raising the sieges in which they were engaged gradually assembled. Soon we learnt a new disaster. Portugal, owing to the imprudence with which Junot had scattered his forces, had been lost to us. Attacked by Sir Arthur Wellesley with superior forces, he had been compelled to capitulate at Vimeira. That day marked the beginning of Wellesley's fame and fortune; he was the junior lieutenant-general in the English army, and commanded that day only in consequence of a delay in the landing of his seniors. The terms of capitulation were that the French army should evacuate Portugal and be taken back to France by sea without being disarmed. They were faithfully executed by the English; but instead of being landed at Bordeaux, the troops were taken to Lorient.

By this time Napoleon had ordered up from Germany three army corps of infantry and much cavalry—all veterans who had fought at Jena, Eylau, and Friedland. To these he added a large portion of his guard, and prepared to set out himself for Spain, at their head. Their number amounted to more than 100,000, which, with the divisions already in Spain, would raise our army to 200,000 men.

Some days before starting, the Emperor, intending to take Augereau with him if the wound he had received at Eylau allowed him to take the command, had summoned him to Saint-Cloud. Being on duty, I accompanied the Marshal, and while Napoleon walked about with Augereau I stayed on one side with his aides-de-camp. It appears that after discussing the matter which they had in hand their conversation turned on the battle of Eylau, and the noble conduct of the 14th. Augereau spoke of the devoted manner in which I had carried orders to that regiment through the swarming Cossacks, and entered into full details of the dangers which I had run in accomplishing that mission, and of the really miraculous manner in which I had escaped death after being stripped and left naked on the snow. The Emperor replied: 'Marbot's conduct was admirable, and I have given him the Cross for it.' The Marshal having quite correctly declared that I had received no reward, Napoleon maintained his statement, and in order to prove it sent for Prince Berthier, the adjutant-general. He looked through the registers, the result of his search being the discovery that the Emperor, on hearing of my exploit at Eylau, had indeed entered the name of Marbot, aide-de-camp to Marshal Augereau, among the officers to be decorated. He had, however, not added my Christian name, not knowing that my brother was on the marshal's staff as supernumerary; so that when the time came to deliver the patents, Prince Berthier, always very busy, had said, to save his secretary trouble, 'The Cross must be given to the elder.' So my brother got decorated, though it was his first action, and, since he was only on temporary leave from the Indies, and his regiment was at the Isle of France, he did not officially even belong to the Grand Army. Thus was fulfilled the prediction which Augereau had expressed to him when he said, 'If you come on the same staff as your brother you will do each other harm.' Anyhow, after scolding Berthier a little, the Emperor came towards me, spoke to me kindly, and, taking the Cross from one of his orderly officers, fastened it on my breast. October 29, 1808, was one of the happiest days of my life. At that time the Legion of Honour had not been lavishly given, and a value was attached to it which since then it has unfortunately lost. Decorated at 26! I was beside myself with joy. The good marshal's satisfaction was equal to mine, and in order to allow my mother to share it he took me to her. No promotion that I ever got pleased her as much. To complete my satisfaction, Marshal Duroc sent for the hat which a cannon-ball had pierced on my head at the battle of Eylau, and which the Emperor wished to see.

By Napoleon's own advice, Augereau declined to go on the campaign. Accordingly, he asked Lannes, who had a command in Spain, kindly to take me with him; not, however, as supernumerary, in which capacity I had been with that marshal in the Friedland campaign, but as a regular member of the staff; but if Augereau returned to duty, I was to go back to him. So in November I set out for Bayonne, where, for the fourth time, I was to report myself to a new chief. My outfit had been left there, and was all ready for me. Indeed, I was able to lend the marshal a horse, as his had not yet come when the Emperor crossed the frontier. I knew the country through which we had to pass, and the ways of it, well; the language a little; so that I was able to be of some use to the marshal, who had never been in these parts before.

Nearly all the officers who had been on Lannes' staff having got promotion at the Peace of Tilsit, the marshal was obliged to form a new staff for Spain. He himself was a man of strong character; but from various causes he was obliged to select officers most of whom, for one reason or another, had had little experience of war. They were all brave enough; but it was the least military staff on which I had ever served. The senior aide-de-camp was Colonel O'Meara, brother-in-law to Clarke, Duke of Feltre. He ended his days as commandant of a small place on the Belgian frontier. Then came Major Gruéhéneuc, brother-in-law to Lannes, who commanded the 26th Light Infantry at the Beresina. Major Saint-Mars was the third. After being taken prisoner in Russia he became general secretary of the Legion of Honour. I was the fourth. The fifth was Marquis Serafino d'Albuquerque, a great Spanish noble, fond of good living, and very plucky. He was killed by a cannon-ball at Essling. Sixth, Captain Watteville, son of the Landammann of the Helvetic Republic, representing the Swiss nation; Lannes being titular colonel of the Swiss troops in the French service. He too went on the Russian campaign as a major of lancers. In spite of my care, he succumbed to cold and fatigue as we got near Wilna. The seventh was the famous Labédoyère. He was a tall and handsome man, brave, cultivated, and witty; a good talker, though with a slight stammer. He became aide-de-camp to Prince Eugene Beauharnais, and was colonel in 1814. The story of his bringing his regiment over to the Emperor at the return of Elba is well known. Under the Restoration he was tried and shot. The eighth aide-de-camp was named de Viry. He belonged to an ancient Savoyard family. So far as I knew, he had no bad qualities, and I became very intimate with him; he was severely wounded at Essling, and died in my arms at Vienna. Besides these the marshal had two supernumerary officers attached to his staff, Captain Dagusan and Sub-lieutenant Le Couteulx de Canteleu.

On my joining the staff, Marshal Lannes warned me that he reckoned very much on my help, both on account of the report of me which he had received from Augereau and from the manner in which I had served under himself in the Friedland campaign. 'If you do not get killed,' said he, 'I will see that your promotion comes quickly.' The marshal never promised in vain, and he was in such high favour with the Emperor that everything was possible to him. I promised to do my duty with unswerving courage and zeal.

We left Bayonne and marched with the troops as far as the Ebro, where we joined King Joseph and the army which had made the recent campaign. Rest in camp life had given these young recruits a military air, which they had been far from having in the previous July. But what most raised their tone was finding themselves under the command of the Emperor in person, and hearing that the veterans of the Grand Army had arrived. The Spaniards on their side were astonished and alarmed at the sight of the old grenadiers of the Grand Army, and realised that a change in the aspect of affairs was going to take place. And, indeed, hardly had the Emperor arrived on the Ebro when he launched numerous columns across the river. All that tried to make head against them were exterminated, or saved themselves only by rapid flight. The Spaniards, however, astonished but not discouraged, rallied several army corps under the walls of Burgos, and made bold to accept battle. It took place on November 9 and did not last long, for the enemy, driven in at the first charge, fled in all directions, pursued by our cavalry, with heavy loss.

During this battle, a remarkable, and, happily, very uncommon incident occurred. Two young infantry lieutenants quarrelled, and fought a duel in front of their battalion under a storm of cannonballs from the enemy. One of them had his cheek laid open by a sword-cut. The colonel put them under arrest and brought them before the marshal, who sent them to the citadel of Burgos, and reported them to the Emperor. He gave them a further punishment, forbidding them to go into action with their company for a month. At the end of this period the regiment to which these two foolish fellows belonged was being reviewed by the Emperor at Madrid. He ordered the colonel to present to him as usual those whom he proposed to promote in the place of officers killed. The sub-lieutenant, who had had the wound in his cheek, was an excellent soldier. His colonel thought that he ought not to lose his promotion for a fault which, though serious, was not dishonourable. He therefore submitted his name to the Emperor, who, perceiving a recent sear on the young man's face, remembered the duel at Burgos, and asked him in a severe tone, 'Where did you get that wound?' Thereupon the sub-lieutenant, wishing neither to tell a lie nor to confess, turned the difficulty very cleverly. Placing his finger on his cheek, he said 'I got it there, sir.' The Emperor understood, and as he liked men of a ready wit, far from being angry at this original repartee, he smiled, and said to the officer, 'Your colonel proposes you for the rank of lieutenant; I grant it you, but in future behave better or I shall cashier you.'

At Burgos I found my brother, who was on the staff of Prince Berthier, chief of the general staff. Lannes' military talent increased every day, and the Emperor, who had a very high opinion of him, no longer gave him any stated command, wishing to keep him about his person and send him wherever things had got into disorder, being sure that he would quickly set them to rights. Thus, considering that he had left the town of Saragossa occupied by the insurgents of Arragon, and supported by the army of Castaños, which had conquered Dupont, and that old General Moncey was only bungling, Napoleon ordered Lannes to go to Logroño, take command of the Army of the Ebro, and attack Castaños. Thus Moncey came under the orders of Lannes. It was the first case in which one marshal of the Empire had commanded another. Lannes showed himself worthy of this mark of confidence and distinction. He started, accompanied by his staff alone, and we travelled by post. You must know that at this time there were no draught horses in Spain, but the post-houses keep the best nags in Europe. We rode, therefore, night and day, escorted from stage to stage by detachments of cavalry. In this way we went back as far as Miranda del Ebro, whence we reached Logroño, following the river. Marshal Moncey appeared much annoyed at finding himself, the senior marshal, placed under the orders of the junior, but he had no choice but to obey.

See what the presence of a single capable and energetic man can do. This army of recruits, which Moncey had not dared to lead against the enemy, were set in motion by Lannes on the day of his arrival, and marched against the enemy with ardour. We came up with him on the following day, the 23rd, in front of Tudela, and after three hours' fighting the conquerors of Baylen were driven in, beaten, completely routed, and fled headlong towards Saragossa, leaving thousands of dead on the field. We captured a great many men, several colours, and all the artillery; a complete victory. During this affair I had a bullet through my sabretache. Just at the outset I had had a lively quarrel with Labédoyère over the following matter. He had just bought a young and ill-broken horse, which at the sound of the cannon reared up and absolutely refused to go on. Labédoyère leapt off in a rage, drew his sword, and hamstrung the unhappy horse, who fell all bleeding on the grass, dragging himself along on his forefeet. I could not contain my indignation, and expressed it to him in strong terms; but Labédoyère took it very ill, and we should have come to blows had we not, been in the presence of the enemy. The report of this incident got about in the staff, and Marshal Lannes, very angry, declared that he would not have Labédoyère any more among his aides-de-camp. The latter, in despair, had seized his pistols to blow his brains out, when our friend de Viry pointed out to him that it would be more honourable to seek death in the ranks of the enemy than to inflict it on himself. Just at that moment, de Viry, who was near the marshal, was ordered to lead a cavalry regiment against the Spanish battery. Labédoyère joined the regiment as it was charging, and was one of the first to dash into the battery. It was carried, and we saw de Viry and Labédoyère bringing back a gun which they had taken together. Neither of them was wounded, but Labédoyère had got a grapeshot through his busby, two inches from his head. The marshal was much touched by this courageous act; all the more so, that, after having handed over the gun to him, Labédoyère was getting ready to hurl himself a second time on the enemy's bayonets. The marshal held him back, and, pardoning his fault, restored him to his place on the staff. That same evening Labédoyère came in the most honourable way to shake hands with me, and we ever afterwards lived on the best of terms. He and de Viry were named in the despatches, and promoted to captains a little time after the battle.

Chapter 5
A Close Encounter with Death

I have now reached one of the most terrible experiences of my military career. Marshal Lannes had just won a great victory, and the next day, after having received the reports of the generals, he wrote his despatch for one of our officers to take to the Emperor. Napoleon's practice was to give a step to the officer who brought him the news of an important success, and the marshals on their side entrusted such tasks to officers for whose speedy promotion they were anxious. It was a form of recommendation which Napoleon never failed to recognise. Marshal Lannes did me the honour of appointing me to carry the news of the victory of Tudela, and I could indulge the hope of being major before long. But, alas! I had yet much blood to lose before I reached that rank.

The high road from Bayonne to Madrid by Vittoria, Miranda del Ebro, Burgos, and Aranda forks off at Miranda from that leading to Saragossa by Logrono. A road from Tudela to Aranda across the mountains about Soria forms the third side of a great triangle. While Lannes was reaching Tudela the Emperor had advanced from Burgos to Aranda. It was, therefore, much shorter for me to go from Tudela to Aranda than by way of Miranda del Ebro. The latter road, however, had the advantage of being covered by the French armies; while the other, no doubt, would be full of Spanish fugitives who had taken refuge after Tudela in the mountains. The Emperor, however, had informed Lannes that he was sending Ney's corps direct from Aranda to Tudela; so, thinking Ney to be at no great distance, and that an advanced force which he had pushed on the day after the battle to get touch of him at Taragona would secure me from attack as far as Aranda, Lannes ordered me to take the shortest road. I may frankly admit that if I had had my choice I should have preferred to make the round by Miranda and Burgos, but the marshal's orders were positive, and how could I express any fear for my own person in the presence of a man who knew no more fear for others than he did for himself?

The duties of marshal's aide-de-camp in Spain were terrible. During the revolutionary wars the generals had couriers paid by the state to carry their despatches; but the Emperor, finding that these men were not capable of giving any intelligible account of what they had seen, did away with them, and ordered that in future despatches should be carried by aides-de-camp. This was all very well as long as we were at war among the good Germans, to whom it never occurred to attack a French messenger; but the Spaniards waged fierce war against them. This was of great advantage to the insurgents, for the contents of our despatches informed them of the movements of our armies. I do not think I am exaggerating when I say that more than 200 staff officers were killed or captured during the Peninsular War. One may regret the death of an ordinary courier, but it is less serious than the loss of a promising officer, who, moreover, is exposed to the risks of the battle-field in addition to those of a posting journey. A great number of vigorous men well skilled in their business begged to be allowed to do this duty, but the Emperor never consented.

Just as I was starting from Tudela, Major Saint-Mars hazarded a remark intended to dissuade Lannes from sending me over the mountains. The marshal, however, answered, 'Oh, he will meet Ney's advance guard to-night, and find troops echelonned all the way to the Emperor's head-quarters.' This was too decided for any opposition, so I left Tudela November 4, at nightfall, with a detachment of cavalry, and got without any trouble as far as Taragona, at the foot of the mountains. In this little town I found Lannes' advance guard. The officer in command, hearing nothing of Ney, had pushed an infantry post six leagues forward towards Agreda. But as this body was detached from its supports, it had been ordered to fall back on Taragona if the night passed without Ney's scouts appearing.

After Taragona there is no more high road. The way lies entirely over mountain paths covered with stones and splinters of rock. The officer commanding our advanced guard had, therefore, only infantry and a score of hussars of the 2nd (Chamborant) Regiment. He gave me a troop horse and two orderlies, and I went on my way in brilliant moon-light. When we had gone two or three leagues we heard several musket-shots, and bullets whistled close past us. We could not see the marksmen, who were hidden among the rocks. A little farther on we found the corpses of two French infantry soldiers, recently killed. They were entirely stripped, but their shakoes were near them, by the numbers on which I could see that they belonged to one of the regiments in Ney's corps. Some little distance farther we saw a horrible sight. A young officer of the 10th Chasseurs a Cheval, still wearing his uniform, was nailed by his hands and feet, head downwards, to a barn door. A small fire had been lighted beneath him. Happily, his tortures had been ended by death; but as the blood was still flowing from his wounds, it was clear that the murderers were not far off. I drew my sword; my two hussars handled their carbines. It was just as well that we were on our guard, for a few moments later seven or eight Spaniards, two of them mounted, fired upon us from behind a bush. We were none of us wounded, and my two hussars replied to the fire, and killed each his man. Then, drawing their swords, they dashed at the rest. I should have been very glad to follow them, but my horse had lost a shoe among the stones and was limping, so that I could not get him into a gallop. I was the more vexed because I feared that the hussars might let themselves be carried away in the pursuit and get killed in some ambush. I called them for five minutes; then I heard the voice of one of them saying, in a strong Alsatian accent, 'Ah! you thieves! you don't know the Chamborant Hussars yet. You shall see that they mean business. My troopers had knocked over two more Spaniards, a Capuchin mounted on the horse of the poor lieutenant, whose haversack he had put over his own neck, and a peasant on a mule, with the clothes of the slaughtered soldiers on his back. It was quite clear that we had got the murderers The Emperor had given strict orders that every Spanish civilian taken in arms should be shot on the spot; and, moreover, what could we do with these two brigands, who were already seriously wounded, and who had just killed three Frenchmen so barbarously? I moved on, therefore, so as not to witness the execution, and the hussars polished off the monk and the peasant, repeating, 'Ah, you don't know the Chamborant!' I could not understand how an officer and two privates of Ney's corps could be so near Taragona, when their regiments had not come that way; but most probably they had been captured elsewhere, and were being taken to Saragossa, when their escort learned the defeat of their countrymen at Tudela, and massacred their prisoners in revenge for it.

After this not very encouraging start I continued my journey. We had gone for some hours, when we saw a bivouac fire of the detachment belonging to the advance guard which I had left at Taragona. The sub-lieutenant in command, having no tidings of Ney, was prepared to return to Taragona at daybreak, in pursuance of his orders. He knew that we were barely two leagues from Agreda, but did not know of which side that town was in possession. This was perplexing for me. The infantry detachment would return in a few hours, and if I went back with it, when it might be that in another league I should fall in with Ney's column, I should be giving a poor display of courage, and laying myself open to reproach from Lannes. On the other hand, if Ney was still a day or two's march away, it was almost certain that I should be murdered by the peasants of the mountains or by fugitive soldiers. What was more, I had to travel alone, for my two brave hussars had orders to return to Taragona when we had found the infantry detachment. No matter; I determined to push on; but then came the difficulty of finding a mount. There was no farm or village in this deserted place where I could procure a horse. That which I was riding was dead lame; and even if the hussars had been able, without incurring severe punishment, to lend me one of theirs, theirs were much fatigued. The horse that had belonged to the officer of chasseurs had received a bullet in the thigh during the fighting. There was only the peasant's mule left. This was a handsome beast, and according to the laws of war, belonged to the two hussars who, no doubt, reckoned on selling her when they got back to the army. Still the good fellows made no demur about lending her to me, and put my saddle on her back. But the infernal beast, more accustomed to the pack than to the saddle, was so restive, that directly I tried to get her away from the group of horses and make her go alone, she fell to kicking, until I had to choose between being sent over a precipice and dismounting.

So I decided to set out on foot. After I had taken farewell of the infantry officer, this excellent young man, M. Tassin by name—he had been a friend of my poor brother Felix at the military school—came running after me, and said that he could not bear to let me thus expose myself all alone, and that though he had no orders, and his men were raw recruits, with little experience in war, he must send one with me, so that I might at least have a musket and some cartridges in case of an attack. We agreed that I should send the man back with Ney's corps; and I went off, with the soldier accompanying me. He was a slow-speaking Norman, with plenty of slyness under an appearance of good-nature. The Normans are for the most part brave, as I learnt when I commanded the 23rd Chasseurs, where I had five or six hundred of them. Still, in order to know how far I could rely on my follower, I chatted with him as we went along, and asked if he would stand his ground if we were attacked. He said neither yes nor no, but answered, 'Well, zur, us shall zee.' Whence I inferred that when the moment of danger arrived my new companion was not unlikely to go and see how things were getting on in the rear.

The moon had just set, and as yet daylight had not appeared. It was pitch-dark, and at every step we stumbled over the great stones with which these mountain paths are covered. It was an unpleasant situation, but I hoped soon to come upon Ney's troops, and the fact of having seen the bodies of soldiers belonging to his corps increased the hope. So I went steadily on, listening for diversion to the Norman's stories of his country. Dawn appeared at last, and I saw the first houses of a large village. It was Agreda. I was alarmed at finding no outposts, for it showed that not only did no troops of the marshal's occupy the place, but that his army corps must be at least half a day farther on. The map showed no village within five or six leagues of Agreda, and it was impossible that the regiments could be quartered in the mountains, far from any inhabited place. So I kept on my guard and before going any farther reconnoitred the position.

Agreda stands in a rather broad valley. It is built at the foot of a lofty hill, steeply escarped on both sides. The southern slope, which reaches the village, is planted with large vineyards. The ridge is rough and rocky, and the northern slope covered with thick coppice, a torrent flowing at the foot. Beyond are seen lofty mountains, uncultivated and uninhabited. The principal street of Agreda runs through the whole length of the place, with narrow lanes leading to the vineyards opening into it. As I entered the village I had these lanes and the vineyards on my right. This detail is important to the understanding of my story. Everybody was asleep in Agreda; the moment was favourable for going through it. Besides, I had some hope—feeble, it is true—that when I reached the farther end I might perhaps see the fires of Marshal Ney's advance guard. So I went forward, sword in hand, bidding my soldier cock his musket. The main street was covered with a thick bed of damp leaves, which the people placed there to make manure; so that our footsteps made no sound, of which I was glad. I walked in the middle of the street, with the soldier on my right; but, finding himself no doubt in a too conspicuous position, he gradually sheered off to the houses, keeping close to the walls so that he might be less visible in case of attack, or better placed for reaching one of the lanes which open into the country. This showed me how little I could rely on the man; but I made no remark to him. The day was beginning to break. We passed the whole of the main street without meeting anyone. Just as I was congratulating myself on reaching the last houses of the village, I found myself at twenty-five paces' distance, face to face with four Royal Spanish Carabineers on horseback, with drawn swords. Under any other circumstances I might have taken them for French gendarmes, their uniforms being exactly similar, but the gendarmes never march with the extreme advanced guard. These men, therefore, could not belong to Ney's corps, and I at once perceived they were the enemy. In a moment I faced about, but just as I had turned round to the direction from which I had come I saw a blade flash six inches from my face. I threw my head sharply back, but nevertheless got a severe sabre-cut on my forehead, of which I carry the scar over my left eyebrow to this day. The man who had wounded me was the corporal of the carabineers, who, having left his four troopers outside the village, had according to military practice gone forward to reconnoitre. That I had not met him was probably due to the fact that he had been in some side lane, while I had passed through the main street. He was now coming back through the street to rejoin his troopers, when, seeing me, he had come up noiselessly over the layer of leaves, and was just going to cleave my head from behind, when, by turning round I presented to him my face and received his blow on my forehead. At the same moment the four carabineers, who seeing that their corporal was all ready for me had not stirred, trotted up to join him, and all five dashed upon me. I ran mechanically towards the houses on the right in order to get my back against a wall; but by good luck I found, two paces off, one of the steep and narrow lanes which went up into the vineyards. The soldier had already reached it. I flew up there too, with the five carabineers after me; but at any rate they could not attack me all at once, for there was only room for one horse to pass. The brigadier went in front; the other four filed after him. My position, although not as unfavourable as it would have been in the street, where I should have been surrounded still remained alarming; the blood flowing freely from my wound had in a moment covered my left eye, with which I could not see at all, and I felt that it was coming towards my right eye, so that I was compelled by fear of getting blinded to keep my head bent over the left shoulder so as to bring the blood to that side. I could not staunch it, being obliged to defend myself against the corporal, who was cutting at me heavily. I parried as well as I could, going up backwards all the time. After getting rid of my scabbard and my busby, the weight of which hampered me, not daring to turn my head for fear of losing sight of my adversary, whose sword was crossed with mine, I told the light-infantry man, whom I believed to be behind me, to place his musket on my shoulder and fire at the Spanish corporal. Seeing no barrel, however, I leapt a pace back and turned my head quickly. Lo and behold, there was my scoundrel of a Norman soldier flying up the hill as fast as his legs would carry him! The corporal thereupon attacked with redoubled vigour, and, seeing that he could not reach me, made his horse rear so that his feet struck me more than once on the breast. Luckily, as the ground went on rising the horse had no good hold with his hind legs, and every time that he came down again I landed a sword-cut on his nose with such effect that the animal presently refused to rear at me any more. Then the brigadier, losing his temper, called out to the trooper behind him, 'Take your carbine: I will stoop down, and you can aim at the Frenchman over my shoulders.' I saw that this order was my death-signal; but as in order to execute it the trooper had to sheathe his sword and unhook his carbine, and that all this time the corporal never ceased thrusting at me, leaning right over his horse's neck, I determined on a desperate action which would be either my salvation or my ruin. Keeping my eye fixed on the Spaniard, and seeing in his that he was on the point of again stooping over his horse to reach me, I did not move until the very instant when he was lowering the upper part of his body towards me; then I took a pace to the right, and, leaning quickly over to that side, I avoided my adversary's blow, and plunged half my sword-blade into his left flank. With a fearful yell the corporal fell back on the croup of his horse; he would probably have rolled to the ground if the trooper behind him had not caught him in his arms. My rapid movement in stooping had caused the despatch which I was carrying to fall out of the pocket of my pelisse. I picked it up quickly, and at once hastened to the end of the lane where the vines began. There I turned round, and saw the carabineers busy round their wounded corporal, and apparently much embarrassed with him and with their horses in the steep and narrow passage.

This fight took less time than I have taken to relate it. Finding myself rid, at least for the moment, of my enemies, I went through the vines and reached the edge of the hill. Then I considered that it would be impossible for me to accomplish my errand and reach the Emperor at Aranda. I resolved, therefore, to return to Marshal Lannes, regaining first the place where I had left M. Tassin and his picket of infantry. I did not hope to find them still there; but at any rate the army which I had left the day before was in that direction. I looked for my soldier in vain, but I saw something that was of more use to me—a spring of clear water. I halted there a moment, and, tearing off a corner of my shirt, I made a compress which I fastened over my wound with my handkerchief. The blood spurting from my forehead had stained the despatches which I held in my hand, but I was too much occupied with my awkward position to mind that.

The agitations of the past night, my long walk over the stony paths in boots and spurs, the fight in which I had just been engaged, the pain in my head, and the loss of blood had exhausted my strength. I had taken no food since leaving Tudela, and here I had nothing but water to refresh myself with. I drank long draughts of it, and should have rested longer by the spring had I not perceived three of the Spanish Carabineers riding out of Agreda and coming towards me through the vines. If they had been sharp enough to dismount and take off their long boots, they would probably have succeeded in reaching me; but the horses, unable to pass between the vinestocks, ascended the steep and rocky paths with difficulty. Indeed, when they reached the upper end of the vineyard, they found themselves brought up by the great rocks, on the top of which I had taken refuge, and unable to climb any farther. Then the troopers, passing along the bottom of the rocks, marched parallel with me a long musket-shot off. They called to me to surrender, saying that as soldiers they would treat me as a prisoner of war, while if the peasants caught me I should infallibly be murdered. This reasoning was sound, and I admit that if I had not been charged with despatches for the Emperor, I was so exhausted that I should perhaps have surrendered.

However, wishing to preserve to the best of my ability the precious charge which had been entrusted to me, I marched on without answering. Then the three troopers, taking their carbines, opened fire upon me. Their bullets struck the rocks at my feet, but none touched me, the distance being too great for a correct aim. I was alarmed, not at the fire, but at the notion that the reports would probably attract the peasants who would be going to their work in the morning, and quite expected to be attacked by these fierce mountaineers. My presentiment seemed to be verified, for I perceived some fifteen men half a league away in the valley advancing towards me at a run. They held in their hands something that flashed in the sun. I made no doubt that they were peasants armed with their spades, and that it was the iron of these that shone thus. I gave myself up for lost, and in my despair I was on the point of letting myself slide down over the rocks on the north side of the hill to the torrent, crossing it as best I could, and hiding myself in some chasm of the great mountains which rise on the farther side of the gorge. Then, if I was not discovered, and if I still had the strength, I should set out when night came in the direction of Taragona.

This plan, though offering many chances of failure, was my last hope. Just as I was about to put it into execution, I perceived that the three carabineers had given up firing on me, and gone forward to reconnoitre the group which I had taken for peasants At their approach the iron instruments which I had taken for spades or mattocks were lowered, and I had the inexpressible joy of seeing a volley fired at the Spanish carabineers. Instantly turning, they took flight towards Agreda, as it seemed, with two of their number wounded. 'The newcomers, then, are French!' I exclaimed. 'Here goes to meet them!' and, regaining a little strength from the joy of being delivered, I descended, leaning on my sword. The French had caught sight of me; they climbed the hill, and I found myself in the arms of the brave Lieutenant Tassin.

This providential rescue had come about as follows. The soldier who had deserted me while I was engaged with the carabineers in the streets of Agreda had quickly reached the vines; thence, leaping across the vinestocks, ditches, rocks, and hedges, he had very quickly run the two leagues which lay between him and the place where we had left M. Tassin's picket. The detachment was on the point of starting for Taragona, and was eating its soup, when my Norman came up all out of breath. Not wishing, however, to lose a mouthful, he seated himself by a cooking-pot and began to make a very tranquil breakfast, without saying a word about what had happened at Agreda. By great good luck he was noticed by M. Tassin, who, surprised at seeing him returned, asked him where he had quitted the officer whom he had been told off to escort 'Good Lord, sir,' replied the Norman, 'I left him in that big village with his head half split open, and fighting with Spanish troopers, and they were cutting away at him with their swords like anything.' At these words Lieutenant Tassin ordered his detachment to arms, picked the fifteen most active, and went off at the double towards Agreda. The little troop had gone a league when they heard shots, and inferred from them that I was still alive but, in urgent need of succour. Stimulated by the hope of saving me, the brave fellows doubled their pace, and finally perceived me on the ridge of the hill, serving as a mark for three Spanish troopers.

M. Tassin and his men were tired, and I was at the end of my strength. We halted, therefore, for a little, and meanwhile you may imagine that I expressed my warmest gratitude to the lieutenant and his men, who were almost as glad as I was. We returned to the bivouac where M. Tassin had left the rest of his people. The cantinière of the company was there with her mule carrying two skins of wine, bread, and ham. I bought the lot and gave them to the soldiers, and we breakfasted, as I was very glad to do, the two hussars whom I had left there the night before sharing in the meal. One of these mounted the monk's mule and lent me his horse, and so we set out for Taragona. I was in horrible pain, because the blood had hardened over my wound. At Taragona I rejoined Lannes' advance guard; the general in command had my wound dressed, and gave me a horse and an escort of two hussars. I reached Tudela at midnight, and was at once received by the marshal, who, though ill himself, seemed much touched by my misfortune. It was necessary, however, that the despatch about the battle of Tudela should be promptly forwarded to the Emperor, who must be impatiently awaiting news from the army on the Ebro. Enlightened by what had befallen me in the mountains, the marshal consented that the officer bearing it should go by Miranda and Burgos, where the presence of French troops on the roads made the way perfectly safe. I should have liked very much to be the bearer, but I was in such pain and so tired that it would have been physically impossible for me to ride hard. The marshal therefore entrusted the duty to his brother-in-law, Major Guéhéneuc. I handed him the despatches stained with my blood. Major Saint-Mars, the secretary, wished to recopy them and change the envelope. 'No, no,' cried the marshal, 'the Emperor ought to see how valiantly Captain Marbot has defended them.' So he sent off the packet just as it was, adding a note to explain the reason of the delay, eulogising me, and asking for a reward to Lieutenant Tassin and his men, who had hastened so zealously to my succour, without reckoning the danger to which they might have been exposed if the enemy had been in force.

The Emperor did, as a matter of fact, a little while after, grant the Cross both to M. Tassin and to his sergeant, and a gratuity of 100 francs to each of the men who had accompanied them. As for the Norman soldier, he was tried by court-martial for deserting his post in the presence of the enemy, and condemned to drag a shot for two years, and to finish his time of service in a pioneer company.

Chapter 6
The Pursuit of the English Army

Lannes advanced to Saragossa; but, having no siege artillery, he was content for the moment to guard the principal approaches, and, leaving Marshal Moncey in command, went to rejoin the Emperor. Being, as I have said, ill, he was obliged to travel in a carriage, relays being furnished by the draught-horses of the army. I anticipated a disagreeable journey; for though we should halt at night, seven or eight hours' riding would increase the pain of my wound, already severe.

But the marshal kindly gave me a place in his carriage, together with his friends Generals Pouzet and Frère. They were fond of chatting, and at times of joking at the expense of their friends, and as they had only known me a short time my presence embarrassed them. But the marshal said, 'He is a good lad; you can talk before him,' and they took advantage freely of his opinion. Although we rested at night, I found the journey very fatiguing. We passed Logrono, Miranda, and Burgos, and went on foot up the celebrated gorge of Somo Sierra, which had been carried a few days before, under the Emperor's eyes, by the Polish lancers of his guard. It was in this fight that General Montbrun, who afterwards became famous, distinguished himself. He was with the head-quarter staff, when the Emperor, who had got some hours in advance of his infantry, reached the foot of Somo Sierra, having only his Polish lancers with him. The high road, at that point very steep, and closed in by mountains was found to be barred by a small earthwork defended by several thousand Spaniards. Napoleon wished to reach Buitrago that day, so, finding his march arrested, and judging that the infantry could not come in for some time, he ordered the Poles to force the passage.

The Poles have only one good quality, but that they possess in the fullest measure—they are very brave. Their commanders, having seen no service, did not know that in passing a defile it is necessary to leave a squadron's distance between every two squadrons, so that if the leaders are repulsed they may find in rear of them an open space in which to re-form and not be driven back upon the squadrons following. The Polish officers therefore launched their regiment into the defile without getting them into a proper formation. Received with a hail of bullets on both flanks, and finding the road barred at the highest point, they suffered considerable loss, increased by the way in which the first squadron fell back in disorder upon the second, the second on the third, and so on, until the regiment, now only a disorganised crowd on an enclosed road, could not wheel about, and was being shot down at almost point-blank range by the Spaniards posted on the rocks. It was difficult to disentangle this mass; when it was at last managed the Poles re-formed in the plain, under the Emperor's eyes. He praised their courage, but blamed their lack of method in attacking. The officers admitted it, and expressed their regret that they had not been led by an experienced general. Then Berthier, wishing to do a good turn to Montbrun, who was out of favour at the moment, but whom he knew to be an excellent cavalry officer, drew Napoleon's attention to his presence. The Emperor called him, and put him in command of the lancers, with orders to renew the attack.

Montbrun was a splendid man, in the same style as Murat; lofty stature, a scarred face, a black beard, of soldierly bearing, and an admirable horseman. The Poles took to him, and promised to follow his instructions; and Montbrun having made the squadrons take their intervals, and seeing that everything was in proper order, placed himself boldly at their head and dashed into the gorge. Some squadrons were at first shaken by the fire, but as the different parts of the column were at sufficient distance to prevent any serious disorder, they recovered, and presently the top of the ascent was reached. General Montbrun dismounted, and was the first to run up to the entrenchments to tear out the palisades under a hail of bullets. The Poles followed his example; the entrenchments were carried and the regiment, remounting, charged the Spaniards, with great slaughter, for the ground, opening out and sloping down, allowed the lancers to reach the enemy's infantry as they fled in disorder. By the time the Emperor reached the top, not only was the French flag to be seen floating over Buitrago, but Montbrun's cavalry was pursuing the routed Spaniards a league beyond the town. That evening Napoleon complimented the Poles, and appointed Montbrun general of division. He commanded a division soon after in Austria, and in 1810 was put in chief command of all the cavalry of the Army of Portugal. He was killed at the battle of the Moskwa.

When Lannes had examined the position we descended to Buitrago, and the next day reached Madrid, which had been occupied by Napoleon only after serious fighting. Lannes presented me to him, and he received me kindly, promising to reward me ere long for my conduct at Agreda. We found M. Guéhéneuc at Madrid in the uniform of a colonel, having been promoted by the Emperor on delivering the despatch stained with my blood. Guéhéneuc was a good fellow; he came to me and said, 'You had the danger, and got the sword-cut, and I have got the step; but I hope that your promotion will not be slow in coming.' I hoped so too; but I will frankly admit that I was a little annoyed with the marshal for the obstinacy with which he had insisted on making me go by Agreda. However, one must submit to one's destiny. Marshal Lannes lodged at Madrid in the same house as Murat had occupied. I found that the kind Senor Hernandez, hearing of my arrival, had come to ask me to stay with him. I was the more glad to accept, since my wound had got poisoned, and good nursing was necessary. This my host gave me in plenty, and I was on the way to get well, when new events compelled me to return to the field.

We had been barely a week at Madrid, when the Emperor learnt, on December 21, that the Portuguese army was daring to march against the Spanish capital, and was only at a few days' distance. Orders were instantly given to march and he left the town at the head of several army corps, going towards Valladolid, from which direction the English, under Sir John Moore, were expected. Marshal Lannes, being quite recovered, was to accompany the Emperor on horse-back. He suggested to me that I should stay at Madrid till my wound was completely healed; but there were two reasons against this. In the first place, I wished to be present at the battle with the English; and secondly, I knew that the Emperor scarcely ever promoted people in their absencey and I was anxious to obtain the promised step to major, so I got ready to start. The only thing that troubled me was that by reason of my wound I could wear neither cocked hat nor busby. The handkerchief bound round my head was not quite a sufficiently military head-gear to appear among a staff closely attached to that of the Emperor. The sight of a mameluke of the guard with his turban and red fez gave me an idea. I had a cap of the same colour; round this I wound a smart silk handkerchief, and placed the whole over my bandages. We marched the first night to the foot of the Guadarrama. There was a sharp frost, and the ice on the roads caused the troops—the cavalry especially—to march with difficulty. The marshal constantly sent officers to see that the column was in good order, but kindly exempted me from this duty. While our colleagues were carrying orders N—— and I were often alone with the marshal. N——beckoned to me and held out a bottle of kirsch. I declined, with thanks; my friend put the neck of the bottle into his mouth, and in less than a quarter of an hour had emptied it. Suddenly, like a Colossus overthrown, he rolled to the ground. The marshal broke out angrily, but N——replied, 'It is not my fault; there is ice between my saddle and my seat!' At this novel and quaint excuse, in spite of his wrath, the marshal could not help laughing. Then he said to me, 'Put him into one of the provision wagons.' I obeyed, and our comrade went to sleep on the sacks of rice, all among the hams and sauce-pans.

Next day a furious snowstorm, with a fierce wind, made the passage of the mountains almost impracticable. Men and horses were hurled over precipices. The leading battalions had actually begun to retreat; but Napoleon was resolved to overtake the English at all costs. He spoke to the men, and ordered that the members of each section should hold one another by the arm. The cavalry, dismounting, did the same. The staff was formed in similar fashion, the Emperor between Lannes and Duroc, we following with locked arms; and so in spite of wind, snow, and ice, we proceeded, though it took us four hours to reach the top. Halfway up, the marshals and generals, who wore jackboots, could go no farther. Napoleon, therefore, got hoisted on to a gun, and bestrode it; the marshals and generals did the same; and in this grotesque order they reached the convent at the summit. There the troops were rested and wine served out. The descent, though awkward, was better. At nightfall we reached the market town of San Rafael, and obtained food and quarters there and in the villages round. My wound had re-opened, the snow had got down my neck, and I was wet through; so I passed a wretched night.

As we continued our march on the following days we came into milder weather. Rain took the place of frost, and the roads became quagmires. At Tordetsillas we came up with some stragglers of the English army, which at our approach was retreating towards the port of Corunna. Anxious to catch it before it could embark, the Emperor forced on the troops, making them do ten or twelve leagues a day. This haste was the cause of a check which Napoleon felt all the more from the fact that it was inflicted on a division of his guard.

When the army was at Villapanda, where it passed the night, the Emperor—who by this time was furious at the protracted pursuit of the English—heard that their rear-guard was only a few leagues from us, at the town of Benavente, beyond the little stream of the Esla. At daybreak he sent forward a column of infantry with cavalry of the guard, under the command of General Lefebvre-Desnouettes, a brave but somewhat imprudent officer. On reaching with his cavalry the banks of the Esla, the general could see no enemy, and proposed to reconnoitre the town of Benavente, half a league beyond the stream. This was all right; but a picket would have sufficed, for twenty-five men can see as far as two thousand, and if they fall into an ambush the loss is less serious. General Desnouettes should, therefore, have awaited his infantry before plunging recklessly into the Esla. But, without listening to any suggestion, he made the whole regiment of chasseurs ford the river, and advanced towards the town, which he ordered the Mamelukes to search. They found not a soul in the place, a pretty certain sign that the enemy was preparing an ambush. The French general ought in prudence to have drawn back, since he was not in sufficient force to fight a strong rear-guard. Instead of this, Desnouettes pushed steadily forward; but as he was going through the town, four thousand or five thousand English cavalry turned it, covered by the houses in the suburbs, and suddenly charged down upon the chasseurs. These, hastening from the town, made so valiant a defence that they cut a great gap through the English, regained the stream, and recrossed without much loss. But when, on reaching the left bank, the regiment reformed, it was seen that General Desnouettes was no longer present. A messenger came with a flag of truce announcing that the general's horse had been killed in the fight, and he himself was a prisoner of war.

At this moment the Emperor came up. Imagine his wrath at hearing that, not only had his favourite regiment undergone a repulse, but that the commander had remained in the hands of the English! Though much displeased with Desnouettes' imprudence, he proposed to the commander on the other side to exchange him against an officer of the same rank among those detained in France; but General Moore was too proud of being able to show to the English people one of the commanders of the imperial guard of France to agree to this; exchange, and, consequently, declined it. General Desnouettes was treated with much kindness, but was sent to London as a trophy, which made Napoleon all the more angry.

In spite of this little victory, the English continued their retreat. We crossed the Esla, and occupied Benavente from this town to Astorga the distance is not less than fifteen or sixteen leagues, with several streams to be crossed; but the Emperor was in such a hurry to overtake the enemy that he required his army to march this distance in one day, though it was the 31st of December and the days were very short. Seldom have I made such a fatiguing march. An icy rain wetted us to the skin; men and horses sank into the marshy ground. We only advanced with the utmost effort; and as all the bridges had been broken by the English, our men were five or six times compelled to strip, place their arms and clothes on their heads, and go naked through the icy water of the streams.

It is painful to relate that I saw three veteran grenadiers of the guard, unable to march any further, and, unwilling to fall to the rear at the risk of being tortured and massacred by the peasants, blow out their brains with their own muskets. A dark and rainy night added to the fatigue of the troops; the exhausted soldiers lay down in the mud. A great number halted at the village of Bañeza; only the leading companies arrived at Astorga, the rest remaining on the road. It was late at night when the Emperor and Lannes, escorted only by their staffs and some hundred cavalry, entered Astorga. So tired and anxious for shelter and warmth was everyone that the place was scarcely searched. If the enemy had had warning of this and returned on their tracks, they might perhaps have carried off the Emperor; fortunately they were in too great a hurry, and we did not find one of them in the town. Every minute fresh bodies of French troops were coming up; and the safety of the imperial headquarters was soon secured.

Astorga is a largish town. We quartered ourselves quickly, placing Marshal Lannes in a handsome house near the Emperor. We were wet through, and near enough to the Asturian mountains to be cold. Our baggage had not yet come up, and the fires which we lighted could not keep the marshal from shivering. I got him to take off all his clothes, roll himself in a woollen rug, and put himself between two mattresses. The houses being well furnished with beds, we all did the like; and in this fashion we saw the year 1808 out.

Chapter 7
The Siege of Saragossa

New Year's Day 1809 was passed at Astorga. The weather continued bad, and it was necessary to allow the army to come together. Food was plentiful, and as there was not an inhabitant in the place we were all the freer to make the most of it. The suicide of the three grenadiers had affected the Emperor keenly; and in spite of rain and wind he visited all the men's quarters, talking to them and restoring their moral. All were awaiting the order to start next day in pursuit of the English, when an aide-de-camp from the Minister for War arrived bringing despatches which decided Napoleon to go no further in person. Doubtless it was the news of the hostile movements which Austria was beginning to make, in order to attack the French Empire while Napoleon and a part of the Grand Army were far away in Spain. The Emperor then resolved to return to France to prepare for this new war with the Austrians; but not wishing to lose the chance of chastising the English, be ordered Ney and Soult to pursue. They set out, their troops marching past the Emperor.

The English troops are excellent; but as they are only raised by voluntary enlistment, and as this becomes difficult in time of war, they are forced to admit married men, who are allowed to be accompanied by their families. Consequently the regiments took along with them a great number of women and children; a serious disadvantage which Great Britain has never been able to remedy. Thus, just as the corps of Soult and Ney were marching past the Emperor outside Astorga, cries were heard from a great barn. The door was opened, and it was found to contain 1000 to 1200 English women and children, who, exhausted by the long march of the previous days through rain, mud, and streams, were unable to keep up with the army and had taken refuge in this place. For forty-eight hours they had lived on raw barley. Most of the women and children were good-looking, in spite of the muddy rags in which they were clad. They flocked round the Emperor, who was touched by their misery and gave them lodging and food in the town; sending a flag of trace to let the English general know that when the weather permitted they would be sent back to him.

Marshal Soult came up with the enemy in the mountains of Leon and beat his rear-guard at Villafranca, where we lost General Colbert and his aide-de-camp Latour-Maubourg. The English army reached the port of Corunna after a hasty march, but a terrible storm made its embarkation very difficult, and it was compelled to give battle to Marshal Soult's troops who were close on its heels. The commander-in-chief, Sir John Moore, was killed, and his army only succeeded in reaching its vessels after immense loss. This event, which the French at first regarded as an advantage, turned out unlucky, for General Moore was replaced by Wellington, who afterwards did us so much harm.

At Astorga my brother, who was on Berthier's staff, was captured by guerrillas when on his way to Madrid with despatches. I shall have more to say about this.

While Soult was pursuing the retreating enemy towards Corunna, the Emperor, accompanied by Marshal Lannes, went back to Valladolid to get on the road to France. He stayed two days in that town, ordering Lannes to go and take command of the two corps which were besieging Saragossa, and after taking that place to rejoin him at Paris. But before leaving us, the Emperor, wishing to show his satisfaction with Lannes' staff, invited the marshal to hand in a scheme of recommendations for promotion with regard to his officers. I was entered for the rank of major and quite expected to get it, especially when I heard that the marshal on leaving the Emperor's study had asked for me. But my hopes were cruelly overthrown. The marshal said to me kindly that when he was asking for a step for me, he thought he ought also to recommend his old friend Captain Dagusan, but that the Emperor had begged him to choose between Dagusan and me. 'I cannot make up my mind,' said the marshal, 'for the wound which you received at Agreda and your behaviour in that difficult business put the right on your side; but Dagusan is old, and is making his last campaign. Still I would not commit an injustice for the world, and I leave it to you to settle which of the two names I shall have entered on the commission which the Emperor is about to sign.' It was an embarrassing position for me; my heart was very full. However, I answered that he must put M. Dagusan's name on the commission. The marshal embraced me with tears in his eyes, promising that after the siege of Saragossa I should certainly get my step. That evening the marshal called his officers together to announce the promotions. Guéhéneuc had his colonelcy confirmed, Saint-Mars was appointed lieutenant-colonel, Dagusan major, d'Albuquerque and Watteville got the Legion of Honour, de Viry and Labédoyère were captains; I got nothing.

Next day we left Valladolid, riding by short stages to Saragossa. Lannes took the command of the whole besieging force to the number of 30,000 men, who were under the orders of Marshal Mortier, Junot replacing Moncey.

Before the great insurrection which followed the captivity of Ferdinand VII., the town of Saragossa had been unfortified, but on learning what had happened at Bayonne, and the violence which Napoleon was doing to Spain in placing his brother Joseph on the throne, Saragossa gave the signal for resistance. Its population rose as one man; monks, women and children took up arms. The town was surrounded by immense and solidly-built convents; these were fortified, and guns placed in them. All the houses were loopholed, and the streets barricaded; powder, cannon-balls, and bullets were manufactured, and great stores of food collected. All the inhabitants enrolled themselves, and took as their commander Count Palafox, one of the colonels of the body-guard and a devoted friend of Ferdinand, whom he had followed to Bayonne, returning to Aragon after the King's arrest. It was during the summer of 1808 that the Emperor heard of the revolt, and the intention to defend Saragossa, but, being still under the delusion to which Murat's despatches had given rise, he regarded the insurrection as a fire of straw which the presence of a few French regiments would put out. Still before employing force he thought to try persuasion. He applied to Prince Pignatelli, the greatest Aragonese noble, who was then in Paris, begging him to use his influence in the province to calm the excitement. Prince Pignatelli accepted this pacific duty, and went to Saragossa. The people ran to meet him, not doubting but that like Palafox he was come to fight the French. But no sooner had he spoken of submission than he was assailed by the mob, who would have hanged him if Palafox had not put him in a dungeon, where he remained eight or nine months.

Meanwhile, several French divisions under General Verdier appeared in June before Saragossa. The fortifications were still incomplete, and an attempt was made to carry the place by assault. But no sooner were our columns in the streets than a murderous fire from windows, towers, roofs, and cellars caused them such losses that they were obliged to retreat. Then our troops surrounded the place, and began a more methodical siege. This would probably have succeeded, had not King Joseph's retreat compelled the army before Saragossa to retreat, also abandoning part of their artillery.

The first siege thus failed, but when our troops had returned to Aragon victorious, the marshal came in 1809 to attack Saragossa afresh. The town was by this time in a much better state of defence, for the fortifications were completed, and all the warlike population of Aragon had thrown itself into the place. The garrison had been further strengthened by a large part of the army of Castaños, which we had beaten at Tudela, so that Saragossa was defended by more than 80,000 men, while the marshal had only 30,000 with which to besiege it. But our officers were excellent, order and discipline reigned in our ranks, while in the town all was inexperience and confusion. The besieged only agreed on one point—to defend themselves to the death. The peasants were the most determined; they had entered the town with their wives, their children, and even their herds, and each party of them had a quarter of the town or a house assigned to it for its dwelling-place, which they were sworn to defend. The people lived mixed up with their beasts in the most disgusting state of filth, the entrails of slaughtered animals lay about in the courtyards and in the rooms, and the besieged did not even take the trouble to remove the bodies of men who had died in consequence of the epidemic which this carelessness speedily developed. Religious fanaticism and the sacred love of country exalted their courage, and they blindly resigned themselves to the will of God. The Spaniards have preserved much of the Arab character; they are fatalists constantly repeating, 'Lo que ha de ser no puede faltar' ('That which is to be cannot fail'). Accordingly they took no precaution.

To attack such men by assault in a town where every house was a fortress would have been to repeat the mistake committed during the first siege, and to incur heavy losses without a chance of success. Accordingly, Marshal Lannes and General Lacoste, the commanding engineer, adopted a prudent method, which, though tedious, was the best way to bring about the surrender or destruction of the town. They began in the usual way by opening trenches, until the first houses were reached, then the houses were mined and blown up, defenders and all; then the next were mined, and so on. These works, however, involved considerable danger for the French, for as soon as one showed himself he was a mark to musket-shots from the Spaniards in the neighbouring buildings. General Lacoste fell in this way, at the moment when he was taking his place in front of a window to examine the interior of the town. Such was the determination of the Spaniards that while a house was being mined, and the dull sound of the rammer warned them that death was at hand, not one left the house which he had sworn to defend. We could hear them singing litanies, then at the moment when the walls flew into the air, and fell back with a crash, crushing the greater part of them, those who had escaped would collect about the ruins, and sheltering themselves behind the slightest cover would recommence their sharpshooting. Our soldiers, however, warned of the moment when the mine was going off, held themselves in readiness, and no sooner had the explosion taken place than they dashed on to the ruins, and, after killing all whom they found, established themselves behind bits of wall, threw up entrenchments with furniture and beams, and in the middle of the ruins constructed passages for the sappers who were going to mine the next house. In this way a good third of the town was destroyed, and the passages established among the ruins formed an inextricable labyrinth, through which one could only find one's way by the help of stakes which the engineer officers placed. Besides the mines, the French used artillery freely, and threw 11,000 shells into the town.

In spite of all Saragossa still held out. In vain did the marshal, touched by the heroism of the defence, send a flag of truce to propose a capitulation. It was refused, and the siege continued. The huge fortified convents could not be destroyed, like the houses, by mining; we, therefore, merely blew up a piece of their thick walls, and when the breach was made sent forward a column to the assault. The besieged would flock to the defence, and in the terrible fighting which resulted from these attacks we suffered our principal losses.

The best fortified convents were those of the Inquisition and of Santa Engracia. A mine had just been completed under the latter when the marshal, sending for me in the middle of the night, told me that in order to hasten my promotion to the rank of major he designed for me a most important duty. 'At daybreak,' said he, 'the mine which is to breach the wall of Santa Engracia will be fired. Eight companies of grenadiers are to assault; I have given orders that the captains should be chosen from those junior to you; I give you the command of the column. Carry the convent, and I feel certain that one of the first messengers from Paris will bring your commission as major.' I accepted with gratitude, though suffering at the moment a good deal from my wound. The flesh in cicatrising had formed a lump which prevented me from wearing military headgear, so Dr. Assalagny, the surgeon-major of the chasseurs, had reduced it with lunar caustic. This painful operation had been performed the day before; I had been feverish all night, and consequently was not in very good condition for leading an assault. No matter; there was no room for hesitation, and I can admit, too, that I was exceedingly proud of the command entrusted to me. Eight companies of grenadiers to a mere captain was magnificent.

I hastened to get ready, and as day dawned I went to the trenches. There I found General Rasout, who, after having handed over the command of the grenadiers to me, observed that, as the mine could not be fired for an hour, I should do well to use this time in examining the wall which was to be blown up, and in calculating the width of the resulting breach so as to arrange my attack. I started, with an adjutant of engineers to show me the way, through the ruins of a whole quarter which had already been thrown down. Finally, I reached the foot of the convent wall where the territory conquered by us came to an end. I found myself in a little court; a light infantry picket, which occupied a sort of cellar hard by, had a sentry in this court, who was sheltered from musket-shots by a heap of planks and doors. The engineer officer, showing me a thick wall in front of us, said that was the one which was to be blown up. In one of the corners of the court whence a pump had been torn away, some stones had fallen out, and left a gap. The sentry showed me that by stooping down one could see through this opening the legs of a stormy force of the enemy posted in the convent garden. In order to verify his statement and notice the lie of the ground on which I was going to fight, I stooped down. At that moment a Spaniard posted on the tower of Santa Engracia fired a shot at me, and I fell on the stones.

I felt no pain at first, and thought that the adjutant standing by me had inadvertently given me a push. Presently, however, the blood flowed copiously; I had got a bullet in the left side very near the heart. The adjutant helped me to rise, and we went into the cellar where the soldiers were. I was losing so much blood that I was on the point of fainting. There were no stretchers, so the soldiers passed a musket under my arms, another under my knees, and thus carried me through the thousand-and-one passages which had been made through the debris of this quarter to the place where I had left General Rasout. There I recovered my senses. The general wished to have me attended to, but I preferred to be under Dr. Assalagny, so, pressing my handkerchief on the wound, I had myself taken to Marshal Lannes' headquarters, a cannon-shot from the town. When they saw me arrive, all covered with blood, carried by soldiers, one of whom was supporting my head, the marshal and my comrades thought I was dead. Dr. Assalagny assured them to the contrary, and hastened to dress my wound. The difficulty was where to put me, for, as all the furniture of the establishment had been burnt during the siege, there was not a bed in the place. We used to sleep on the bricks wherewith the rooms were paved. The marshal and all my comrades at once gave their cloaks: these were piled up, and I was laid on them. The doctor examined my wound, and found that I had been struck by a projectile which must have been flat because it had passed between two ribs without breaking them, which an ordinary bullet would not have done. To find the object Assalagny put a probe into the wound, but when he found nothing his face grew anxious. Finding that I complained of severe pain in the loins, he turned me on my face, and examined my back.

Hardly had he touched the spot where the ribs are connected to the spine than I involuntarily gave a cry. The projectile was there. Assalagny then took a knife, made a large incision, perceived a metallic body showing between two ribs and tried to extract it with the forceps. He did not, however, succeed, though his violent efforts lifted me up, until he made one of my comrades sit on my shoulders, and another on my legs. At length he succeeded in extracting a lead bullet of the largest calibre. The Spaniards had hammered it flat till it had the shape of a half-crown, across was scratched on each face and small notches all round gave it the appearance of the wheel of a watch. It was these teeth which had caught in the muscles, and rendered the extraction so difficult. Thus crushed out, the ball presented too large a surface to enter a musket, and must have been fired from a blunderbuss. Striking edgewise, it had acted like a cutting instrument, passed between two ribs, and travelled round the interior of the chest to make its exit in the same way as its entry, fortunately preserving sufficient force to make its way through the muscles of the back. The marshal, wishing to let the Emperor know with what fanatical determination the inhabitants of Saragossa were defending themselves, sent him the bullet extracted from my body. Napoleon, after examining it, had it brought to my mother, at the same time announcing to her that I was about to be promoted to major.

Assalagny was one of the first surgeons of the day, and thanks to him, my wound, which might have been mortal, was a case of rapid cure. The marshal had a folding bedstead which he took on campaign. This he lent me, with mattress and sheets; my valise served me for pillow, my cloak for blankets. Still, I was not well off, for my room had neither door nor window, and wind and rain entered. The ground floor of the house, too, was used for a hospital, the sounds and odours of which reached my room; more than two hundred sutlers had set up their booths round the head-quarters. The camp was close by; so that there was eternal singing, shouting, drumming, and the bass to this fiendish concert was supplied by numerous cannon, booming night and day. I got no sleep; but at the end of a fortnight my vigorous constitution got the upper hand, and I was able to leave my bed.

The climate being mild, I was also able to take short walks, leaning on the arm of Dr. Assalagny or my friend, de Viry; but their duties did not allow of their staying with me long, and I suffered much from ennui. One day my servant came in to say that an old hussar, with tears streaming down his face, was asking to see me. As you will guess, it was my old tutor, Sergeant Pertelay. His regiment had just come to Spain, and hearing that I had been wounded, he came straight to me. I was glad to see the good man again, and gave him a cordial greeting. After this he often came to visit me, and divert me by his interminable yarns and the quaint advice which he still thought himself entitled to give me. My convalescence did not last long, and by March 15 I was nearly well, though weak.

Typhus, famine, fire, and sword had destroyed nearly a third of the inhabitants and garrison of Saragossa, and still no thought of surrender entered the minds of the survivors. The principal forts had been taken, and the mines had destroyed a very large portion of the town. The monks had persuaded the poor folk that the French would massacre them, and none dared come out. Good luck and Lannes' kindness at last put an end to this memorable siege. On March 20 the French carried a nunnery by assault. Besides the nuns, they found three hundred women of all classes who had taken refuge in the church. They were treated with respect, and brought to the marshal. The poor creatures, having been surrounded for several days, had received no food, and were famishing. Lannes led them himself to the camp market, where, summoning the carabiniers, he ordered them to bring food for the women, making himself responsible for payment. Nor did his generosity stop there; he had them all taken back to Saragossa. On their return the inhabitants, who had followed their movements from roofs and towers, rushed forward to hear their adventures. They all spoke well of the French marshal and soldiers, and from that moment the excitement subsided and a surrender was decided upon. That evening Saragossa capitulated.

Lannes' first condition was, that Prince Fuentes-Pignatelli should be given up to him alive. The poor man arrived escorted by a savage-looking gaoler with pistols in his sash, who had the impudence to bring him to the marshal's room, demanding a receipt from the hand of the French commander-in-chief. The marshal had him turned out; but as the man would not go without his receipt, Labédoyère, never very patient, lost his temper, and literally kicked him downstairs. As for Prince Pignatelli, he was indeed a painful sight, owing to his sufferings in prison. He was devoured by fever, and we had not a bed to offer him; for, as I have said, the marshal was lodging in a house utterly unfurnished, the sole advantage of which was that it lay near the point of attack. Junot meanwhile, being less conscientious, had established himself a league away in a rich convent, where he lived very comfortably. He offered hospitality to the prince, who, fatally for himself, accepted it. Junot gave him such a 'blow-out' that his stomach, undermined by prison diet, gave way under the sudden change, and Prince Pignatelli died just as he was restored to freedom and happiness. He left an income of more than 900,000 francs to a collateral relation who had hardly a farthing.

When a place capitulates it is usual for the officers to retain their swords. This practice was followed at Saragossa, except in the case of the governor, Palafox, touching whom the marshal had received special instructions from the Emperor, on the following grounds:—

Count Palafox, a devoted friend of Ferdinand, had followed him to Bayonne. Thrown into consternation by the abdication of that prince and his father, the Spanish grandees summoned by Napoleon to a national assembly, finding themselves in France and in Napoleon's power, for the most part recognised Joseph as their king. Palafox, it appears, under the same pressure, did the same; but hardly had he returned to Spain when he promptly protested against the moral violence which, he asserted, had been used towards him, and hastened to put himself at the head of the insurgents at Saragossa. The Emperor regarded this conduct as perfidious, and ordered that, when the town was taken, Count Palafox should be treated, not as a prisoner of war, but as a state prisoner, and accordingly disarmed and sent to prison at Vincennes. Marshal Lannes, therefore, found himself under the necessity of sending an officer to arrest the governor and demand his sword. He entrusted the duty to d'Albuquerque, who found it all the more painful that he was not only a Spaniard, but a relation and old friend of Palafox's. I have never been able to divine the marshal's motive in selecting him for such a duty. D'Albuquerque, however, had to obey, and entered Saragossa more dead than alive. He presented himself to Palafox, who handed him his sword, saying, with a noble pride: 'If your ancestors, the famous d'Albuquerques, could return to life, there is not one of them who would not sooner be in the place of the prisoner who is surrendering this sword, covered with honour, than in that of the renegade who is receiving it on behalf of the enemies of his country. 'Poor d'Albuquerque, terrified and almost fainting, had to lean against a piece of furniture to avoid falling. The scene was related to us by Captain Pasqual, who, having been ordered to take charge of Palafox after his arrest, was present at the interview. Count Palafox remained in France till 1814.

How strange are human affairs! Palafox having been proclaimed governor of Saragossa when the insurrection broke out, has received both from fame and history the credit of the heroic defence. He really contributed little to it, for he fell ill early in the siege, and handed over the command to General Saint-Marc, a Belgian in the Spanish service, and it was he who sustained all our attacks with such remarkable courage and ability. But as he was a foreigner, Spanish pride assigned all the glory of the defence to Palafox, whose name will go down to posterity, while that of the brave and ardent General Saint-Marc is mentioned in no history, and remains forgotten.

The garrison, 40,000 in number, were forwarded to France as prisoners of war, but two-thirds of them escaped and recommenced the slaughter of Frenchmen as members of guerrilla bands. They had carried away the germs or typhus, and died later. The ruined streets of the city were a perfect charnel-house, and the contagion spread to the French troops who formed the new garrison.

Chapter 8
Landshut and Eckmühl

With the capture of Saragossa, Marshal Lannes' work was done, and he started to rejoin the Emperor at Paris and accompany him into Germany. We rode the distance from Aragon to Bidassoa. The celebrated guerilla prince attacked our escort in the Pyrenees near Pampeluna, and a servant of the marshal's who acted as outrider was killed. At Saint-Jean de Luz the marshal found his carriage and offered places in it to Saint-Mars, Le Couteulx, and myself. I sold my horses, and de Viry took my servant back. One of the marshal's valets having vainly tried to act as outrider, and there being no postilions, we three offered to do three stages apiece. I admit that this riding post cost me a good deal, hardly healed as I was of my two wounds, but I reckoned on my youth and my strong constitution. I began my duties on the darkest of nights and under a violent storm, and besides, as I was not preceded by a postilion as the outrider who carries despatches usually is, I got into bad places, and rode my horse into holes; the carriage was at my heels, I did not know the position of the post-houses, which are hard to find at night and in such weather. To finish my misfortunes, I had to wait for some time for the ferry-boat across the Adour at Peyrehorade. I took cold and was shivering, and in a good deal of pain from my wound when I took my place in the carriage. You may see from these details that an aide-de-camp's life is not all rosewater. We stayed forty-eight hours at Lectoure, where the marshal had a comfortable house in the buildings of the old bishop's palace. Then we continued our journey towards Paris. As the marshal travelled night and day and could not bear the smell of cooked food, we were obliged to fast pretty well for six stages, and then only to eat as we galloped. I was, therefore, much surprised when one evening the marshal begged me to stop at Pétignac or Le Roulet, and to announce that he would halt an hour for supper. I was especially surprised when I saw that the house to which I was directed was not an inn; but when the marshal's coming was announced, the inhabitants displayed the most lively joy, laid the table, prepared a succulent repast, and flew out to meet the carriage. The marshal, with tears in his eyes, kissed them all round, including the smallest brats, and showed every sign of the warmest friendship towards the postmaster. After dinner he bade Saint-Mars take out of his pocketbook a superb gold watch and a chain of the same metal clasped with a big diamond, presented these to the postmaster and his wife, gave 300 or 400 francs to the maids, and departed after most tender embraces.

I supposed that this family were the marshal's relations, but when we were in the carriage he said to us, 'You are doubtless astonished at the interest I take in these good people, but the husband did me a great service, for he saved my life in Syria.' Then the marshal related to us how, when he was a general of division at Acre, he was leading an assault against the tower when he received a bullet through his neck, and fell senseless. His soldiers, deeming him dead, were retiring in disorder before thousands of Turks, who cut off the heads of such as they could catch and placed them on the points of the palisades. A brave captain appealed to the men to bring away the body of their general, carried him off, and, when exhausted, dragged him by one leg to the back of the trenches. The soil being sandy, the general's head received no injury, and his senses being restored by the shaking he was tended by Larrey, who quite brought him back to life. The captain having been severely wounded left the army with a small pension, and married a wife without much money. But the marshal became a second Providence for the family. He purchased for them a postmastership, some fields, some horses, and a house and had the eldest son educated at his own expense until the others were old enough to leave their parents. So naturally these good people were as grateful to the marshal, as he to his rescuer. The ex-captain no doubt lost a good deal when Marshal Lannes died. He never saw him again after that day.

We continued our journey, with the cold always increasing, which made the way from Orleans to Paris wretched enough. I arrived on April 2, terribly tired and in much pain. The joy with which I met my mother again was mingled with bitter, for she had just heard that my brother had been taken prisoner by Spanish guerrillas, and I was about to start on a new campaign.

The moment I got to Paris the marshal took me to the minister of war to find out what he had done for me. My commission as major lacked only the Emperor's signature, but Napoleon being much occupied with the movements of the Austrian army did not ask the minister for the document, which was all ready, and made no promotion. An evil fate pursued me.

The capital was much excited. The English, seeing us occupied in Spain, thought that the moment had come to raise the whole North of Europe against Napoleon. The plan was premature, for the Emperor still could dispose of vast influence and a strong force in Germany. Prussia did not dare to stir; the princes of the Germanic Confederation placed their armies at the service of Napoleon; even Russia sent a corps of 25,000 men. In spite of this, the Austrians in the pay of England had just declared war, and their armies were advancing on our ally, Bavaria. The Emperor was making ready to go to Germany, whither Lannes was to follow him. All the carriages had been reserved by the hundreds of generals and others, and I was in a difficulty, for both the Emperor and the marshal were to leave Paris on April 13, and I had orders to start a day before them. I had therefore to make up my mind to ride post once more. Luckily, a week's rest had reduced the irritation of the wound in my side. That in my forehead was healed over, and I was careful to wear a cocked hat instead of my heavy busby. My servant, Woirland, went with me, but being a very bad rider, he often fell off, only saying, as he got up again, 'How tough you are! Oh, yes; you are tough!'

In forty-eight hours I covered the hundred and twenty leagues between Paris and Strasburg, in spite of rain and snow. Woirland could do no more; we had to change our mode of travelling. Besides, I knew that in Germany nobody posted on horseback, and we were still only half-way to Augsburg, our rendezvous. At last I found a carriage, and reached Augsburg, where I joined my comrades. The Emperor, the marshal, and nearly all the troops were already in the field. I managed to buy a horse in the town. I exchanged my carriage for another, and we set off in the saddle. In the course of a few weeks we had sold our horses cheap, and spent a great deal of money—all to go and meet the bullets which were to take away many of our lives. You may call the feeling which urged us love of glory, or perhaps madness; it was an imperious master, and we marched without looking back.

We reached head-quarters on April 20, during the action at Abensberg. Marshal Lannes complimented us on our zeal, and sent us off at once into the thick of the fire to bear his orders. The Austrians, under the Archduke Charles, withdrew behind the Danube at Landshut, beyond the Iser, as usual omitting to destroy the bridges. Napoleon attacked Landshut with the infantry. They crossed the bridge twice under a hail of bullets, but on reaching the other side were stopped by a huge gate, which the enemy's rear-guard was defending with a brisk fire from the walls of the town. Twice our columns were repulsed with loss, but the Emperor, who set very much by the capture of Landshut, that he might cross the Iser before the archduke could organise his resistance more thoroughly, ordered a third attack. The troops told off for this were getting ready to march when Napoleon, seeing his aide-de-camp, General Mouton, who was coming to report the result of a mission which he had given him that morning, said, 'You come just in time; put yourself at the head of that column, and carry the town of Landshut. So perilous a task set him without notice would have astonished a man less brave than General Mouton. He was in no way perturbed by it. Dismounting and drawing his sword, he ordered the charge to be sounded. He was the first to dash over the bridge at the head of the grenadiers. Finding the gate of Landshut in his way, he had it broken down with hatchets, put all who resisted to the sword, took the town, and came calmly back to the Emperor with his report of the mission which he had undertaken in the morning. Strangely enough, during their conversation not a word was said about the capture of Landshut, and the Emperor never spoke of it to General Mouton; but after the campaign he sent him a remarkable picture by Hersant, in which the general is represented marching to the attack of the place at the head of his column. This keepsake from Napoleon was worth more than the highest eulogies.

Crossing the Iser, the French army marched on Eckmühl, where the bulk of the Austrian army was massed. The Emperor and Marshal Lannes passed the night at Landshut; a battle on the following day appeared imminent. The town and neighbourhood were full of troops. In every direction staff officers were carrying orders and returning. My comrades and I were fully occupied, and as we only had very second-rate horses, picked up anyhow, and they were pretty thoroughly tired, we foresaw that it would be difficult for us to perform our duties satisfactorily in the battle of the morrow.

When I came in about ten o'clock, on returning from an errand three or four leagues from Landshut, Marshal Lannes gave me an order to carry to General Gudin. His division being a long way off, I was to remain with him till the marshal arrived in the field. This was embarrassing, for the horse which I had been riding was knocked up, the marshal had not one to lend me, and there was no French cavalry at Landshut which might be required to supply me with one. I could not go to the Emperor's quarters to tell the marshal that I was practically horseless, yet without a good steed how was I to carry an order on which perhaps the safety of the army depended? I got out of the difficulty by what I admit was a wicked act, but perhaps excusable in the circumstances. You shall decide. I called my servant, Woirland, a practised 'snapper-up of unconsidered trifles,' who had served his apprenticeship in Humbert's Black Legion, and was never at a loss. I imparted my difficulty to him, and bade him procure me a horse at any price; I simply must have one. 'You shall have it,' said he, and leaving the town he made for the camp of the Wurtemberg cavalry. The men were all asleep, sentries and all; Woirland inspected the horses at his ease, saw one that he liked, unfastened it, and, at the risk of getting knocked on the head if anyone saw him, he brought it out of the camp, turned everything off its back, came back to the town, put my saddle on it, and informed me that it was all ready. Now the horses of the Wurtemberg cavalry are marked on the near thigh with a pair of stag's horns, so I could easily recognise whence the new mount, which my Figaro had brought me, was procured. He did not deny it; the horse, to put it plainly, had been stolen. But see how a difficult situation stretches the conscience! To silence mine, I said to myself: 'If I do not take this animal, which belongs to the King of Wurtemberg, it is impossible for me to bear to General Gudin the orders which he has got to execute at daybreak. This may involve the loss of a battle, and cost the King of Wurtemberg his crown. Therefore, in making use of a horse from his army I am indirectly doing him a service. Besides, as the Emperor gave him a kingdom, he may very well lend the Emperor a horse, which I shall return when I have made use of it to their joint advantage.' Whether this reasoning would satisfy a casuist I know not, but matters were pressing; I leapt into the saddle, and galloped off. Master Woirland knew his business, it was an excellent horse. The only thing which disturbed me was that the infernal pair of horns stamped on its thigh, showing whence it came, exposed me to the chance of having it claimed by some Wurtemberg officer. Finally, at daybreak, I reached General Gudin, just as his troops were marching. I went with him until the Emperor and Marshal Lannes overtook us with the main body. The battle was fought, victory was never for a moment in doubt. Marshal Davout distinguished himself, earning the title which was given him later on of Prince of Eckmühl.

My horse behaved splendidly, but his last day had come. In the hottest of the action, Marshal Lannes sent one of his least experienced aides-de-camp to General Saint-Sulpice with orders to charge with his cuirassiers a brigade of the enemy's cavalry. The aide-de-camp explained matters so badly that the general was going off in quite a different direction, and the marshal perceiving this told me to place myself at the head of the division, and to guide it towards the enemy by the high road which runs through the village of Eckmühl. While Lannes was explaining his wishes to me, studying a map which he, I, and General Cervoni were holding each by one side, a cannon-ball came across it, and threw General Cervoni stone dead against the marshal's shoulder. He was covered with the blood of his friend, who had come from Corsica only the day before on purpose to make this campaign. Deeply grieved as he was, he continued to give me his orders with perfect clearness, and I hastened to General Saint-Sulpice, and rode beside him at the head of the cuirassiers towards Eckmühl.

The village was occupied by a regiment of Croats, who instead of firing upon us out of the windows where they were out of reach of our sabres, bravely but stupidly left their excellent position, and came down into the street, intending to form close column, and stop our squadrons with their bayonets. The French cuirassiers gave them no time for this; they came up so quickly that the Croats, caught in disarray just as they were coming out of the houses, were driven in and sabred, and soon the street was piled with their bodies. They did not, however, yield without a valiant defence. One battalion especially made a vigorous resistance, and my horse having received in the scuffle the point of a bayonet in his heart went forward a few steps, and fell dead against a corner stone in such wise that one of my legs was caught under the poor animal's body, and my knee pressed against the stone, so that I was quite unable to move. Woe to the dismounted horseman in such cases! No one stops to pick him up, nor, indeed, could he if he would; so the first regiment of our cuirassiers, after cutting down all the Croats who did not lay down their arms promptly, continued the charge, and passed through the village followed by the whole division at a gallop.

Horses, unless very tired, seldom set their feet on the body of a man lying on the ground. Thus the whole division of cuirassiers passed over me without doing the slightest injury. Still, I could not free myself, and my situation became more unpleasant when I foresaw that our cuirassiers would be repulsed and driven back through the village by a very strong force of the enemy's cavalry, which I had seen before the charge on the further side of Eckmühl. I was afraid that the Austrian troopers would serve me out by way of revenging the Croats. During the moment of quiet which succeeded the uproar of the street fighting and the passage of cavalry, I perceived at no great distance two grenadiers of the enemy's who had laid aside their pieces, and were helping their wounded comrades to rise. I beckoned them to come to me and assist me in getting my leg free; whether from good nature or from fear that I might have them killed, although at that moment I had no Frenchmen at my orders, they obeyed. They knew that our cuirassiers were in front, and probably regarded themselves as prisoners; anyhow, these kind of soldiers do not reflect much. They came up, and I admit that when I saw one of them pull from his pocket a knife to cut the leather of the stirrup which held my foot under the horse, I was afraid that the fancy might seize him of sticking it, as he might quite safely have done, into me. But he was honest, and with the help of his comrade succeeded in setting me on my feet. I made them take my saddle and bridle, and left Eckmühl to rejoin our infantry, which was still outside.

The two Croats followed me in the most docile manner, and it was lucky for them they did, for hardly were we out of the village when a fearful noise arose behind us. It was caused by the return of our squadrons, who, as I expected, were driven back by the enemy's superior force, and these in their turn were sabring all who lagged behind. Our cuirassiers, furious at their repulse, tried as they galloped past me to run through the Croats who were carrying my saddle. The men had helped me; I objected, therefore, to their being killed, and ordered them by signs to lie down in a ditch, where the sabres could not reach them. I should have put myself there if I had not observed at the head of the Austrian force some Uhlans, who could easily have reached me with their lances. Luckily for us, help came to Saint-Sulpice's division before it had gone 300 or 400 paces, for, seeing it in retreat, the Emperor sent forward two divisions of cavalry, which were rapidly hastening to meet us. But short as was the distance which I had to traverse to escape the Austrian lances, it was a long way for a dismounted man. Two cuirassiers took me between them, and each giving me a hand carried me along so well that with the help of long strides, I could keep up for a couple of minutes with their galloping horses. This was all that mattered, the supports came up promptly, the enemy stayed their pursuit and were even driven back beyond Eckmühl, which our troops re-occupied. I was glad to be at the end of my more than double-quick march, for I was out of breath, and could not have kept it up. I had a good opportunity of observing how ill-suited for war are such big and heavy boots as our cuirassiers then wore. A young officer of the squadron which saved me had his horse killed, and two of his men stretched out their hands to help him to run as I had done, but although he was tall and slight and far more active than I, his stiff and heavy foot-gear prevented him from moving his legs quickly enough to keep up with the horses. He was compelled to let go of the helping hands, and the next time we saw the ground which we had so rapidly crossed, we found the lieutenant killed by the stroke of a lance. We could see that he had been trying to get rid of his large boots, one of which was pulled half off. My little hussar boots, being light and flexible, had been no hindrance to me.

Hoping to recover my saddle and bridle, I returned to the ditch, where I had made the two Croats hide, and found them, quietly lying there. Several charges had taken place across their lair without their receiving the least scratch. I rewarded them, and marched them in front of me to the hillock, where the Emperor and Marshal Lannes were, knowing well that my chief would not wish to lose my services during the rest of the battle, and would make one of the regiments which were near him lend me a horse. He gave orders accordingly, but as at the moment there were none but cuirassiers in the neighbourhood, they brought me an immense heavy animal, quite unfit to carry an aide-de-camp rapidly from point to point. The marshal having remarked this, a colonel of Wurtemberg Light Horse, who happened to be behind the Emperor, eager to do a polite thing, bade his orderly dismount; and there I was again on an excellent horse, marked with the stag's horns. The colonel's kindness renewed, in some measure, my remorse for the crime I had committed in the morning, but I silenced it by repeating my somewhat Jesuitical arguments. The joke of the thing was that, as I was bearing an order to the reserve, I fell in with my servant, Woirland, who, coming up to give me some provisions out of his always well-filled saddle-bags, exclaimed, 'Why, that horse is the devil! He was grey this morning, and now he's black!'

The battle of Eckmühl began and lasted all day on broken ground, covered with small hills and copse-wood; but, as one advances towards the Danube, the country grows level and bare until one enters the immense plain which extends to Ratisbon. The Austrian cavalry is one of the best in Europe, but under the plea that they must reserve it to cover their retreat in the event of their being beaten, they employ it not at all, or very little, during the fight. This leads to their defeat, and compels a retreat which they might have avoided. Then, however, their cavalry does cover their retrograde movement admirably. This happened at Eckmühl, for, as soon as the Archduke Charles saw that the battle was lost, and that his infantry, driven out of the hilly ground, were exposed to the

French squadrons, while making it difficult to retreat in the plain, he caused the whole of his cavalry to take the offensive. They came bravely forward to check us, while the Austrian infantry, artillery, and baggage were retiring upon Ratisbon. The Emperor, on his side, advanced our hussars and chasseurs, supported by the strong brigades of Saint-Sulpice and Nansouty, to which the enemy opposed two brigades of the same arm. The light cavalry on both sides drew off promptly to the flank, to avoid being crushed by these formidable steel-clad masses, who advanced rapidly upon each other, met with a shock, penetrated each other, and became one immense mêlée. A faint twilight, and the beams of a rising moon, alone gave light for this terrible and majestic combat. The shouts of the fighters were drowned by the sound of repeated blows of heavy sabres upon thousands of helmets and cuirasses, from which the sparks flew in numbers. Austrians and French both wished to remain masters of the field. Courage, tenacity, and strength were well matched, but the defensive arms were unequal, for the Austrian cuirasses only covered them in front, and gave no protection to the back in a crowd. In this way, the French troopers, who, having double cuirasses and no fear of being wounded from behind, had only to think of thrusting, were able to give point at the enemy's backs, and slew a great many of them with small loss to themselves. This unequal fight lasted some minutes; finally the Austrians, with immense loss in killed and wounded, were compelled, for all their bravery, to abandon the ground. When they had wheeled about, they understood still better what a disadvantage it is not to have a cuirass behind as well as in front. The fight became a butchery, as our cuirassiers pursued the enemy, and for the space of half a league the ground was piled with killed and wounded cuirassiers. Few would have escaped, had not our men stayed to charge some battalions of Hungarian grenadiers, which they broke up and captured almost entirely. This fight settled a question which had been long debated, as to the necessity of double cuirasses, for the proportion of Austrians wounded and killed amounted respectively to eight and thirteen for one Frenchman.

After this terrible charge, the enemy, unable to resist any further, fled in the greatest disorder, briskly pursued along the road—fugitives pell-mell with victors. Marshal Lannes proposed to the Emperor that he should profit by the rout of the Austrians to destroy their army completely, hurling it back on the Danube, and entering Ratisbon with it. But the other marshals pointed out that we were still three leagues from that place, that our infantry was weary, and that it would be dangerous to risk a night engagement against an enemy which had shown such obstinate courage. The Emperor therefore ordered the pursuit to cease, and the army bivouacked in the plain. The Austrians admitted a loss of 5,000 killed, and 15,000 prisoners, twelve colours, and sixteen guns; of ours they only captured a few men, and killed 1,500. In such disorder did the enemy retreat that in the night one of their cavalry regiments was straying about our camp, unable to find any line of retreat open. Colonel Guéhéneuc, bearing an order, stumbled upon this force, and the commander, after having seized M. Guéhéneuc, said, 'You were my prisoner, now I am yours,' and we saw Guéhéneuc come up, much to the Emperor's amusement, and the Austrian regiment which had surrendered to him.

After such a success, captured horses were, as you may suppose, plentiful in the camp. I bought three capital animals for a few louis, and being thus completely mounted for the rest of the campaign I gave up the two screws which I had previously acquired, and returned to the Wurtembergers the horse which they had lent me.

Chapter 9
Ratisbon

The archduke had made use of the darkness to reach Ratisbon, where the bridge enabled him to transport his baggage and the greater part of his army to the left bank of the Danube. Then we were able to perceive the extent of the Emperor's foresight in having at the outset of the campaign ordered Davout—coming up from Hamburg and Hanover, with a view of joining the Grand Army on the right bank of the Danube—to secure possession of Ratisbon and his bridge by leaving a regiment there. Davout had, accordingly, left the 65th of the line, commanded by a relative of his, Colonel Coutard, wishing to give him an opportunity of distinguishing himself. But Coutard could not hold the place, and, after some hours' fighting, surrendered it to the Austrians, who, but for the means of retreat afforded by the bridge, would have been compelled to lay down their arms. Colonel Coutard having stipulated for the return to France of himself and his officers alone, the Emperor decreed that in future the officers of a corps which had been compelled to capitulate should share the fate of their men, hoping thereby to encourage commanders to resist more stubbornly.

The Emperor could not, however, march on to Vienna until Ratisbon was retaken, otherwise, as soon as he had moved forward, the archduke would have crossed the Danube by the bridge, and, bringing his army back to the right bank, would have attacked us in rear. We had then, at all costs, to take possession of the place. Marshal Lannes was charged with this difficult duty. The enemy had 6,000 men in Ratisbon, whom they could reinforce to any extent by help of the bridge; many guns were in position on the ramparts, and the parapet was garnished with infantry. The fortifications of Ratisbon were old and bad, the ditches were dry and used as kitchen gardens. Still, although the means of defence were not such as could have resisted a regular siege, the town was in a position—especially as the garrison could communicate with an army of more than 80,000 men—to repel a assault. To get into the place it was necessary to descend a deep ditch with the help of ladders, cross it under fire from the enemy, and scale the rampart, the angles of which were commanded by a flanking fire.

The Emperor, having dismounted, took up his position on a hillock a short cannon-shot from the town. Having noticed near the Straubing gate a house which had imprudently been built against the rampart, he sent forward some twelve-pounders and howitzers, and ordering them to concentrate their fire upon this house, so that its ruins, falling into the ditch, might partially fill it, and form at the foot of the wall an incline by which our troops might mount to the assault. While the artillery was executing this order, Lannes brought Morand's division close up to the promenade which goes round the town; and, in order to shelter his troops from the enemy's fire, up to the last moment he placed them in rear of a large stone store-house, which appeared to have been placed there on purpose to aid our undertaking. Carts laden with ladders taken from the neighbouring villages were brought up to this point, where perfect protection was obtained against the Austrian projectiles. While waiting till everything was ready, Marshal Lannes had gone back to the Emperor to receive his final orders. As they were chatting, a bullet—fired, in all probability, from one of the long-range Tyrolese rifles—struck Napoleon on the right ankle. The pain was at first so sharp that the Emperor had to lean upon Lannes, but Dr. Larrey, who quickly arrived, declared that the wound was trifling. If it had been severe enough to require an operation, the event would certainly have been considered a great misfortune for France; yet it might perhaps have spared her many calamities. However, the report that the Emperor had been wounded spread through the army. Officers and men ran up from all sides; in a moment Napoleon was surrounded by thousands of men, in spite of the fire which the enemy's guns concentrated on the vast group. The Emperor, wishing to withdraw his troops from this useless danger, and to calm the anxiety of the more distant corps, who were getting unsteady in their desire to come and see what was the matter, mounted his horse the instant his wound was dressed, and rode down the front of the whole line, amid loud cheers.

It was at this extempore review held in presence of the enemy that Napoleon first granted gratuities to private soldiers, appointing them knights of the Empire and members, at the same time, of the Legion of Honour. The regimental commanders recommended, but the Emperor also allowed soldiers who thought they had claims to come and represent them before him; then he decided upon them by himself. Now it befell that an old grenadier who had made the campaigns of Italy and Egypt, not hearing his name called, came up, and, in a calm tone of voice, asked for the Cross. 'But,' said Napoleon, 'what have you done to deserve it?' 'It was I, sir, who, in the desert of Joppa, when it was so terribly hot, gave you a water-melon.' 'I thank you for it again; but the gift of the fruit is hardly worth the Cross of the Legion of Honour.' Then the grenadier, who till then had been as cool as ice, working himself up into a frenzy, shouted, with the utmost volubility, 'Well, and don't you reckon seven wounds received at the bridge of Arcola, at Lodi and Castiglione, at the Pyramids, at Acre, Austerlitz, Friedland; eleven campaigns in Italy, Egypt, Austria, Prussia, Poland —' but the Emperor cut him short, laughing, and mimicking his excited manner, cried: 'There, there—how you work yourself up when you come to the essential point! That is where you ought to have begun; it is worth much more than your melon. I make you a knight of the Empire, with a pension of 1,200 francs. Does that satisfy you?' 'But, your majesty, I prefer the Cross.' 'You have both one and the other, since I make you knight.' ' Well, I would rather have the Cross.' The worthy grenadier could not be moved from that point, and it took all manner of trouble to make him understand that the title of knight of the Empire carried with it the Legion of Honour. He was not appeased on this point until the Emperor had fastened the decoration on his breast, and he seemed to think a great deal more of this than of his annuity of 1,200 francs. It was by familiarities of this kind that the Emperor made the soldiers adore him, but it was a means that was only available to a commander whom frequent victories had made illustrious; any other general would have injured his reputation by it.

As soon as Lannes gave notice that all was ready for the assault, we returned towards Ratisbon, the Emperor meanwhile going back to his hillock to witness the operations. The various army corps round him awaited events in silence. Our artillery had completely destroyed the house by the rampart, and its fragments falling into the ditch had made a slope practicable enough, but not reaching higher than to ten or twelve feet from the top of the wall; to reach this, therefore, ladders had to be placed on the rubbish no less than to descend into the ditch. On reaching the building, behind which Morand's division were taking shelter from the fire, Lannes called for fifty volunteers to go forward and plant the ladders. Many more than that number came forward, and the number had to be reduced. The brave fellows, led by picked officers, set out with admirable spirit; but they were hardly clear of the building when they met the hail of bullets, and were nearly all laid low. A few only continued to descend into the ditch, where the guns soon disabled them, and the remains of this first column fell back, streaming with blood, to the place where the division was sheltered. Nevertheless at the call of Lannes and Morand, fifty more volunteers appeared, and, seizing the ladders, made for the ditch. No sooner, however, did they show themselves than a still hotter fire nearly annihilated them. Cooled by these two repulses, the troops made no response to the marshal's third call for volunteers. If he had ordered one or more companies to march, they would, no doubt, have obeyed; but he knew well what a difference there is in point of effect between obedience on the soldiers' part and dash; and for the present danger volunteers were much better than troops obeying orders. Vainly, however, did the marshal renew his appeal to the bravest of a brave division; vainly did he call upon them to observe that the eyes of the Emperor and all the Grand Army were on them. A gloomy silence was the only reply, the men being convinced that to pass beyond the walls of the building into the enemy's fire was certain death. At length, Lannes exclaiming, 'Well, I will let you see that I was a grenadier before I was a marshal, and still am one,' seized a ladder, lifted it, and would have carried it towards the breach. His aides-de-camp tried to stop him; he resisted, and got angry with us. I ventured to say, 'Monsieur le Maréchal, you would not wish us to be disgraced, and that we should be if you were to receive the slightest wound in carrying that ladder to the ramparts as long as one of your aides-de-camp was left alive.' Then, in spite of his efforts, I dragged the end of the ladder from him, and put it on my shoulder, while de Viry took the other end, and our comrades by pairs took up other ladders.

At the sight of a marshal disputing with his aides-de-camp for the lead of the assault, a shout of enthusiasm went up from the whole division. Officers and soldiers wished to lead the column, and in their eagerness for this honour they pushed my comrades and me about, trying to get hold of the ladders. If however we had given them up, we should seem to have been playing a comedy to stimulate the troops. The wine had been drawn, and we had to drink it, bitter as it might be. Understanding this, the marshal let us have our way, though fully expecting to see the greater part of his staff exterminated as they marched at the head of this perilous attack.

I have said already that my comrades, although as brave as possible, lacked experience, and more especially what is called military tact. I made, therefore, no demur about taking the command of the little column. The matter was important enough to warrant it, and no one contested my right. Behind the building I organised the detachment which was to follow us. The destruction of the two former columns I ascribed to the imprudence with which their leaders had massed together the soldiers composing them. This arrangement was unsuitable in two ways. First, it gave the enemy the advantage of firing upon a mass instead of upon isolated men, and secondly, our grenadiers, who were laden with ladders, having formed a single group and getting in each other's way, had not been able to move fast enough to get quickly clear of the Austrian fire. I settled, therefore, that de Viry and I, carrying the first ladder, should start off at a run; that the second ladder should follow at twenty paces distant, and the rest in due course; that when we reached the promenade the ladders should be placed five feet apart to avoid confusion; that when we descended into the ditch we should leave every second ladder against the wall towards the promenade so that the troops might follow without delay; that the others should be lifted and carried quickly to the breach, where we should place them only a foot apart, both on account of the want of space and in order that we might reach the top of the rampart close together and push back the besieged when they tried to throw us down. This plan having been expounded and comprehended, the marshal, who approved it, cried, 'Off with you, my boys, and Ratisbon is taken.' At the word, de Viry and I darted out, crossed the promenade at a run, and, lowering our ladder, descended into the ditch. Our comrades followed with fifty grenadiers. In vain did the cannon thunder, the musketry rattle, grape-shot and bullets strike trees and walls. It is very difficult to take aim at isolated individuals moving very fast and twenty paces apart, and we got into the ditch without one man of our little column being wounded. The ladders already indicated were lifted, we carried them to the top of the rubbish from the ruined house, and placing them against the parapet, we ran up them to the rampart. I was first up one of the first ladders, Labédoyère, who was climbing the one beside me, feeling that the lower end of it was not very steadily placed on the rubbish, asked me to give him my hand to steady him, and we both reached the top of the rampart in full view of the Emperor and the whole army, who saluted us with a mighty cheer. It was one of the finest days of my life. De Viry and d'Albuquerque joined us in a moment with the other aides-de-camp and fifty grenadiers and by this time a regiment of Morand's division was coming towards the ditch at the double.

The chances of war are often strange. The two first detachments had been annihilated before reaching the foot of the breach, and yet the third suffered no loss whatever. Only my friend de Viry had a button of his pelisse carried away by a bullet; yet if the enemy on the parapet had had the presence of mind to charge with the bayonet on Labédoyère and me, it is probable that we should have been overwhelmed by their number, and either killed or hurled back into the ditch. But Austrians lose their heads very quickly; the boldness and rapidity of our attack astonished them to such a point that when they saw us swarming over the breach they first slackened their fire and soon ceased firing altogether. Not only did none of their companies march against us, but all went off in the opposite direction to the point which we had just carried.

As I said, the attack took place close to the Straubing gate. Marshal Lannes had ordered me to get it opened or break it down, so that he could enter the town with Morand's division. Accordingly, as soon as I saw my fifty grenadiers on the ramparts, and the head of the supporting regiment already arrived in the ditch, where their passage was secured by a further supply of ladders, I went down into the town without further delay, every moment being precious. We marched steadily towards the Straubing gate, only a hundred paces from the breach, and great was my surprise to find an Austrian battalion massed under the immense archway, all the men facing towards the gate, so as to be ready to defend it if the French broke it in. The major in command, thinking only of the duty which was entrusted him and taking no heed of the noise which he heard on the ramparts close by, was so confident that the French attack would fail that he had not even placed a sentry outside the archway to let him know what was going on, so he was thunderstruck at seeing us come up in his rear.

He had taken up his position behind his men, so that having faced about on seeing us approach, he found himself fronting the little French column, the strength of which he was quite unable to judge, for I had formed it in two squads which rested on the sides of the arch and closed it completely. At their major's cry of surprise, the battalion all faced round, and the rear sections, which had become the front, presented their muskets at us. Our grenadiers also raised theirs, and as only one pace separated the two parties, you may imagine what a horrible massacre would have resulted if a shot had been fired. The situation was very dangerous for both sides, but their greater number gave the Austrians an immense advantage, for if we had opened fire muzzle to muzzle, our little column would have been destroyed as well as the enemy's company which was in front of our muskets. But the rest of the battalion would have been cleared. It was lucky that our adversaries could not tell the weakness of our force, and I hastened to tell the major that as the town had been taken by assault and occupied by our troops, nothing remained for him but to lay down his arms under pain of being put to the sword.

The assured tone in which I spoke intimidated the officer; all the more so that he could hear the tumult produced by the successive arrival of our soldiers who had followed us over the breach, and hastened to form in front of the archway. We harangued his battalion, and, after having explained the situation to them, ordered them to lay down their arms. The companies who were close to our muzzles obeyed, but those who were at the other end of the archway, close to the gate and sheltered from our shot, fell to shouting, refused to surrender, and pushed forward the mass of the battalion till we were nearly upset. The officers, however, succeeded in quieting them, and everything seemed in a fair way to be settled, when the impetuous Labédoyère, impatient at the delay, lost his temper, and was on the point of ruining the whole thing; for, seizing the Austrian major by the throat, he was just about to run him through if the rest had not turned his sword aside. The other side then resumed their arms, and a bloody battle was about to take place, when the gate began to resound on the outside under the powerful blows which the axes of the pioneers of Morand's division, led by Marshal Lannes in person, were delivering upon it. Then the enemy, understanding that they would be between two fires, surrendered, and we made them march disarmed from under the archway towards the town. The gate thus cleared, we opened it to the marshal, whose troops rushed into the place like a torrent.

After complimenting us, the marshal gave the order to march towards the bridge, in order to cut off such of the enemy's regiments as were in Ratisbon, and prevent the Archduke from sending reinforcements. Hardly, however, had we entered the main street when we were threatened by a new danger. Our shells had set several houses on fire, and the fire was on the point of reaching some thirty wagons, which the enemy had abandoned after taking out the horses. If these had caught fire, the passage of our troops would certainly have been hindered, but we hoped to avoid the obstacle by slipping along close to the walls. Suddenly, however, the Austrian major whom I had presented to the marshal cried out in a tone of most profound despair, 'Conquerors and conquered, we are all lost; those wagons are full of powder!' We all turned pale, including the marshal, but, quickly recovering his calm in presence of imminent death, he made the French column take open order, and fire their muskets against the houses, and ordered the soldiers to push the wagons along from hand to hand until they were under the arch and out of the town. He himself set the example, and generals, officers, and men all went to work. The Austrian prisoners worked with the French, for it was a question of life and death with them also. Many pieces of burning wood were already falling on the wagons, and if one of them had taken fire, we should have been all blown up, and the town entirely destroyed. But they worked with such energy that in a few minutes all the powder-wagons were pushed outside the town, whence the prisoners were made to draw them to our main park of artillery.

The tumbrils being safely out of the way, and the danger over, the marshal, with the infantry brigade, advanced to the centre of the town. Having reached this point, and wishing to make the quarters which he had already captured secure against any renewed attack, he followed the Spanish practice and occupied all the windows in the principal streets. After this prudent arrangement, the marshal ordered that the column should continue its route towards the bridge, and ordered me to march at the head and guide it. I obeyed, though it seemed a difficult task, for I had never been in Ratisbon before, and, naturally, did not know the streets.

As the town belonged to our ally, the King of Bavaria, it might have been expected that the inhabitants would be sufficiently devoted to our cause to point out the way to the bridge; but they were too frightened to come out, and we did not see one. All the doors and windows were shut, and we were in too great a hurry to drive them in, for at every cross-road appeared groups of Austrians who retreated firing. The only retreat open to the enemy was across the bridge, and I thought that I might get there by following them, but there was so little concerted action among the Austrians that most of the squads of sharpshooters who were posted in front of us took flight at our approach in different directions. As I was thus lost in the labyrinth of unknown streets, with no idea of the direction that the column should take, suddenly a door opened, and a young woman, pale and with wild eyes, came flying towards us, crying, 'I am French, save me!' It was a Parisian milliner in business at Ratisbon, who, fearing that, as a Frenchwoman, she might be ill-treated by the Austrians, had, as soon as she heard the sound of French voices, come to throw herself headlong into the arms of her compatriots. At sight of her a bright idea flashed into my mind. 'Do you know where the bridge is?' said I. 'Certainly.' 'Show us the way, then.' 'Great Heavens! In the middle of this shooting? I am frightened to death already, and was going to ask you to let me have some soldiers to defend my house. I am going back this moment.' 'Very sorry, but you will show us the bridge before you go back.

Two men took the lady's arms, and marched her along at the head of the column.' This was done, in spite of the tears and cries of our fair compatriot. At every turning I asked her which direction we must take. The nearer we got to the Danube, the more skirmishers we met; the bullets whistled round the frightened milliner's ears, but, not being familiar with the sound, she was much less alarmed at the faint whistle than at the reports of the muskets. But suddenly one of the grenadiers who was supporting her got a bullet through his arm; the blood spurted on to her, her knees gave way, and we had to carry her. What had befallen her neighbour made me more cautious for her, so I put her in rear of the first section, so as to be in some measure sheltered from bullets by the men. At last we reached a little square facing the bridge. The enemy, who held the further end of it, as well as the suburb on the right bank named Stadt-am-Hof, no sooner caught sight of the column than they opened artillery fire. I thought it was useless to expose the lady from Paris any longer, and let her go free. But as the poor woman, who was more dead than alive, knew not where to take shelter, I advised her to enter a little chapel of Our Lady at the further end of the square. She agreed, the grenadiers lifted her over the little grating which closed the entry, and she hastened to get out of reach of shot, crouching down behind the statue of the Virgin, where, I can assure you, she made herself pretty small.

On hearing that we had reached the bank of the river, the marshal came to the head of the column and recognised for himself the impossibility of crossing the bridge, the suburb on the left bank being on fire. While the assault was taking place, six Austrian battalions, posted on the ramparts at some distance from the point of attack, had remained tranquilly looking out to see if anyone was coming from the country. They were roused from their stolid inaction by the sound of firing in the direction of the bridge. Hastening thither, they found their retreat cut off both by us and by the burning suburb, and had to surrender.

The same day the Emperor entered Ratisbon, and ordered the troops who had not fought to assist the inhabitants in getting the fire under control; still a great many houses were burnt. After having visited and rewarded the wounded, the glorious remains of the two first columns who had failed in their attempt, Napoleon wished also to see the third column, which had carried Ratisbon under his eyes. He testified his satisfaction, and decorated several. On the marshal reminding him of my old and new claims to the rank of major, Napoleon replied, 'You may consider the thing done.' Then, turning to Berthier, 'Make me sign his commission the first time you bring up any papers.' I could only congratulate myself, I could not reasonably expect the Emperor to suspend his important work that I might have my commission a few days earlier. Indeed, I was almost beside myself at the marks of satisfaction which the Emperor and the marshal had shown towards me, and at the praises which my comrades and I received on all hands.

As you may suppose, before leaving the neighbourhood of the bridge, I had the Paris lady fetched from the chapel and taken to her house by an officer. The marshal, seeing the soldiers helping her to re-cross the grating, asked me how she got there. I told him the story, which he passed on to the Emperor, who laughed a good deal, and said that he should like to see the lady.

Among the many spectators of our attack—which, as I have said, was delivered in full view of the Grand Army—were Marshal Masséna and his staff. One of them, M. Pelet, now Director-General of Military Stores, has written in his excellent work on the campaign of 1809: 'Marshal Lannes seized a ladder, and was starting to fix it himself; his aides-de-camp struggled to stop him. At the sight of this generous contest, the mass of our soldiers fell on the ladders, caught them up, and crossed the intervening span, preceded by the aides-de-camp. In the twinkling of an eye the ladders were fixed, the ditch crossed. On the top the first seen to appear, holding each other's hand, were Labédoyère and Marbot; the grenadiers followed. This account of an eye-witness is quite correct; he rightly gives equal credit to my comrade and myself. But the biographer of poor Labédoyère has not been so fair. After copying General Pelet's account, he has thought fit to suppress my name and give Labédoyère the sole credit of having been the leader of the assault at Ratisbon. However, I saw no occasion to put him right; and, after all, General Pelet's work establishes the fact, to which 150,000 men could testify.

Ratisbon was taken April 23. The Emperor passed the next two days in the town, ordering all repairs to be done at his cost. As Napoleon, accompanied by Lannes, was going about the streets, I saw the milliner whom I had compelled to act as our guide to the bridge, and pointed her out to the marshal. He showed her to the Emperor, who spoke to her, with many jocose compliments on her courage; and subsequently sent her a handsome ring in memory of the assault. The crowd of soldiers and civilians who were about the Emperor, having made inquiries about the action of this little scene, the facts were somewhat distorted. The lady was represented as a heroine, who of her own accord had faced death to ensure the safety of her compatriots. In this form the tale was told, not only in the army, but throughout Germany. Even General Pelet was misled by the popular report. If the Parisian lady was for a time under fire from the enemy, love of glory had very little to do with it.

During our short stay at Ratisbon, the marshal appointed on his staff Lieutenant de la Bourdonnaye, an intelligent and brave young officer, who had been recommended to him by his father-in-law, M. de Gluéhéneuc. La Bourdonnaye was distressed at missing the assault, but he had plenty more opportunities of showing his courage. A comical adventure befell him in this connection. The dandies in the army had taken to trousers of inordinate width, which looked very well on horseback, but were a great hindrance to walking. During the action at Wels, La Bourdonnaye had been ordered by the marshal to dismount, and run across the bridge with an order for the troops. His spurs caught in his trousers, he fell, and we thought he was killed. But he picked himself up nimbly, and as he started off again, he heard the marshal call out, 'Is it not absurd to go to fight with six yards of cloth about your legs?' La Bourdonnaye wishing, in his first battle under Lannes' eyes, to show his zeal, drew his sword, hacked and tore his trousers off at mid-thigh, and being thus released, set off running bare-kneed. Although we were under fire, the marshal and the staff laughed at the new-fashioned costume till they cried; and when La Bourdonnaye came back, he was complimented on his ready ingenuity.

Leaving a strong garrison in Ratisbon, the Emperor marched on Vienna by the right bank of the Danube, while the enemy followed the left bank in the same direction. I need not relate all the engagements which we had with Austrian forces trying to bar our road. I will only mention that Masséna, whose division had hitherto been held by circumstances aloof from all the fighting, was imprudent enough on May 3 to attack the bridge of Ebersberg over the Traun, which was defended by 40,000 men with a fortress in their rear. The attack was utterly useless, since before it began Lannes' division had crossed the Traun five leagues higher up, and was marching to take the Austrians in rear. They would certainly have retired at our approach without Masséna's losing a single man. His attack, made in order to pass a river already passed, succeeded, but with a loss of more than 1,000 killed and 2,000 wounded. The Emperor blamed this waste of human life, and, doubtless to give Masséna a lesson, he sent from Wels a brigade of light cavalry under the command of General Durosnel, who descended the left bank of the Traun, and reached Ebersberg without firing a shot, at the same time as Masséna's troops entered after considerable loss. Napoleon went from Wels to Ebersberg by the right bank, which showed that the road was perfectly clear. On reaching the field of battle, he was deeply grieved at the sight of so many men uselessly killed, and would see no one for the whole evening. If any other than Masséna had ventured without orders to deliver an attack so imprudently, he would probably have been sent to the rear, but Masséna was the spoilt child of victory, and the Emperor limited himself to some severe remarks. The army was less indulgent, and criticised Masséna's conduct loudly. In excuse he said that as the Austrians who were defending the place under General Hiller had the bridge across the Danube at Mauth-hausen, there was reason to fear that if they were not promptly attacked without awaiting the returning force from Wels, General Hiller might cross the Danube and join the Archduke on the other side. But this would have involved no inconvenience for us: it would have been to our advantage, for we should have found the right bank of the river entirely undefended. Furthermore, the object that Masséna had in view was not attained, for General Hiller actually did cross the Danube at Stein, and made all haste to reach Vienna.

After crossing the Traun, burning the bridge at Mauth-hausen, and passing the Enns, the army advanced to Mölk, without knowing what had become of General Hiller. Some spies assured us that the Archduke had crossed the Danube and joined him, and that we should on the morrow meet the whole Austrian army, strongly posted in front of Saint-Pölten. In that case, we must make ready to fight a great battle; but if it were otherwise, we had to march quickly on Vienna in order to get there before the enemy could reach it by the other bank. For want of positive information the Emperor was very undecided. The question to be solved was, Had General Hiller crossed the Danube, or was he still in front of us, masked by a swarm of light cavalry, which, always flying, never let us get near enough to take a prisoner from whom one might get some enlightentent?

Chapter 10
I Become a Sailor

Still knowing nothing for certain, we reached, on May 7, the pretty little town of Mölk, standing on the bank of the Danube, and overhung by an immense rock, on the summit of which rises a Benedictine convent, said to be the finest and richest in Christendom. From the rooms of the monastery, a wide view is obtained over both banks of the Danube. There the Emperor and many marshals, including Lannes, took up their quarters, while our staff lodged with the parish priest. Much rain had fallen during the week, and it had not ceased for twenty-four hours, and still was falling, so that the Danube and its tributaries were over their banks. That night, as my comrades and I, delighted at being sheltered from the bad weather, were having a merry supper with the parson, a jolly fellow, who gave us an excellent meal, the aide-de-camp on duty with the marshal came to tell me that I was wanted, and must go up to the convent that moment. I was so comfortable where I was that I found it annoying to have to leave a good supper and good quarters to go and get wet again, but I had to obey.

All the passages and the lower rooms of the monastery were full of soldiers, forgetting the fatigues of the previous days in the monks' good wine. On reaching the dwelling-rooms, I saw that I had been sent for about some serious matter, for generals, chamberlains, orderly officers, said to me repeatedly, 'The Emperor has sent for you.' Some added, 'It is probably to give you your commission as major.' This I did not believe, for I did not think I was yet of sufficient importance to the sovereign for him to send for me at such an hour to give me my commission with his own hands. I was shown into a vast and handsome gallery, with a balcony looking over the Danube; there I found the Emperor at dinner with several marshals and the abbot of the convent, who has the title of bishop. On seeing me, the

Emperor left the table, and went towards the balcony, followed by Lannes. I heard him say in a low tone, 'The execution of this plan is almost impossible; it would be sending a brave officer for no purpose to almost certain death.' 'He will go, sir,' replied the marshal; 'I am certain he will go, at any rate we can but propose it to him.' Then, taking me by the hand, the marshal opened the window of the balcony over the Danube. The river at this moment, trebled in volume by the strong flood, was nearly a league wide; it was lashed by a fierce wind, and we could hear the waves roaring. It was pitch-dark, and the rain fell in torrents, but we could see on the other side a long line of bivouac fires. Napoleon, Marshal Lannes, and I, being alone on the balcony, the marshal said, 'On the other side of the river, you see an Austrian camp. Now, the Emperor is keenly desirous to know whether General Hiller's corps is there, or still on this bank. In order to make sure, he wants a stout-hearted man, bold enough to cross the Danube, and bring away some soldier of the enemy's, and I have assured him that you will go.' Then Napoleon said to me, 'Take notice that I am not giving you an order; I am only expressing a wish. I am aware that the enterprise is as dangerous as it can be, and you can decline it without any fear of displeasing me. Go, and think it over for a few moments in the next room; come back and tell us frankly your decision.'

I admit that when I heard Marshal Lannes' proposal I had broken out all over in a cold sweat; but at the same moment, a feeling, which I cannot define, but in which a love of glory and of my country was mingled, perhaps, with a noble pride, raised my ardour to the highest point, and I said to myself, 'The Emperor has here an army of 150,000 devoted warriors, besides 25,000 men of his guard, all selected from the bravest. He is surrounded with aides-de-camp and orderly officers, and yet when an expedition is on foot, requiring intelligence no less than boldness, it is I whom the Emperor and Marshal Lannes choose.' 'I will go, sir!' I cried without hesitation. 'I will go; and if I perish, I leave my mother to your Majesty's care.' The Emperor pulled my ear to mark his satisfaction; the marshal shook my hand, exclaiming, 'I was quite right to tell your Majesty that he would go. There's what you may call a brave soldier.'

My expedition being thus decided on, I had to think about the means of executing it. The Emperor called General Bertrand, his aide-de-camp, General Dorsenne, of the guard, and the commandant of the imperial head-quarters, and ordered them to put at my disposal whatever I might require. At my request an infantry picket went into the town to find the burgomaster, the syndic of the boatmen, and five of his best hands. A corporal and five grenadiers of the old guard who could all speak German, and had still to earn their decorations, were also summoned, and voluntarily agreed to go with me. The Emperor had them brought in first, and promised that on their return they should receive the Cross at once. The brave men replied by a 'Vive l'Empereur!' and went to get ready. As for the five boatmen, on its being explained to them through the interpreter that they had to take a boat across the Danube, they fell on their knees and began to weep. The syndic declared that they might just as well be shot at once, as sent to certain death. The expedition was absolutely impossible, not only from the strength of the current, but because the tributaries had brought into the Danube a great quantity of fir-trees recently cut down in the mountains, which could not be avoided in the dark, and would certainly come against the boat and sink it. Besides, how could one land on the opposite bank among willows which would scuttle the boat, and with a flood of unknown extent? The syndic concluded, then, that the operation was physically impossible. In vain did the Emperor tempt them with an offer of 6,000 francs per man; even this could not persuade them, though, as they said, they were poor boatmen with families, and this sum would be a fortune to them. But, as I have already said, some lives must be sacrificed to save those of the greater number, and the knowledge of this makes commanders sometimes pitiless. The Emperor was inflexible, and the grenadiers received orders to take the poor men, whether they would or not, and we went down to the town.

The corporal who had been assigned to me was an intelligent man. Taking him for my interpreter, I charged him as we went along to tell the syndic of the boatmen that as he had got to come along with us, he had better in his own interest show us his best boat, and point out everything that we should require for her fitting. The poor man obeyed; so we got an excellent vessel, and we took all that we wanted from the others. We had two anchors, but as I did not think we should be able to make use of them, I had sewn to the end of each cable a piece of canvas with a large stone wrapped in it. I had seen in the south of France the fishermen use an apparatus of this kind to hold their boats by throwing the cord over the willows at the water's edge. I put on a cap, the grenadiers took their forage-caps, we had provisions, ropes, axes, saws, a ladder—everything, in short, which I could think of to take.

Our preparations ended, I was going to give the signal to start, when the five boatmen implored me with tears to let the soldiers escort them to their houses to take, perhaps, the last farewell of their wives and children; but, fearing that a tender scene of this kind would further reduce their small stock of courage, I refused. Then the syndic said, 'Well, as we have only a short time to live, allow us five minutes to commend our souls to God, and do you do the same, for you also are going to your death.' They all fell on their knees, the grenadiers and I following their example, which seemed to please the worthy people much. When their prayer was over, I gave each man a glass of the monks' excellent wine, and we pushed out into the stream.

I had bidden the grenadiers follow in silence all the orders of the syndic who was steering; the current was too strong for us to cross over straight from Mölk: we went up, therefore, along the bank under sail for more than a league and although the wind and the waves made the boat jump, this part was accomplished without accident. But when the time came to take to our oars and row out from the land, the mast on being lowered fell over to one side, and the sail, dragging in the water, offered a strong resistance to the current and nearly capsized us. The master ordered the ropes to be cut and the masts to be sent overboard; but the boatmen, losing their heads, began to pray without stirring. Then the corporal, drawing his sword, said, 'You can pray and work too; obey at once, or I will kill you.' Compelled to choose between possible and certain death, the poor fellows took up their hatchets, and with the help of the grenadiers, the mast was promptly cut away and sent floating. It was high time, for hardly were we free from this dangerous burden when we felt a fearful shock. A pine-stem borne down by the stream had struck the boat. We all shuddered, but luckily the planks were not driven in this time. Would the boat, however, resist more shocks of this kind? We could not see the stems, and only knew that they were near by the heavier tumble of the waves. Several touched us, but no serious accident resulted. Meantime the current bore us along, and as our oars could make very little way against it to give us the necessary slant, I feared for a moment that it would sweep us below the enemy's camp, and that my expedition would fail. By dint of hard rowing, however, we had got three-quarters of the way over, when I saw an immense black mass looming over the water. Then a sharp scratching was heard, branches caught us in the face, and the boat stopped. To our questions the owner replied that we were on an island covered with willows and poplars, of which the flood had nearly reached the top. We had to grope about with our hatchets to clear a passage through the branches, and when we had succeeded in passing the obstacle, we found the stream much less furious than in the middle of the river, and finally reached the left bank in front of the Austrian camp. This shore was bordered with very thick trees, which, overhanging the bank like a dome, made the approach difficult no doubt, but at the same time concealed our boat from the camp. The whole shore was lighted up by the bivouac fires, while we remained in the shadow thrown by the branches of the willows. I let the boat float downwards, looking for a suitable landing-place. Presently I perceived that a sloping path had been made down the bank by the enemy to allow the men and horses to get to the water. The corporal adroitly threw into the willows one of the stones that I had made ready, the cord caught in a tree, and the boat brought up against the land a foot or two from the slope. It must have been just about midnight. The Austrians, having the swollen Danube between them and the French, felt themselves so secure that except the sentry the whole camp was asleep.

It is usual in war for the guns and the sentinels always to face towards the enemy, however far off he may be. A battery placed in advance of the camp was therefore turned towards the river, and sentries were walking on the top of the bank. The trees prevented them from seeing the extreme edge, while from the boat I could see through the branches a great part of the bivouac. So far my mission had been more successful than I had ventured to hope, but in order to make the success complete I had to bring away a prisoner, and to execute such an operation fifty paces away from several thousand enemies, whom a single cry would rouse, seemed very difficult. Still, I had to do something. I made the five sailors lie down at the bottom of the boat under guard of two grenadiers, another grenadier I posted at the bow of the boat, which was close to the bank, and myself disembarked, sword in hand, followed by the corporal and two grenadiers. The boat was a few feet from dry land; we had to walk in the water, but at last we were on the slope. We went up, and I was making ready to rush upon the nearest sentry, disarm him, gag him, and drag him off to the boat, when the ring of metal and the sound of singing in a low voice fell on my ears. A man, carrying a great tin pail, was coming to draw water, humming a song as he went; we quickly went down again to the river to hide under the branches, and as the Austrian stooped to fill his pail my grenadiers seized him by the throat, put a handkerchief full of wet sand over his mouth, and placing their sword-points against his body threatened him with death if he resisted or uttered a sound. Utterly bewildered, the man obeyed, and let us take him to the boat; we hoisted him into the hands of the grenadiers posted there, who made him lie down beside the sailors. While this Austrian was lying captured, I saw by his clothes that he was not strictly speaking a soldier, but an officer's servant. I should have preferred to catch a combatant, who could have given me more precise information; but I was going to content myself with this capture for want of a better, when I saw at the top of the slope two soldiers carrying a cauldron between them, on a pole. They were only a few paces off. It was impossible for us to re-embark without being seen. I therefore signed to my grenadiers to hide themselves again, and as soon as the two Austrians stooped to fill their vessel powerful arms seized them from behind, and plunged their heads under water. We had to stupefy them a little, since they had their swords, and I feared that they might resist. Then they were picked up in turn, their mouths covered with a handkerchief full of sand, and sword-points against their breasts constrained them to follow us. They were shipped as the servant had been, and my men and I got on board again.

So far all had gone well. I made the sailors get up and take their oars, and ordered the corporal to cast loose the rope which held us to the bank. It was, however, so wet, and the knot had been drawn so tight by the force of the stream, that it was impossible to unfasten. We had to saw the rope, which took us some minutes. Meanwhile, the rope, shaking with our efforts, imparted its movement to the branches of the willow round which it was wrapped, and the rustling became loud enough to attract the notice of the sentry. He drew near, unable to see the boat, but perceiving that the agitation of the branches increased, he called out, 'Who goes there?' No answer. Further challenge from the sentry. We held our tongues, and worked away. I was in deadly fear; after facing so many dangers, it would have been too cruel if we were wrecked in sight of port. At last, the rope was cut and the boat pushed off. But hardly was it clear of the overhanging willows than the light of the bivouac fires made it visible to the sentry, who, shouting, 'To arms,' fired at us. No one was hit; but at the sound the whole camp was astir in a moment, and the gunners, whose pieces were ready loaded and trained on the river, honoured my boat with some cannon-shots. At the report my heart leapt for joy, for I knew that the Emperor and marshal would hear it. I turned my eyes towards the convent, with its lighted windows, of which I had, in spite of the distance, never lost sight. Probably all were opened at this moment, but in one only could I perceive any increase of brilliancy; it was the great balcony window, which was as large as the doorway of a church, and sent from afar a flood of light over the stream. Evidently it had just been opened at the thunder of the cannon, and I said to myself, 'The Emperor and the marshals are doubtless on the balcony; they know that I have reached the enemy's camp, and are making vows for my safe return.' This thought raised my courage, and I heeded the cannon-balls not a bit. Indeed, they were not very dangerous, for the stream swept us along at such a pace that the gunners could not aim with any accuracy, and we must have been very unlucky to get hit. One shot would have done for us, but all fell harmless into the Danube. Soon I was out of range, and could reckon a successful issue to my enterprise. Still, all danger was not yet at an end. We had still to cross among the floating pine-stems, and more than once we struck on sub-merged islands, and were delayed by the branches of the poplars. At last we reached the right bank, more than two leagues below Mölk, and a new terror assailed me. I could see bivouac fires, and had no means of learning whether they belonged to a French regiment. The enemy had troops on both banks, and I knew that on the right bank Marshal Lannes' outposts were not far from Mölk, facing an Austrian corps, posted at Saint-Pölten.

Our army would doubtless go forward at daybreak, but was it already occupying this place? And were the fires that I saw those of friends or enemies? I was afraid that the current had taken me too far down, but the problem was solved by French cavalry trumpets sounding the reveille. Our uncertainty being at an end, we rowed with all our strength to the shore, where in the dawning light we could see a village. As we drew near, the report of a carbine was heard, and a bullet whistled by our ears. It was evident that the French sentries took us for a hostile crew. I had not foreseen this possibility, and hardly knew how we were to succeed in getting recognised, till the happy thought struck me of making my six grenadiers shout, 'Vive l'Empereur Napoleon!' This was, of course, no certain evidence that we were French, but it would attract the attention of the officers, who would have no fear of our small numbers, and would no doubt prevent the men from firing on us before they knew whether we were French or Austrians. A few moments later I came ashore, and I was received by Colonel Gautrin and the 9th Hussars, forming part of Lannes' division. If we had landed half a league lower down we should have tumbled into the enemy's pickets. The colonel lent me a horse, and gave me several wagons, in which I placed the grenadiers, the boatmen, and the prisoners, and the little cavalcade went off towards Mölk. As we went along, the corporal, at my orders, questioned the three Austrians, and I learnt with satisfaction that the camp whence I had brought them away belonged to the very division, General Hiller's, the position of which the Emperor was so anxious to learn. There was, therefore, no further doubt that that general had joined the Archduke on the other side of the Danube. There was no longer any question of a battle on the road which we held, and Napoleon, having only the enemy's cavalry in front of him, could in perfect safety push his troops forward towards Vienna, from which we were but three easy marches distant. With this information I galloped forward, in order to bring it to the Emperor with the least possible delay.

When I reached the gate of the monastery, it was broad day. I found the approach blocked by the whole population of the little town of Mölk, and heard among the crowd the cries of the wives, children, and friends of the sailors whom I had carried off. In a moment I was surrounded by them, and was able to calm their anxiety by saying, in shocking bad German, 'Your friends are alive, and you will see them in a few moments.' A great cry of joy went up from the crowd, bringing out the officer in command of the guard at the gate. On seeing me he ran off in pursuance of orders to warn the aides-de-camp to let the Emperor know of my return. In an instant the whole palace was up. The good Marshal Lannes came to me, embraced me cordially, and carried me straight off to the Emperor, crying out, 'Here he is, sir; I knew he would come back. He has brought three prisoners from General Hiller's division.' Napoleon received me warmly, and though I was wet and muddy all over, he laid his hand on my shoulder, and did not forget to give his greatest sign of satisfaction by pinching my ear. I leave you to imagine how I was questioned! The Emperor wanted to know every incident of the adventure in detail, and when I had finished my story said, 'I am very well pleased with you, 'Major' Marbot. These words were equivalent to a commission, and my joy was full. At that moment, a chamberlain announced that breakfast was served, and as I was calculating on having to wait in the gallery until the Emperor had finished, he pointed with his finger towards the dining-room, and said, 'You will breakfast with me.' As this honour had never been paid to any officer of my rank, I was the more flattered. During breakfast I learnt that the Emperor and the marshal had not been to bed all night, and that when they heard the cannon on the opposite bank they had all rushed on to the balcony. The Emperor made me tell again the way in which I had surprised the three prisoners, and laughed much at the fright and surprise which they must have felt.

At last, the arrival of the wagons was announced, but they

had much difficulty in making their way through the crowd, so eager were the people to see the boatmen. Napoleon, thinking this very natural gave orders to open the gates, and let everybody come into the court. Soon after, the grenadiers, the boatmen, and the prisoners were led into the gallery. The Emperor, through his interpreter, first questioned the three Austrian soldiers, and learning with satisfaction that not only General Hiller's corps, but the whole of the Archduke's army, were on the other bank he told Berthier to give the order for the troops to march at once on Saint-Pölten. Then, calling up the corporal and the five soldiers, he fastened the Cross on their breast, appointed them knights of the Empire, and gave them an annuity of 1,200 francs apiece. All the veterans wept for joy. Next came the boatmen's turn. The Emperor told them that, as the danger they had run was a good deal more than he had expected, it was only fair that he should increase their reward; so, instead of the 6,000 francs promised, 12,000 in gold were given to them on the spot. Nothing could express their delight; they kissed the hands of the Emperor and all present, crying, 'Now we are rich!' Napoleon laughingly asked the syndic if he would go the same journey for the same price the next night. But the man answered that, having escaped by miracle what seemed certain death, he would not undertake such a journey again even if his lordship, the abbot of Mölk, would give him the monastery and all its possessions. The boatmen withdrew, blessing the generosity of the French Emperor, and the grenadiers, eager to show off their decoration before their comrades, were about to go off with their three prisoners, when Napoleon perceived that the Austrian servant was weeping bitterly. He reassured him as to his safety, but the poor lad replied, sobbing, that he knew the French treated their prisoners well, but that, as he had on him a belt, containing nearly all his captain's money, he was afraid that the officer would accuse him of deserting in order to rob him, and he was heart-broken at the thought. Touched by the worthy fellow's distress, the Emperor told him that he was free, and as soon as we were before Vienna, he would be passed through the outposts, and be able to return to his master. Then, taking a rouleau of 1,000 francs, he put it in the man's hand, saying, 'One must honour goodness wherever it is shown.' Lastly, the Emperor gave some pieces of gold to each of the other two prisoners, and ordered that they too should be sent back to the Austrian outposts, so that they might forget the fright which we had caused them, and that it might not be said that any soldiers, even enemies, had spoken to the Emperor of the French without receiving some benefit.

Chapter 11
Major Marbot at Vienna

On leaving the gallery I found the ante-room filled with generals and officers of the guard. My comrades were there also, and all congratulated me, both on the success of my expedition, and on the step which the Emperor had granted to me by addressing me as 'major.' It was not, however, till next month that I got my commission, by which time I had another wound to show for it. Do not, however, accuse the Emperor of ingratitude; during May his time was taken up by the events of the war, and as he always gave me the title of major he would naturally think that I considered myself as such.

As we moved from Mölk to Saint-Pölten, the Emperor and Marshal Lannes put many further questions to me as to the doings of that night. They halted opposite to the old castle of Dürrenstein, on the further bank. This place had a double interest for us, both as commanding the scene of the memorable fight when Marshal Mortier, separated from the rest of the French army in 1805, had to cut his way through the Russian troops, and as having, in the middle ages, been the prison of Richard Cœur de Lion. While studying these ruins, and meditating on the fate of the royal warrior who was so long shut up there, Napoleon fell into a deep reverie. Had he a presentiment that his enemies would one day shut him up, and that he would end his life as a captive?

Marshal Lannes, hearing several cannon-shots in the direction of Saint-Pölten, moved rapidly on that town, and a few charges took place in the streets between our advanced guard and a small force of light cavalry which the enemy still had on the right bank. All my colleagues being at the moment on duty, I happened to be alone with the marshal when we entered Saint-Pölten. Passing in front of a nunnery we saw the abbess come out with a crozier in her hand, followed by all her nuns. The holy women, terrified, were coming to seek protection. The marshal reassured them, and, as the enemy were flying and our troops in the occupation of the town, he thought he might safely dismount. A scorching sun had followed the tempest of the previous night. The marshal had just covered three leagues at a gallop, and was very hot. The abbess invited him to come and take some refreshment. He accepted; and suddenly there were two of us in the convent surrounded by some fifty nuns! In a moment the table was laid and a splendid luncheon served. I never saw such a profusion of syrups, preserves, sweetmeats of all sorts. We did them full justice, and the nuns filled our pockets with them, presenting several boxes to the marshal, who said that he would take them as a present from these ladies to his children. Alas! he was never to see his dear children again.

That night the Emperor and the marshal slept at Saint-Pölten; two days more brought us to Vienna, which we reached very early on May 10. The Emperor made his way at once to the royal palace at Schönbrunn, thus being at the gates of the Austrian capital twenty-seven days after leaving Paris. We had thought that the Archduke Charles would have hastened his march on the left bank, and crossed the river by the bridge of Spitz, so as to reach Vienna before us; but he was several days behind, and only a feeble garrison defended the capital. The city proper of Vienna is very small, but is surrounded by immense suburbs, which are enclosed by a single wall too weak to stop an army. The Archduke Maximilian, who commanded in Vienna, abandoned the suburbs, therefore, and withdrew with all the combatants behind the old fortifications of the town. If he had chosen to make use of the assistance offered by the courageous population, he might have held out for some time, but he did not do so, and on their arrival the French troops occupied the suburbs without striking a blow. Marshal Lannes, deceived by an incorrect report, and thinking that the enemy had also abandoned the city, sent Colonel Guéhéneuc in a hurry to tell the Emperor that we occupied Vienna, and Napoleon, eager to announce this great news, ordered M. Guéhéneuc to set out at once for Paris. But the place still held out, and when Lannes tried to enter at the head of a division, we were received with cannon-shots. General Tharreau was wounded and several soldiers killed. The marshal withdrew the troops into the suburbs, and decided to send Colonel Saint-Mars with a summons to the governor. He was accompanied by M. de la

Grange, who, having been for a long time attached to the French embassy at Vienna, knew his way perfectly. A flag of truce ought to go forward alone, accompanied by a trumpeter; but instead of acting according to this custom, Colonel Saint-Mars took three orderlies, and M. de la Grange the same number, so that with the trumpeter there were nine of them, which was far too many. The enemy thought, or pretended to think, that they were coming to inspect the fortifications rather than to bring a summons to surrender. A gate suddenly opened, and there came out a squad of Hungarian hussars, who charged sword in hand upon the party, wounded them all severely, and carried them prisoners into the town. The troopers who committed this act of barbarism belonged to the Szekler regiment, the same which, in 1799, had murdered the French plenipotentiaries, Roberjot and Bonnier, and severely wounded Jean Debry outside Rastadt.

On hearing of the unworthy manner in which the Austrians had shed the blood of the party sent with a flag of truce, the Emperor came up indignantly, and sent for a great number of howitzers to bombard Vienna in the night. The defenders, meanwhile, had opened a terrible fire on the suburbs, and kept it up for twenty-four hours at the risk of killing their fellow-citizens.

On the morning of the 11th, the Emperor went round the outskirts of Vienna, and noticing that the Archduke Maximilian had committed the serious mistake of not lining the Prater with troops, he resolved to take possession of it by throwing a bridge over the small arm of the Danube. To this end two companies of voltigeurs crossed in boats and occupied the 'Lusthaus,' with the neighbouring wood to protect the construction of the bridge. This was finished during the night, and as soon as it was known in Vienna that the French held the Prater and could march thence towards the Spitz bridge, the only way of retreat open to the garrison, there was great agitation, which fresh events soon increased. By ten o'clock in the evening our gunners, covered by the solid buildings of the imperial stables, began to throw shells into the town, which soon was on fire in several quarters, and notably in the Graben.

It has been said, and repeated though wrongly by General Pelet, that the Archduchess Louisa lying ill at that time in her father's palace, the commander of the garrison gave notice of this to the

Emperor of the French, and that orders were given to change the positions of the batteries. This story is quite fictitious, for Marie Louise was not in Vienna during the attack, and if she had been the Austrian generals would certainly not have exposed their Emperor's daughter to the hazards of war, when she could with proper care have been taken in a few minutes to the other side of the Danube. But there are some people who will discover the marvellous everywhere, and have pleased themselves by making out that the life of the archduchess was saved by him whose throne she was shortly to share.

Our shells continued to pour upon the town till midnight, when Napoleon, leaving the task of directing the fire to the artillery generals, started with Marshal Lannes to return to Schönbrunn. It was bright moonlight, and, the road being good, the Emperor set off as usual at a gallop. He was riding for the first time a handsome horse presented to him by the King of Bavaria. His equerry, M. de Canisy, among whose duties was that of trying the Emperor's horses, had doubtless neglected this precaution, but affirmed that the horse was perfect. After a few paces the horse fell; the Emperor rolled off and lay at full length without giving a sign of life. We thought he was dead, but he had only fainted. He was quickly picked up, and, in spite of all that Marshal Lannes could say, insisted on riding the rest of the way. He took another mount, and started again at a gallop. On reaching the great court of the palace, he made all the staff and the squadron of his guard who had witnessed the accident draw up in a circle round him, and forbade anyone to speak of it. The secret, though entrusted to more than two hundred persons, half of whom were common troopers, was so religiously kept that the army and Europe never knew that Napoleon had nearly lost his life. The equerry, Count de Canisy, expected a severe reprimand, but Napoleon only punished him by ordering him to ride the Bavarian horse every day, and after the next day, when he had been off several times owing to the weakness of the animal's legs, the Emperor pardoned him, bidding him only examine better in future horses which he gave him to ride.

Finding his retreat threatened, and the capital in danger of being burnt to the ground, the Archduke evacuated Vienna in the night and retired behind the main branch of the Danube, destroying the

Spitz bridge. It was by this very bridge that the French army crossed the Danube in 1805, when, as I have related, Marshals Lannes and Murat got possession of it by a trick. After the departure of the troops, the populace were beginning to pillage the town, and the authorities sent General O'Reilly and the Archbishop, with some of the principal officials, to ask for aid from Napoleon. Upon this, several regiments entered as protectors rather than as conquerors. The citizens were disarmed, with the exception of the civic guard, who showed themselves as worthy of this mark of confidence as they were in 1805.

Marshal Lannes' headquarters were in the magnificent palace of Prince Albert of Sachs-Teschen near the Kärnthner Thor. Prince Murat had occupied this during the Austerlitz campaign, but the marshal did not stay there, preferring to be lodged in a private house at Schönbrunn, where he could more readily communicate with the Emperor. In Vienna we found MM. Saint-Mars and de la Grange, with their escort all severely wounded. The marshal had M. Saint-Mars taken to Prince Albert's palace.

From the opening of the campaign of 1809, the English had done all in their power to stir up fresh enemies for Napoleon by raising the German populations against him and his allies. The first to rise in revolt were the Tyrolese, who, taken from Austria and given to Bavaria by the treaties of 1805, saw an opportunity of returning to their former master. The Bavarians, under Marshal Lefebvre, fought many bloody engagements with the mountaineers, who, led by a simple innkeeper named Hofer, fought with heroic courage. But after some brilliant successes they were beaten by French troops coming from Italy, and their commandant, Hofer, was taken and shot.

Prussia, humiliated by the defeat of Jena, but not daring, in spite of pressure from England, to run the risks of a fresh war with Napoleon, was willing enough to put a fresh spoke in his wheel by adopting a middle term between peace and war, such as is reprobated among all civilised nations. Major Schill, leaving Berlin in open day at the head of his regiment of hussars, swept the north of Germany killing and plundering the French, and calling on the people to revolt. In this way he succeeded in forming a band of more than 600 men, at whose head he had the hardihood to attack, with support from the English fleet, the fortress of Stralsund, defended by the brave General Gratien. There was fighting in the streets, and Major Schill was killed. Many young men belonging to the best families of Prussia, who were taken fighting with him, were brought to trial by the Emperor's order, and sent off to Brest, condemned as thieves and assassins to penal servitude for life. The Prussian nation was angry enough at this treatment, but the Government, realising the true character of such acts of brigandage, did not venture to make any remonstrance, and contented itself with disavowing Schill and his troops, whom it would have rewarded had their enterprise brought about the rising of Germany.

The Prince of Brunswick-Oels, who had lost his states under the treaty of Tilsit and taken refuge in England, went to Lusatia, and, raising a band of 2,000 men, carried on a guerilla war against the French and their allies, the Saxons. In Westphalia, Colonel Derneberg. an officer of King Jerome's guard, spread sedition in several districts, and even marched upon Cassel, with the intention of carrying off Jerome. Katt and several other Prussian officers raised bands in different places, as it was afterwards proved, with the tacit consent of the Prussian Government. If these various insurgent bodies, led by able and enterprising chiefs, had combined, the consequences to us might have been very awkward; but they all broke up when the news came of the battle of Eckmühl and the capture of Vienna. The moment had not yet come to unite all the forces of Germany against Napoleon; Russia was then our ally, and her agreement was lacking. She had even furnished us with a contingent of 20,000 men, who were acting, though very slackly, in Galicia. Russia, however, had no scruple at the peace about claiming her share of the Austrian spoils, with which she never again parted.

Chapter 12
The Battle of Aspern-Essling

Napoleon had now concentrated the bulk of his forces around Vienna. Less fortunate, however, than in 1805, he found the Spitz bridge broken, and could not finish the war nor reach his enemy, without passing the mighty stream of the Danube. At this period of the spring, the melting snow swells the stream till it becomes immense, and each of its branches is equal to a large river. The crossing consequently presented many difficulties, but as the stream flows among a great number of islands, some of which are very spacious, points can be found there on which to support bridges. After inspecting the bank closely, both above and below Vienna, the Emperor observed two spots favourable for the passage. The first by the isle of Schwarzelaken, opposite Nussdorf, half a league above Vienna; the second, the same distance below the town, opposite the village of Kaiserbersdorf, and crossing the great island of Lobau. Napoleon had both bridges set to work upon at once in order to distract the attention of the enemy. The first was entrusted to Lannes, the other to Masséna.

Marshal Lannes ordered General Saint-Hilaire to send 500 men to the island of Schwarzelaken, which is separated from the left bank by a small arm of the river, and almost reaches the end of the Spitz bridge. General Saint-Hilaire composed this force of men from two regiments under two majors, which was likely to interfere with combined action. Thus, on reaching the island these officers, not acting in concert, committed the great mistake of having no reserve in a large house well placed for protecting the landing of more troops. Then dashing on blindly, without organisation, they pursued some detachments of the enemy who were defending the island. These shortly received reinforcements from the left bank, and though our soldiers repulsed the first attacks with vigour, forming square and fighting with the bayonet, they were overwhelmed by numbers, more than half being killed and all the rest wounded and taken before support could reach them. The Emperor and Marshal Lannes arrived on the river-bank just in time to witness this disaster. They bitterly reproached General Saint-Hilaire, who, though he had much experience of war, had made the mistake of first composing his detachment badly, and then of letting it go before he was in a position to support it promptly by successive reinforcements. It is true he had few boats at his disposal, but plenty more were coming up, for which he might have waited, and not acted precipitately. In this affair the Austrian troops were commanded by a French émigré, General Nordmann. He was very soon punished for having borne arms against his country, for he was killed by a cannon-ball at the battle of Wagram.

In despair at having caused the deaths of so many brave men, the Emperor and Marshal Lannes were hastening along the bank in a state of great agitation, when the marshal, catching his foot in a rope, fell into the Danube. Napoleon, who was alone with him at the moment, dashed into the water up to his waist, and had got the marshal out when we ran up to his assistance. This accident did not improve their tempers, already tried by the check which we had received, and which compelled the idea of a passage by the Schwarzelaken island to be given up. Having ascertained our purpose, the enemy had occupied it with several thousand men. Ebersdorf was now the only point at which we could cross the Danube. The village lies on the left bank, and in order to reach it we had to cross four branches of the river; the first being 500 yards in breadth, from which may be judged the immense length of the bridge that we had to throw across. Then comes an island, and then the second branch, the most rapid of all, 320 yards wide. The third stream is not more than 40. After passing these obstacles the huge island of Lobau is reached, which again is separated from the main land by the fourth branch, 140 yards across. We therefore had over 1,000 yards of water to traverse, and four bridges to build. The advantage of the crossing opposite Ebersdorf was that the Lobau island served as an immense place of arms, from which one could reach the left bank with more security, and further, as it formed a re-entering angle, offered a very advantageous debouchment upon the middle of the plain, which stretches between the villages of Gross-Aspern and Essling. No better configuration could be desired for the passage of an army.

Finding, when he arrived opposite Vienna, that Napoleon was checked by the river, the Archduke Charles hoped to prevent his crossing it by threatening his rear. He attacked our forces at Linz, and at Krems made arrangements to cross the river with all his army. But his troops were everywhere repulsed, and he confined himself to resisting our passage opposite Ebersdorf. Many obstacles were in the way of our building the bridges; we had to use boats of different shapes and dimensions, and materials lacking the necessary strength; we had no anchors, and had to supply their place with boxes full of cannon-balls. The works were carried on under cover of the plantations, and protected by Masséna's division. Lannes' division, posted over against Nussdorf, was to make apparent preparations for a crossing, in order to distract the enemy's attention. But this demonstration was merely a feint; and the marshal himself accompanied the Emperor on the 19th, when he went to Ebersdorf to direct the establishment of the bridges. After examining everything most thoroughly, and ascertaining that everything had been procured that was possible under the circumstances, Napoleon caused a brigade of Molitor's division to cross to the island of Lobau in eighty large boats and ten rafts. The breadth of the river and its roughness made this difficult, but once on the island the troops met with no obstacle; the enemy, pre-occupied with the idea that we meant to cross above Vienna, having omitted to guard that point. The construction of the bridges lasted all night, and, the weather being fine, was completed by noon on the 20th, when all the divisions of Masséna's corps crossed to the island. Probably, such great works have never been completed in so short a time. By four o'clock in the afternoon the fourth branch of the Danube was bridged by Masséna's infantry divisions, commanded by Generals Legrand, Boudet, Carra-Saint-Cyr, and Molitor, followed by the light cavalry divisions under Lasalle and Marulaz, with General Espagne's cuirassiers, 25,000 men in all, debouched from the island, with the intention of occupying the villages of Essling and Aspern. Only a few squadrons of the enemy appeared on the horizon; the bulk of the Austrian army was still at Gerhardsdorf, but was about to march to prevent us from establishing ourselves on the left bank. Marshal Lannes' corps was to leave Nussdorf for Ebersdorf, but, being delayed in its passage through Vienna, it did not come up till late the next day. The infantry of the guard followed.

On the evening of May 20, the Emperor and Marshal Lannes being lodged in the only house which existed on the island, my comrades and I took up our quarters close by, in brilliant moonlight, on beautiful turf. It was a delicious night, and with the carelessness of soldiers, thinking nothing of the morrow's dangers, we chatted gaily, and sang the last new airs—among others, two which were then very popular in the army, being attributed to Queen Hortense. The words were very appropriate to our circumstances; there was:—

'You leave me, dear, to go where glory waits you;
My loving heart accompanies your steps.'
And then again:—
'The gentle radiance of the evening star
Illumined with its beams the tents of France.'

Captain d'Albuquerque was the most joyous of us all, and after charming us with his fine voice, he sent us into fits of laughing by relating the most comical adventures of his adventurous life. Poor fellow! he little thought that the next day's sun would be his last—as little as we guessed that the plain which lay over against us on the other bank was soon to be watered with the blood of our kind marshal, and with that of almost every one of us.

On the morning of the 21st the Austrian lines showed themselves, and took up their position facing ours in front of Essling and Aspern. Marshal Masséna ought to have loopholed the houses of these villages, and covered the approaches by field-works, but unluckily he had neglected to take this precaution. The Emperor found fault with him, but as the enemy was approaching, and there was no time to repair the omission, Napoleon did his best to supply it by covering the last bridge with a tête de pont, which he traced himself. If Marshal Lannes' corps, the imperial guard, and the other expected troops had been present, Napoleon would certainly not have given the Archduke time to deploy, but would have attacked him on the spot. Having, however, only three divisions of infantry and four of cavalry to oppose to the enemy's large force, he was constrained, for the moment, to act on the defensive. To this end he rested his left wing, consisting of three divisions of infantry under Masséna, on the village of Aspern. The right wing, formed by Boudet's division, rested on the Danube, near the great wood lying between the river and the village of Essling, and occupied that village also. Lastly, the three cavalry divisions, and part of the artillery, under the orders of Marshal Bessières, formed the centre, spreading over the space which remained empty between Essling and Aspern. The Emperor compared his position to an entrenched camp, of which Aspern and Essling represented the bastions, united by a curtain formed by the cavalry and the artillery. The two villages, though not entrenched, were capable of a good defence, being built of masonry surrounded by low banks, which protected them against the inundation of the Danube. The church and churchyard of Aspern could hold out for a long time. Essling had for its citadel a large enclosure and an immense stone house built of hewn stone. We found these points very useful.

Although the troops composing the right and centre did not form any part of Lannes' corps, the Emperor wished in this difficulty to make use of the marshal's talents, and had entrusted the command-in-chief of them to him. He was heard to say to Marshal Bessières, much, as it appeared, to Bessières' annoyance, 'You are under the orders of Marshal Lannes.' I shall relate directly the serious quarrel to which this declaration gave rise, and how, greatly against my will, I got mixed up in it.

About 2 P.M. the Austrian army advanced upon us, and we were very hotly engaged. The cannonade was terrible; the enemy's force was so much superior to ours that they might easily have hurled us into the Danube by piercing the cavalry line which formed our only centre, and if the Emperor had been in the Archduke's place he would certainly have taken that course. But the Austrian commander-in-chief was too methodical to act in this determined way, therefore instead of boldly massing a strong force in the direction of our tête de pont, he occupied the whole of the first day in attacking Aspern and Essling, which he carried and lost five or six times after murderous combats. As soon as one of these villages was occupied by the enemy, the

Emperor sent up reserves to retake it, and if we were again driven from it, he took it again, though both places were on fire. During this alternation of successes and reverses, the Austrian cavalry several times threatened our centre, but ours repulsed it and returned to its place between the two villages, though terribly cut up by the enemy's artillery. Thus the action continued till ten in the evening, the French remaining masters of Essling and Aspern, while the Austrians, withdrawing their left and centre, did nothing but make some fruitless attacks on Aspern. They brought up, however, strong reinforcements for the morrow's action.

During this first day of the battle, though Marshal Lannes' staff, being always engaged in carrying orders to the most exposed points, had incurred great danger, we had yet no loss to deplore, and we were beginning to congratulate ourselves when, as the sun went down, the enemy, wishing to cover his retreat by a redoubled fire, sent a hail of projectiles at us. At that moment d'Albuquerque, La Bourdonnaye, and I, standing facing the marshal, were reporting to him upon orders which we had been sent to convey, having our backs consequently towards the enemy's guns. A ball struck poor d'Albuquerque in the loins, flinging him over the head of his horse, and laying him stone dead at the marshal's feet. 'There,' he exclaimed, 'is the end of the poor lad's romance! But he has at any rate died nobly.' A second ball passed between La Bourdonnaye's saddle and the spine of his horse without touching either horse or rider, a really miraculous shot. But the front of the saddle-tree was so violently smashed between La Bourdonnaye's thigh, that the wood and the iron were forced into his flesh, and he suffered for a long time from this extraordinary wound.

I had been between my two comrades, and saw them both fall at the same moment. I went towards the escort to order some troopers to come and carry La Bourdonnaye away, but I had hardly gone a few steps when an aide-de-camp of General Boudet, having come forward to speak to the marshal, had his head taken off by a cannon-ball in the very spot which I had just left. Clearly this place was no longer tenable. We were right in front of one of the enemy's batteries, so the marshal, for all his courage, thought it advisable to move a couple of hundred yards to the right.

The last order which Marshal Lannes had given me to carry was addressed to Marshal Bessières, and gave rise to a brisk altercation between the two marshals, who hated each other cordially. In order to understand the scene which I am about to relate, it is necessary that you should know the reasons of this hatred.

General Bonaparte, when on his way to assume the command of the Army of Italy in 1796, took as his senior aide-de-camp Murat, whom he had just promoted to colonel, and for whom he had a great liking. Having, however, in the first actions noticed the military capacity, zeal, and courage of Lannes, then commanding the 4th of the line, he granted to that officer an equally large share of his esteem and friendship, thus exciting Murat's jealousy. When the two colonels had become generals of brigade, Bonaparte was accustomed, on critical occasions, to entrust to Murat the direction of the cavalry charges and put Lannes in command of the reserve of the grenadiers. Both did splendidly, and the army had nothing but praise for either. But between these gallant officers there grew up a rivalry which, if the truth must be told, was not at all displeasing to the commander-in-chief, as tending to stimulate their zeal and their desire of distinction. He would extol before Murat the achievements of General Lannes, and enlarge in Lannes' presence on the merits of Murat. The rivalry soon led to altercations, in which Bessières, then merely captain in General Bonaparte's Guides and in high favour with the commander, always took the part of his compatriot Murat; while taking every opportunity, as Lannes was well aware, of depreciating him. After the Italian campaigns Lannes and Murat accompanied Bonaparte to Egypt. About this time both conceived a wish to marry Caroline Bonaparte, and Bessières found an opportunity to injure Lannes' suit irretrievably. As a member of the administrative council, charged with the distribution of the military fund, he became aware that Lannes had exceeded the allowance for the outfit of his regiment, the consular guard; by 300,000 francs. He revealed this to Murat, who brought it to the ears of the First Consul. Lannes was dismissed from the command of the guard, and allowed a month to make up the deficit, which, without the generous aid of Augereau, he would have found it hard to do. Napoleon afterwards received him back into favour; but meantime Murat had married Caroline Bonaparte. As may be supposed, Lannes never forgave Bessières, and the antipathy was in full vigour when they came in contact at the battle of Essling.

At the moment of the brisk cannonade which had just killed poor d'Albequerque, Lannes, observing that the Austrians were making a retrograde movement, thought it a good opening for a cavalry charge. He called me to carry the order to Marshal Bessières, who, as I have said, had just been placed under his command by the Emperor. I was on duty; so the next aide-de-camp in course for service came up. It was de Viry. Marshal Lannes gave him the following order: 'Go and tell Marshal Bessières that I order him to charge home.' This expression, conveying that the charge must be pushed till the sabres are in the enemy's bodies, obviously is very like a reprimand; as implying that hitherto the cavalry has not acted with sufficient vigour. The expression 'I order,' employed by one marshal to another, was also very rough. Lannes used the two phrases intentionally.

Off went de Viry, fulfilled his instructions, and returned to the marshal, who asked, 'What did you say to Marshal Bessières?' 'I informed him that your excellency begged him to order a general charge of the cavalry.' Lannes shrugged his shoulders, and cried, 'You are a baby; send another officer!' This time it was Labédoyère. The marshal knew he was of firmer character than de Viry, and gave him the same message, emphasising the expressions 'I order' and 'charge home.' Labédoyère did not see Lannes' intention, and did not like to repeat the words verbatim to Bessières; so he too employed a circumlocution. Accordingly when he came back and reported the words he had used, Lannes turned his back on him. At that moment I galloped up to the staff. It was not my turn for duty, but the marshal called me and said, 'Marbot, Marshal Augereau assured me that you were a man I could count on. So far I have found his words justified by your conduct. I should like a further proof. Go and tell Marshal Bessières that I order him to charge home. You understand, sir, home.' As he spoke he poked me in the ribs with his finger. I perfectly understood that Lannes wished to mortify Bessières, first by taking a harsh way of reminding him that the Emperor had put him in a subordinate post to himself, and further by finding fault with his management of the cavalry. I was perturbed at being obliged to transmit offensive expressions to the other marshal. It was easy to foresee that they might have awkward results; but my immediate chief must be obeyed.

So I galloped off to the centre, wishing that one of the shots which were dropping thickly about might bowl over my horse, and give me a good excuse for not accomplishing my disagreeable mission! I approached Marshal Bessières with much respect, and begged to speak with him in private. 'Speak up, sir,' he replied stiffly. So I had to say in presence of his staff and a crowd of superior officers, 'Marshal Lannes directs me to tell your Excellency that he orders you to charge home.' Bessières angrily exclaimed, 'Is that the way to speak to a marshal, sir? Orders! charge home! You shall be severely punished for this rudeness.' I answered, 'Marshal, the more offensive the terms I have used seem to your Excellency, the more sure you may be that in using them I only obeyed my orders.' I saluted and returned to Lannes. 'Well, what did you say to Marshal Bessières?' 'That your Excellency ordered him to charge home.' 'Right; here is one aide-de-camp at any rate who understands me.' In spite of this compliment, you may imagine that I was very sorry to have had to deliver such a message. However, the cavalry charge came off; General d'Espagne was killed, but the result was very good. Whereon Lannes said, 'You see that my stern injunction has produced an excellent effect; but for it M. le Maréchal Bessières would have fiddled about all day.'

Night came on, and the battle ceased both in the centre and on our right, on which Lannes determined to join the Emperor, who was bivouacking within the works of the tête de pont. But hardly had we started, when the marshal, hearing brisk firing in Aspern, where Masséna was in command, wished to go and see what was taking place in the village. He bade his staff go on to the Emperor's bivouac, and, taking only myself and an orderly, bade me guide him to Aspern, where I had been several times in the course of the day. I went in that direction; with the moon and the blaze of Essling and Aspern we had plenty of light. Still, as the frequent paths were apt to be hidden by the tall corn, and I was afraid of losing myself in it, I dismounted in order to find the way better. Soon the marshal dismounted also, and walked by my side chatting about the day's fighting and the chances of that which would take place on the morrow. A quarter of an hour brought us close to Aspern, the approaches to which were lined by the bivouac fires of Masséna's troops. Wishing to speak to him, Marshal Lannes bade me go forward to ascertain his quarters. Before we had gone many steps, I perceived Masséna walking in front of the camp with Marshal Bessières. The wound in my forehead which I had received in Spain prevented me from wearing a busby, and I was the only one among the marshal's aides-de-camp who had a cocked hat. Bessières, recognising me by this, but not yet noticing Marshal Lannes, came towards me, saying, 'Ah! it is you, sir; if what you said recently came from you alone, I will teach you to choose your expressions better when speaking to your superiors; if you were only obeying your marshal, he shall give me satisfaction, and I bid you tell him so.' Then Marshal Lannes, leaping forward like a lion, passed in front of me, and seizing my arm, cried: 'Marbot, I owe you an apology; for though I believed I could be certain of your attachment, I had some doubts remaining as to the manner in which you had transmitted my orders to this gentleman; but I see that I was unfair to you.' Then, addressing Bessières, 'I wonder how you dare to find fault with one of my aides-de-camp. He was the first to mount on the walls at Ratisbon, he crossed the Danube at the risk of almost certain death, he has just been twice wounded in Spain, while there are some so-called soldiers who haven't had a scratch in their lives, and have got their promotion by playing the spy and informer on their comrades. What fault have you to find with this officer?' 'Sir,' said Bessières, 'your aide-de-camp came and told me that you ordered me to charge home; it appears to me that such expressions are unseemly!' 'They are quite right, sir, and it was I who dictated them; did not the Emperor tell you that you were under my orders?' Bessières replied with hesitation, 'The Emperor warned me that I must comply with your opinion.' 'Know, sir,' cried the marshal, ' that in military matters people do not comply, they obey orders. If the Emperor had thought fit to place me under your command, I should have offered him my resignation. But so long as you are under mine, I shall give you orders and you will obey; otherwise I shall withdraw the command of the troops from you. As for charging home, I gave you the order because you did not do it, and because all the morning you were parading before the enemy without approaching him boldly.' 'But that's an insult,' cried Bessières, angrily; 'you shall give me satisfaction!' 'This very moment if you like!' cried Lannes, laying his hand on his sword. During this discussion, old Masséna, interposing between the adversaries, sought to calm them, and not succeeding, he took the high tone in his turn. 'I am your senior, gentlemen; you are in my camp, and I shall not permit you to give my troops the scandalous spectacle of seeing two marshals draw on each other, and that in presence of the enemy. I summon you, therefore, in the name of the Emperor, to separate at once.' Then, adopting a gentler manner, he took Marshal Lannes by the arm, and led him to the further end of the bivouac, while Bessières returned to his own. You may suppose how distressed I was by this deplorable scene. Finally, Marshal Lannes, remounting, set off for the Emperor's bivouac where my comrades were already established. On reaching it, he took Napoleon aside, and related what had happened. The Emperor at once sent for Marshal Bessières, whom he received sternly; then they went some distance away, and walked rapidly, the Emperor appearing to be reprimanding him severely. Marshal Bessières looked confused, and must have felt still more so when the Emperor sat down to dinner without inviting him, while he made Marshal Lannes take a seat at his right hand. My comrades and I were as sad this evening as we had been cheerful the night before. We had just seen poor d'Albuquerque killed; we had close beside us La Bourdonnaye horribly wounded, and groaning so as to break our hearts; and we were, besides, agitated with sad presentiments with regard to the result of the battle, of which we had seen only the first part. Moreover, we were on our legs all night, seeing Marshal Lannes' corps across the Danube, followed by the imperial guard. Meanwhile, the river was rising visibly; great trees, borne down by the flood, kept striking the bridges of boats, more than once breaking them. They were, however, promptly repaired, and, in spite of accidents, the troops which I have mentioned crossed the river, and were assembled on the battle-field by the time that the dawn of May 22 appeared, and the roar of cannon announced that the fight was being renewed.

Having at his disposal twice as many troops as on the previous day, the Emperor took steps to attack. Marshal Masséna and three of his infantry divisions remained in Aspern; the fourth, that of General Boudet, was left at Essling, under the command of Marshal Lannes, whose corps occupied the space between the two villages, having as its second line Bessières' cavalry, still under the orders of Lannes. The imperial guard formed the reserve. The Emperor's reprimand to Marshal Bessières had been so severe that, as soon as he saw Lannes, he came to ask him how he wished his troops to be placed. The marshal, wishing to establish his authority, replied, 'As you await my orders, sir, I order you to place them at such a point.' The expression was harsh, but one must remember how Bessières had behaved to Lannes in the days of the Consulate. He appeared hurt, but obeyed in silence.

The Archduke, who might, by a vigorous attack, have pierced our weak line between Essling and Aspern the day before, renewed his efforts against those villages. But, as we had then resisted his whole army, with only Masséna's corps and part of our cavalry, we were all the more able to do so now that we had been joined by the imperial guard, Marshal Lannes' corps, and a division of cuirassiers. The Austrians were repulsed at all points; one of their columns, consisting of 1,000 men under General Weber, with six guns, was actually cut off and captured in Aspern.

So far the Emperor had been acting on the defensive while the troops were crossing the river, but now that the numbers whom he had on the battle-field were doubled, and Marshal Davout's corps had assembled at Ebersdorf, and begun to cross, Napoleon judged that the time had come for assuming the offensive, and ordered Marshal Lannes at the head of the infantry divisions of Saint-Hilaire, Tharreau, Claparède, and Demont, followed by two divisions of cuirassiers, to break the enemy's centre. Lannes advanced proudly into the plain; nothing could resist him. In a moment he captured a battalion, five guns, and a flag. At first the Austrians retreated in good order, but as their centre was obliged to extend in proportion as we advanced, it was at last broken through. Their troops fell into such disorder that we could see the officers and sergeants striking their soldiers with sticks, without being able to keep them in the ranks. If our advance had continued a few moments longer, it would have been all up with the Archduke's army.

Chapter 13
Aspern-Essling (2)

Everything foretold a complete victory for us. Masséna and General Boudet were making ready to issue from Aspern and Essling, and to fall upon the Austrians, when, to our surprise, an aide-de-camp from the Emperor came up with orders to Marshal Lannes to suspend his attacking movement. Trees and other objects floating in the Danube had caused a new breach in the bridge, and the arrival of Davout's troops and of the ammunition was delayed. After an hour's waiting the passage was repaired, and, though the enemy had profited by the delay to reinforce his centre, we renewed our attack. Again the Austrians were giving ground, when we heard that an immense piece of the great bridge had been carried away, and would take forty-eight hours to replace. The Emperor accordingly ordered Lannes to halt on the ground which he had taken.

This mishap, which hindered us from winning a brilliant victory, came about as follows. An Austrian officer, posted on look-out duty with some companies of Jägers in the islands above Aspern, had embarked in a small boat and gone out to the middle of the river to get a distant view of our troops crossing the bridges. Thus he witnessed the first breach caused by the floating trees, and the idea struck him that the same accident might be repeated as fast as we repaired the damages. So he had a number of beams and some fire-boats launched down the stream, destroying some of our pontoons. But seeing that the engineers quickly replaced them, the officer caused a large floating mill to be set on fire and towed out into mid-stream. Borne down upon our principal bridge, it broke away a large part of it. Perceiving instantly that all hope of restoring the passage, and enabling Davout to reach the field of battle was abandoned for that day; the Emperor ordered Lannes to withdraw his troops by degrees to their former position, between Aspern and Essling so that, resting on those villages, they might hold their ground against the enemy. The movement was being carried out in perfect order, when the Archduke, who had at first been puzzled by our retreat, heard that the bridge was broken, and saw a chance of driving the French army into the Danube. With this view he sent his cavalry against the most advanced of our divisions, that of Saint-Hilaire. Our battalions repulsed the charge, and the enemy then opened upon them with a heavy artillery fire. Just then I was bearing an order from Lannes to General Saint-Hilaire. Hardly had I reached him when a storm of grape struck his staff, killing several officers and smashing the general's leg. He died under amputation. I was myself struck in the thigh by a grape-shot, which tore out a piece of flesh as large as an egg, but the wound was not dangerous, and I was able to return and report to the marshal. I found him with the Emperor, who, seeing me covered with blood, remarked, 'Your turn comes round pretty often!' Both he and the marshal felt the loss of General Saint-Hilaire keenly.

Seeing the division attacked at all points, the marshal went to take command of it. He withdrew it slowly, often facing towards the enemy, until our right rested on Essling, which was still held by Boudet's division. Though my wound was not yet dressed, I thought I ought to go with the marshal. In the course of the retreat, my friend de Viry had his shoulder smashed by a bullet, and I had some difficulty in getting him brought to the entrenchments.

The position was very critical. Compelled to act on the defensive, the Emperor posted his army in an arc, having the Danube for its chord, our right resting on the river in rear of Essling, our left in rear of Aspern. Under pain of being driven into the river we had to keep up the flight for the rest of the day; it was now 9 A.M., and not till nightfall should we be able to retire to the island of Lobau by the weak bridge over the small branch. The Archduke, recognising the weakness of our position, repeatedly attacked the two villages and the centre, but, fortunately for us, did not think of forcing our weakest point, between Essling and the Danube, by which a strong column pushed vigorously forward might have reached the tête de pont and destroyed us. All along our lines the slaughter was terrible, but absolutely necessary to save the honour of France and the portion of the army which had crossed the Danube.

To check the energy of the enemy's attacks, Marshal Lannes frequently resumed the offensive against their centre, and forced it back, but they soon returned with reinforcements. On one of these occasions, Labédoyère got a grapeshot in his foot, and Watteville a dislocated shoulder, his horse being killed under him by a cannon-ball. Thus of all the staff Sub-lieutenant Le Couteulx and I remained, and I could not leave the marshal alone with that young officer, who, though brave enough, had no experience. Wishing to retain me, he said, 'Go, and get dressed; if you can then sit your horse, come back to me.' I went to the first field-hospital; the crowd of wounded was enormous, and lint had run short. A doctor put into my wound some of the coarse tow which is used as wadding for cannon, and the rough fibres gave me a good deal of pain. Under other circumstances I should have gone to the rear, but now every man had to display all his energy, and I went back to the marshal. I found him very anxious, having just heard that the Austrians had taken half of Aspern from Masséna. That village was taken and re-taken many times. Essling was being vigorously attacked at that very instant, and bravely defended by Boudet's division. So fierce were both sides that they were fighting in the midst of the burning houses, and barricading themselves with the hacked corpses which blocked the streets. Five times the Hungarian grenadiers were driven back, but their sixth attack succeeded. They got possession of the village, all but the great granary, into which General Boudet withdrew, as into a citadel.

While this fighting was going on, the marshal sent me several times into Essling. The danger was considerable, but in the excitement I even forgot the pain of my wound.

At length, perceiving that, repeating his fault of the day before, he was wasting his forces against our two bastions Essling and Aspern, and neglecting our centre, where a well-sustained attack with his reserve would bring him to our bridge and secure the destruction of the French army, the Archduke launched large masses of cavalry, supported by heavy columns of infantry, on this point. Marshal Lannes, not surprised by this display of force, gave orders that the Austrians should be allowed to approach within gun-shot range and received them with such a furious fire of musketry and grape that they halted, nor could the stimulating presence of the Archduke induce them to come a single pace nearer. They could perceive behind our line the bearskin caps of the Old Guard, which was advancing in a stately column, with shouldered arms.

Cleverly profiting by the enemy's hesitation, Marshal Lannes caused Bessières to charge them at the head of two divisions of cavalry. Part of the Austrian battalions and squadrons were overthrown, and the Archduke, finding his attack on our centre unsuccessful, thought to profit at least by the advantage which the capture of Essling offered. At that moment, however, the Emperor ordered his aide-de-camp, General Mouton, to retake the village. Hurling himself upon the Hungarian grenadiers, he drove them out, and remained master of Essling, a feat which covered himself and the Young Guard with glory, and earned him later on the title of Count of Lobau.

These successes on our part having slackened the enemy's ardour, the Archduke, whose losses were enormous, abandoned the hope of forcing our position, and for the rest of the day only kept up an ineffectual combat. This terrible thirty hours' battle was drawing to its end. It was high time, for our ammunition was nearly exhausted. Had it not been for the activity with which Davout kept sending it over in small boats from the right bank, it would have failed utterly. As, however, the boats came few and far between, the Emperor bade us economise, and our fire became mere sharpshooting practice, the enemy at the same time reducing his.

While the two armies were mutually watching each other but not moving, and the commanders in groups in rear of the battalions were discussing the events of the day, Marshal Lannes, weary with riding, had dismounted, and was walking about with Major-General Pouzet. Just then a spent ball struck the general on the head, laying him dead at the marshal's feet. He had been formerly a sergeant in the Champagne Regiment, and at the beginning of the Revolution was at the camp of Le Miral when my father commanded there. At the same time the battalion of volunteers from the Gers, in which Lannes was sub-lieutenant, formed part of the division. The sergeants of the old line regiments having the task of instructing the volunteers, that of Gers fell to the share of Pouzet.

Quickly perceiving the young sub-lieutenant's talents, he did not confine himself to teaching him the manual exercise, but gave him such instruction in manœuvres that he became an excellent tactician. Attributing his first promotion to Pouzet's instruction, Lannes was much attached to him, and in proportion as he got on himself he used his interest to advance his friend. His grief, then, at seeing him fall dead was very great.

At that moment we were a little in advance of the tile-works, to the left, near Essling. In his emotion, wishing to get away from the corpse, the marshal went a hundred paces in the direction of Enzersdorf, and seated himself, deep in thought, on the further side of a ditch, from which he could watch the troops. A quarter of an hour later, four soldiers laboriously carrying in a cloak a dead officer whose face could not be seen stopped to rest in front of the marshal. The cloak fell open, and Lannes recognised Pouzet. 'Oh!' he cried, 'is this terrible sight going to follow me everywhere?' Getting up, he went and sat down at the edge of another ditch, his hand over his eyes and his legs crossed. As he sat there, plunged in gloomy meditation, a small three-pound shot, fired from a gun at Enzersdorf, ricochetted, and struck him just where his legs crossed. The knee-pan of one was smashed, and the back sinews of the other torn. Instantly I rushed towards the marshal, who said, 'I am wounded; it's nothing much; give me your hand to help me up.' He tried to rise, but could not. The infantry regiments in front of us sent some men at once to carry the marshal to an ambulance, but, having neither stretcher nor cloak, we had to take him in our arms, an attitude which caused him horrible pain. Then a sergeant, seeing in the distance the soldiers who were carrying General Pouzet's body, ran and asked them for the cloak in which he was wrapped. We were about to lay the marshal on it, so as to carry him with less pain; but he recognised the cloak, and said to me, 'This is my poor friend's; it is covered with his blood; I will not use it. Drag me along rather how you can.' Not far off I saw a clump of trees; I sent M. le Couteulx and some grenadiers there, and they presently returned with a stretcher covered with boughs. We carried the marshal to the tête de port, where the chief surgeons proceeded to dress his wound, first holding a private consultation, in which they could not agree as to what should be done. Dr. Larrey was in favour of amputating the leg of which the knee-pan was broken; another, whose name I forget, wanted to cut off both; while Dr. Yvan, from whom I heard these details, was against any amputation. This surgeon, who had long known the marshal, asserted that his firmness of character gave some chance of a cure, while an operation performed in such hot weather would inevitably bring him to the grave. Larrey was the senior surgeon of the army, and his opinion prevailed. One of the marshal's legs was amputated. He bore the operation with great courage; it was hardly over when the Emperor came up. The interview was most touching. The Emperor, kneeling beside the stretcher, wept as he embraced the marshal, whose blood soon stained his white kerseymere waistcoast.

Some evil-disposed persons have written that Marshal Lannes addressed the Emperor reproachfully, and implored him to make war no longer; but as I was at that moment supporting the marshal's shoulders and heard everything that he said, I can assert that this was not the case. On the contrary, the marshal felt the proofs of the Emperor's concern very deeply, and when the latter was obliged to go away to give the orders required for the safety of the army, and said, 'You will live, my friend, you will live,' the marshal replied, pressing his hand, 'I trust I may, if I can still be of use to France and to your Majesty.'

In spite of his cruel sufferings the marshal did not forget the position of his troops, but every moment asked for news of them. He learnt with pleasure that as the enemy did not venture to pursue they were profiting by nightfall to return to the island of Lobau. His anxiety extended to his aides-de-camp who had been wounded near him; he asked how they were going on, and when he knew that I had been dressed with coarse tow, he asked Dr. Larrey to examine my wound. I should have liked to carry the marshal to Ebersdorf, on the right bank, but the broken bridge prevented this, and we did not dare to put him on board of a frail boat. He was therefore compelled to pass the night on the island, where, for want of a mattress, I borrowed a dozen cavalry cloaks to make him a bed. We were short of everything and had not even good water to give the marshal, who was parched with thirst. We offered him Danube water, but the flood had made this so muddy that he could not drink it, and said, resignedly, 'We are like sailors who die of thirst with water all round them.'

My desire to soothe his sufferings led me to devise a new kind of filter. One of the marshal's valets, who had remained on the island, had with him a small portmanteau containing linen. I took one of the marshal's shirts of fine material; we tied all the openings with string except one, and, plunging into the Danube the kind of bag thus made, we drew it out full, and then hung it over a large can, so that the water filtering through the linen was cleared of nearly all the earthy particles. The poor marshal, who had followed my operations with eager eyes, was at last able to get a draught, which, if not perfect, was at least fresh and clear, and was very grateful for my invention. The care which I was bestowing on my illustrious patient could not avert my fears for the fate which might befall him if the Austrians were to cross the small arm of the river and attack us on the island. What could I then do for him? I thought for a moment that my fears were going to be realised, for a battery near Enzersdorf sent several shots at us; but the fire did not last long.

In the Archduke's position two courses were open to him: either to make a fierce attack upon the French divisions which remained on the field of battle, or, if this seemed too bold a move, he might without risk to his troops place his artillery on the bank of the small arm from Enzersdorf to Aspern, and by bombarding the island annihilate the 40,000 French who were crowded on it. Happily for us, the enemy's commander-in-chief took neither of these courses; and Masséna, to whom Napoleon had entrusted the command of so much of the army as was still on the left bank, was able during the night to evacuate the villages of Aspern and Essling unmolested, and bring his wounded, all his troops, and all his artillery over to the island. The bridge across the small arm was taken up, and by daybreak on the 23rd all our regiments who had been engaged were safe on the island; nor during the forty-five days which Masséna's occupation of it lasted did the enemy fire another shot in that direction.

A boat of some size was sent by the Emperor on the 23rd to bring Marshal Lannes to the right bank. I put him and our wounded comrades into it and, when we reached Ebersdorf, sent the latter to Vienna in the charge of M. le Couteulx, remaining myself alone with the marshal. He was taken to one of the best houses in Ebersdorf, and I sent for all his people to come and join him there.

Meanwhile our troops massed on the island of Lobau, short of food and ammunition, reduced to live on horseflesh, and cut off from the right bank by the great breadth of the river, were in a most critical position. It was feared that the Archduke's inaction was feigned, and it was expected that at any moment he might ascend the Danube to a point, above Vienna, and, crossing the river, attack us in rear by the right bank, at the same time raising the capital against us. In that case, Marshal Davout's corps, which was guarding Vienna and Ebersdorf, would certainly have made a stout resistance. But could it have beaten the whole of the enemy's army? And, meanwhile, what would have become of the troops shut up on the island?

The Emperor profited cleverly by the time which the Austrians left him, and never was his prodigious activity better employed. Aided by the indefatigable Davout and his divisions, he did on the 23rd alone more than another general could have got done in a week. A well-organised service of boats brought provisions and ammunition to the island; the wounded were all got away to Vienna; hospitals were established; materials in great quantity collected to repair the bridges, build fresh ones, and protect them by a stockade; a hundred guns of the largest calibre, captured in Vienna, were taken to Ebersdorf. By the 24th, communication with the island was re-established, and the Emperor marched Lannes' division, the guard, and all the cavalry on to the right bank, leaving only Masséna's corps to fortify the island, and put in battery the big guns which had been brought up. This point being secured, the Emperor ordered Bernadotte's army corps, and the various divisions of the Germanic Confederation to come on to Vienna, which would enable him to repulse the Archduke in the event of his venturing across the river to attack us. A few days later we received a powerful reinforcement. A French army under Eugene Beauharnais, coming from Italy, took up its position on our right. I have not yet mentioned this army. At the beginning of the campaign it had experienced a check at Sacile; but a renewed attack on the part of the French resulted in the defeat of the enemy, who were driven across the Alps. The Archduke John had been thrown back across the Danube into Hungary, which opened the communications between the Viceroy and the Grand Army, of which his troops henceforward formed the right wing, posted opposite Pressburg.

Chapter 14
I Attend to My Wounds

I have promised not to weary you with details of strategy, but as the battle of Essling and the unforeseen events which hindered us from winning a brilliant victory have been widely discussed, I think I ought to make some remarks upon the causes which led to that result, all the more so that they have been misdescribed by a Frenchman, who has imputed to the Emperor mistakes which he did not commit. General Rogniart, in his work 'Considerations on the Art of War' asserts that at Essling Napoleon fell thoughtlessly into a trap which the Archduke set for him when he ordered the centre of his army to retire and draw the French forward while he was having the bridges broken, their destruction having been already arranged. Not only is this assertion contrary to the truth, but, it is absurd. As a matter of fact if the Archduke knew that he had under his hand the means of destroying the bridges, why did he not have them broken on the evening of the 21st, when not more than 25,000 French troops had crossed to the left bank, whom with the 125,000 at his disposal, he could make sure of destroying or capturing? Would not this have been better than leaving the passage of the river open to Napoleon all night, thus enabling him to double the force which he could oppose to the enemy? If, again, he had arranged the destruction of the bridges, why did he during the afternoon of the 21st lose four or five thousand men in attacking the villages of Essling and Aspern? It would have been much wiser to wait till Masséna's corps, having its retreat cut off, should be obliged to capitulate. Why, finally, did he on the morning of the 22nd renew his furious attacks upon Essling and Aspern instead of waiting till the bridges were broken? Clearly, because he did not know that it was in his power to destroy them. It was only chance and the flooded state of the river which brought down upon the pontoons the floating trees which caused the first partial breaches, while later on the quick wit of an Austrian officer arranged for the destruction of the great bridge by launching into the current boats laden with burning wood, and lastly, a huge floating mill, which carried away nearly the whole bridge. But nothing had been arranged beforehand, and this was admitted to us afterwards by several of the enemy's generals, whom we saw on the occasion of the armistice at Znaym.

If any doubt remained on the subject it would be entirely destroyed by the following irresistible argument. Of all the military decorations in the Austrian Empire, the most difficult to obtain was that of Maria Theresa, for it was only granted to an officer who could show that he had done more than his duty. He had to ask for the decoration himself, and if he failed he was for ever debarred from demanding it again. Now, in spite of the strictness of this regulation, the officer of the Austrian Jägers obtained the Cross of Maria Theresa, which shows undoubtedly that he had acted on an inspiration of his own, and not by the Archduke's orders.

As soon as the troops had effected their retreat into the island of Lobau, and on to the right bank of the Danube, the Emperor took up his quarters at Ebersdorf in order to survey the arrangements for a fresh crossing. Not one bridge, but three, were to be constructed, all having a strong stockade of piles up stream from them to withstand any floating objects which the enemy might launch at them. The care which the Emperor bestowed on these important works did not prevent him from coming twice a day to visit Marshal Lannes. For the first four days after his wound the marshal went on as well as possible; he preserved perfect equanimity, and conversed very calmly. So far was he from renouncing the service of his country, as some writers have stated, that he made plans for the future. Learning that Mesler, the celebrated Viennese mechanician, had made for the Austrian General, Count Palfy, an artificial leg with which he could walk and ride as well as ever, the marshal asked me to write to that artist, asking him to come and measure him for a leg. But the oppressive heat which we had experienced for some time became more intense, with disastrous results to the wounded man. He was attacked by high fever, accompanied with terrible delirium. The critical situation in which he had left the army was always on his mind, and he fancied himself still on the battle-field. He would call his aides-de-camp in a loud voice, bidding one tell the cuirassiers to charge, another to bring the artillery to such and such a point, and so on. In vain did Dr. Yvan and I try to soothe him; he did not understand us. His excitement kept increasing; he no longer recognised even the Emperor. This condition lasted several days without his getting a moment's sleep or resting from his imaginary combats. At length, in the night between the 29th and 30th, he left off giving his orders; a great weakness succeeded the delirium; he recovered all his mental faculties, recognised me, pressed my hand, spoke of his wife, his five children, his father, and, as I was very near his pillow, he rested his head on my shoulder, appeared to be falling asleep, and passed away with a sigh. It was daybreak on May 30. A few moments later the Emperor arrived for his morning visit. I thought it my duty to meet him and let him know of the sad event, cautioning him not to enter the infected atmosphere of the room. But Napoleon, putting me aside, advanced to the marshal's body, which he embraced, bathing it with tears, and saying repeatedly, 'What a loss for France and for me!' Berthier tried in vain to draw him away from the sad sight; he remained for more than an hour, and only yielded when Berthier pointed out that General Bertrand and the engineer officers were waiting to execute an important piece of work, for which he had himself fixed the time. As he went away he expressed his satisfaction with the unremitting care which I had taken of the marshal, and bade me have the body embalmed, and everything got ready for its transport to France.

My grief, already very keen, was increased by the necessity of attending the operation in order to draw up a report of it, and of superintending the removal of the body. It was a sad day for me, and I reflected much on the destiny of this man, who, gifted only with a quick intelligence and a dauntless courage, had raised himself by merit from the lowest to the highest rank of society, and now, in full enjoyment of his honours and vast wealth, had just ended his career in a foreign land, far from his family, in the arms of none but his aide-de-camp. Both physical and moral shocks had impaired my health. My wound, a slight one at first, and easy to cure if I could have had a few days' rest of mind and body, had become terribly inflamed during these ten days of anxiety and fatigue; for no one, not even his valets, had rendered me any efficient help in tending the marshal. One of them, a kind of dandy, had gone off the first day, under the plea that the stench of the wounds made him ill. The other was more zealous, but really fell ill from this cause, and I was obliged to send for a hospital man, who was as willing as possible, but whose unfamiliar face and dress seemed to displease the marshal, so that I had to give him everything. This day and night watching made my wound worse; my thigh was much swollen, and I could hardly stand, when I determined at length to go to Vienna and get proper treatment. In the Archduke Albert's palace I found all my wounded comrades. The Emperor had not lost sight of us, for he instructed the chief court surgeon, who lodged at Schönbrunn, to look after Marshal Lannes' aides-de-camp, and this good Dr. Franck came to see us twice daily. On examining my wound he thought it in a very bad state, and prescribed entire rest. But in spite of his advice I often walked through the passages to see my friend de Viry, who was kept in bed by a much worse wound than mine. Indeed I soon had the grief of losing this excellent comrade, to my infinite regret; and as I was the only aide-de-camp who knew his father, the duty of announcing to him the fatal news fell to me. The poor old man, broken-hearted, survived his son but a short time.

After the death of Marshal Lannes I had gone to Vienna to get my wound attended to. I lay on my bed deep in sad meditations; for not only did I regret for his own sake the marshal who had been so kind to me, but I could not disguise from myself that the loss of such a supporter changed my position vastly. The Emperor had, indeed, told me at Mölk that he appointed me major and both he and Berthier addressed me as such; but, as in the bustle of the war, no commissions had been drawn out, I was actually still only a captain. My fears for my future were terminated by a piece of good luck. My comrade, La Bourdonnaye, far more severely wounded than I, lay in the next room to mine, and we often chatted through the open door. M. Mounier, the Emperor's secretary, afterwards peer of France, often came to see La Bourdonnaye, and I made his acquaintance. Having often heard my performances and my wounds spoken of at headquarters, and seeing me with a fresh mark of the enemy's fire, he asked what reward I had got. ' None,' said I. 'It can only be by an oversight,' replied he, 'for I am sure I saw your name for one of the commissions lying in the Emperor's portfolio.' Next day I learnt from him that he had placed the commission under the Emperor's eyes, and that the Emperor had written on the margin, 'This officer shall enter the mounted chasseurs of my guard as major'; thus granting me a great and unprecedented favour, for the officers of the guard had army rank superior to that which they held in the corps. In thus admitting me as major, Napoleon raised me two steps at once, and gave me the rank of major, or lieutenant-colonel in the line, which was magnificent. I was not, however, dazzled by this advantage, although, as the guard did garrison duty in Paris, I should be able to see more of my mother; but Marshal Bessières was general in command of the guard, and not only did he give a bad reception to officers whom he had not recommended himself, but I feared his ill-will on account of the incident at Essling.

I was in a painful state of uncertainty when Prince Eugene, Viceroy of Italy, arrived at Vienna, and took up his quarters in the Archduke Albert's palace. One day Masséna came to visit him, and, wishing to show kindness to Marshal Lannes' aides-de-camp, came up to our rooms and stayed some time with me, as he had known me at the time of the siege of Genoa. I told him my difficulty, and he replied, 'No doubt it would be a great advantage to you to enter the guard, but you would expose yourself to Marshal Bessières' vengeance. Come and be my aide-de-camp, and you shall be received like a child of my family, as the son of a good general who died when fighting under me, and I will take care of your promotion.' Enticed by these promises, I accepted; Masséna went off at once to the Emperor, who finally agreed to his request, and sent me on June 18 my commission as major to be aide-de-camp to Masséna.

Delighted though I was at being at length a field-officer, it was not long before I was sorry for having accepted Masséna's offer. An hour after my appointment as aide-de-camp came Marshal Bessières bringing with his own hands my nomination to the guard; he assured me that he would have much pleasure in receiving me in the corps, as he knew that in bearing the order to him on the field of Essling I was only obeying the instructions of Marshal Lannes. I was deeply grateful for this kind and straightforward action, and much regretted that I had been so prompt in engaging myself to

Masséna; but it was too late to go back on my decision. I feared at the time that my promotion would suffer, but luckily it was not so, for M. Mounier, who took my place in the guard, was still only major when I became colonel. It is true that he passed the next two years in Paris, while I was in the thick of the fire and got two more wounds.

Napoleon rewarded Marshal Lannes' staff plentifully. Among others, Saint-Mars became colonel of the 3rd Chasseurs, and Labédoyère aide-de-camp to Prince Eugene. As for me, as soon as I could get to Schönbrunn to thank the Emperor for my promotion, his Majesty did me the honour of saying, 'I should have liked to have you in my guard; however, as Marshal Masséna wants you for his aide-de-camp, and that suits you, I have no objection; but in order to show in a special way how pleased I am with you, I appoint you knight of the Empire, with an annuity of 2,000 francs.' If I had dared, I should have begged the Emperor to return to his first purpose, and admit me into his guard; but how could I tell him the reason why I had originally declined? That being impossible, I confined myself to thanking him, but it was with a sore heart. However, having to resign myself to the position into which my own hot-headedness had brought me, I put aside useless regrets, and took all the more care of my wound, so that I might be fit to accompany my new marshal in the fighting which was sure to follow our next passage of the Danube.

Chapter 15
The Island of Lobau

By the end of June I was well enough to join Masséna's headquarters on the isle of Lobau, and was greeted in friendly fashion by my new comrades. The staff was numerous, and contained several officers of distinction. Before resuming my tale of the campaign of 1809 I should like to make you acquainted with one of them who played an important part in the events preceding the battle of Wagram—Colonel de Sainte-Croix.

Charles d'Escorches de Sainte-Croix, son of the marquis of that name, once Louis XVI.'s ambassador to the Porte, was in all respects a most remarkable man. His military career was short enough, but of wonderful brilliancy. His family and mine were connected, and we were most intimate friends; indeed, the desire of serving with him had been a strong inducement to me to accept Masséna's proposal. Keen as was Sainte-Croix's natural love of war, it was late before he could gratify it, since he was destined for diplomacy, and all through the Peace of Amiens was employed under Talleyrand in the Foreign Office. When the campaign of 1805 opened he was twenty-three, and therefore too old to enter the École Militaire, so that but for a lucky circumstance he might never have entered the army.

After Austerlitz Napoleon formed from the prisoners there taken two foreign regiments for the French service. These not being governed by the same regulations as the national forces, he was able to officer them as he pleased, appointing even to field rank men who had had no military experience, but belonging to good families, and showing a zeal for the service. By this abnormal system of promotion Napoleon got the benefit of attaching to himself some hundred and fifty young men of education and fortune who otherwise would have been corrupted by a slothful life at Paris. The first foreign regiment was commanded by the nephew of the famous La Tour d'Auvergne; the second, by a great German noble, the Prince of Eisenburg; and they were known by the names of their chiefs. They were organised on the model of the foreign regiments in the French service before the Revolution, and as the Foreign Minister had always been responsible for the levying of these troops, Napoleon ordered Talleyrand to search the archives for precedents. Knowing young Sainte-Croix's military tastes, the Minister assigned the work to him, and, in addition to tracing the history of the old regiments, he proposed modifications to suit the altered conditions. Struck with the good sense displayed in this scheme, and knowing the author's desire to serve in the new corps, the Emperor appointed him first major, and, soon after, lieutenant colonel in the La Tour d'Auvergne Regiment. It was a great favour, as the Emperor had never seen Sainte-Croix; but it went near to spoil his prospects at the outset.

A M. de M——, cousin to the Emperor, had hoped for the rank of lieutenant-colonel, but only got that of major. Hurt in his vanity, he sought a quarrel with Sainte-Croix on a frivolous pretext. As he was a first-rate performer with every kind of weapon, his friends were sure of his victory, and escorted him in a cavalcade to the Bois de Boulogne; but only one accompanied him to the spot where his adversary, with one second, awaited him. They fought with pistols, and M. de M—— received a bullet in the breast which laid him dead; upon which, his second, instead of going to fetch help, and thinking only of the consequences which this tragic end of a relation of the Emperor might entail on himself, fled through the wood and far away from Paris, without returning for his horse or informing the dead man's friends. Sainte-Croix and his friends also returned to the city, and the body was left alone on the ground. Meanwhile, those who were awaiting M. de M——'s return, hearing the shots but seeing no more of him, went into the wood, and found the poor young man's body. It happened that in falling he had fractured his skull on a hard stump, and when his friends after examining the wound in the breast, saw another in the head, they thought that Sainte-Croix, after wounding his opponent with a bullet from his pistol, had finished him by smashing his skull with the butt. This seemed to explain the disappearance of the dead man's second, on the supposition that he lacked either strength or courage to prevent the assassination. With this notion in their minds, they hastened to Saint-Cloud, and imparted it to the Empress, who went to the Emperor demanding justice. An order was given to arrest Sainte-Croix, and, as he had in no way concealed himself, he was locked up. Doubtless he would have lain in prison while a long inquiry was held had not Fouché, a family friend, being sure that he would not have committed such a crime, made an active search for the missing second. Being found and brought to Paris, he honestly reported what had happened, and further, the officials charged with the inquiry discovered near the corpse a stump of a root stained with blood and having hair adhering to it. Sainte-Croix's innocence was admitted; he was set free, and went to join his regiment in Italy.

M. de La Tour d'Auvergne was an estimable man, but with no great turn for military matters. Sainte-Croix, therefore, had the organising of the new regiment, and did it with such zeal that he made it one of the finest corps in the army. He distinguished himself in Calabria, and earned the great regard of Masséna, who, after the battle of Eylau, sent for him to Poland, though it was quite against the regulations to take an officer, especially a major, from his regiment. When he reached Warsaw he was presented by Masséna to the Emperor, who, recalling the death of M. de M——, received him coldly, expressing to the marshal his dissatisfaction at his having been brought away from his regiment. The Emperor had another reason for his unfriendly welcome. Although of short stature himself, Napoleon had a great preference for tall, strong, masculine men; but Sainte-Croix was small, slight, and with the face of a pretty fair-complexioned woman. In this feeble-seeming body, however, there was a soul of steel, an heroic courage, and a restless activity. The Emperor soon recognised these qualities, but, thinking that it was enough for Sainte-Croix to have started with the rank of major, he did nothing for him during that campaign. When, however, in 1809, Masséna was put in command of an army corps, he remembered how the Emperor had reproved him for attaching Sainte-Croix to his staff without leave, and asked and obtained him for his aide-de-camp.

In one of the actions preceding our entry into Vienna Sainte-Croix took a flag from the enemy, and the Emperor made him colonel; at Essling he showed wonderful courage and intelligence, and the Emperor's prejudice against him was completely destroyed by the important services which he rendered to Masséna's corps when acting as advanced guard on the isle of Lobau. The Emperor went every day to inspect the fortifications on the island, remaining on foot for seven or eight hours. These long walks fatigued Masséna, who was already a little infirm, and General Becker, chief of the staff, often could not answer the Emperor's questions, while Sainte-Croix, with his wonderful activity and intelligence, knew everything, foresaw everything, and could give the most exact information. Thus Napoleon fell into the way of applying to him, and gradually Sainte-Croix became, if not de jure, certainly de facto chief of the staff to the army corps which was defending the island of Lobau.

It would have been so easy for the Austrians to bombard us out of this island, that the Emperor went away each evening with regret, and passed each night in cruel anxiety. As soon as he awoke he wished to have news of Masséna's corps, and Sainte-Croix had orders to report to him in his room every morning at daybreak. Thus, every night the colonel went on foot round the vast island, visiting our outposts and examining those of the enemy; then, mounting his horse, he hurried over the two leagues to Schönbrunn. The aides-de-camp had orders to bring him at once to the Emperor's bedroom, and the Emperor, dressing in his presence, would discuss the position of the two armies. Then they would gallop off to the island; the Emperor would inspect the works all day, often mounting a high double ladder, which the ingenious Sainte-Croix had had set up as an observatory, and whence the movements of the enemy's troops on the left bank could be seen, and in the evening Sainte-Croix would escort the Emperor back to Schönbrunn. For forty-four days in extreme heat he worked in this way, without being weary or slackening his activity for a moment. Often Napoleon would call him to council, when discussing with Marshals Masséna and Berthier the best way of getting the army across to the left bank. The passage would have to be made at a different point to the former one, since it was known that that place had been strongly entrenched by the Archduke. Sainte-Croix proposed to turn the enemy's defences by crossing opposite Enzersdorf, which course was adopted.

In short, Napoleon's opinion of his merit was so high that he said one day to the Russian envoy, M. de Czernicheff, 'I have never since I have been in command of armies met a more capable officer, nor one who understood my thought quicker and executed it better. He reminds me of Marshal Lannes and General Desaix, and if he is not struck down by a thunderbolt France and Europe will be astonished at the distance which I shall take him.' These words were very soon known everywhere, and it was expected that Sainte-Croix would quickly be a marshal. But, unhappily, the thunderbolt did strike him; he was killed the next year by a cannon-ball at the gates of Lisbon.

Napoleon, though he usually kept at a distance the commanders whom he most esteemed, now and again was familiar with one of them, and even amused himself by inciting him to frank repartees. Thus Lasalle, Junot, and Rapp used to say to the Emperor whatever came into their heads. The two first, who used to ruin themselves every other year, would thus relate their pranks to Napoleon, who always paid their debts. Sainte-Croix was too clever and too decorous to abuse the favour which he enjoyed; still, when the Emperor drove him to it, he was capable of prompt and decisive repartee. Thus, when Napoleon, who would often take his arm, as they walked through the sands of the isle of Lobau, said to him, on one of their numerous expeditions, 'I remember that after your duel with my wife's cousin I wanted to shoot you; I admit that it would have been a mistake and a very great loss.' 'That is quite true, sir,' answered Sainte-Croix, 'and I am certain that now, when your Majesty knows me better, you wouldn't exchange me for one of the Empress's cousins.' 'For one, indeed!' said the Emperor; 'you may say for the lot of them.' Another day, when Sainte-Croix was present, as Napoleon got up the latter said, as he drank a glass of cold water, 'I believe that Schönbrunn in German means "beautiful spring"; it was rightly named, for the spring in the park produces delicious water, which I drink every morning. Do you like cold water?' 'No, indeed, sir; I prefer a good glass of bordeaux or champagne.' Then the Emperor, turning to his valet, said, 'Send the colonel a hundred bottles of bordeaux and the same number of champagne,' and that very evening, as Masséna's aides-de-camp were dining in their bivouac under the trees, we saw several mules, from the imperial stables, arriving with two hundred bottles of excellent wine for Sainte-Croix, and we drank the Emperor's health therein.

Chapter 16
The Battle of Wagram

As the moment approached for crossing the Danube again, the Austrians watched more assiduously the bank of the small arm of the river which lay between us and them. They fortified Enzersdorf, and if a group of French soldiers came too near the part of the island opposite that village their outposts would fire upon them; but they took no notice of parties of two or three. The Emperor wished to have a near view of the enemy's preparations, and it has been said that in order to do so without danger he disguised himself as a private, and did sentry's duty. This report is incorrect; the real fact was as follows. The Emperor and Marshal Masséna, wearing sergeants' great-coats, and followed by Sainte-Croix in a private's uniform, went close up to the bank. The colonel stripped himself, and went into the water, while Napoleon and Masséna, to still any suspicion on the part of the enemy, took off their coats as though they too proposed to bathe, and then examined at their ease the point where they wished to throw the bridges across. The Austrians were so accustomed to see our soldiers come in little parties to bathe at that place that they remained quietly lying on the grass. This fact shows that in war commanders ought strictly to forbid this kind of truce, and marking off all neutral points, which the troops on either side often establish for their respective convenience.

Having settled to cross the river at this spot, the Emperor decided that several bridges should be constructed there; but as it was more than probable that on the alarm being given by the outposts the Austrian troops posted at Enzersdorf would hasten up to oppose the construction of the bridges, it was arranged that 2,500 grenadiers should first be transported to the other bank, and should at once attack Enzersdorf to occupy the garrison, and prevent their interfering with our works and hindering our passage. This being settled, the Emperor said to Masséna, 'As this leading column will be specially exposed, we must compose it of our best troops, and select a brave and capable colonel to command them.' 'But, sir, that is my job,' said Sainte-Croix. 'How so?' replied the Emperor, who probably asked the question only to draw the answer which he got. 'Why,' said the colonel, 'because of all the officers on the island I am the one who has had the most tiring work for six weeks past. I have been on my legs carrying out your orders day and night; and I beg that your Majesty will be kind enough to give me in return the command of the 2,500 grenadiers who are to make the first landing on the enemy's bank.' 'Well, you shall have it,' replied Napoleon, much pleased with this noble daring; and the final arrangements for the crossing having been made, the attack was fixed for the night of July 4.

Before that time came two important events happened in our army corps. Lieutenant-General Becker was a good officer, though indolent, but it was his fault to criticise everything, and he allowed himself openly to disapprove Napoleon's plan of attack. On hearing of it the Emperor sent him back to France. General Fririon became chief of the staff; a capable man, but without the firmness required in one acting under Masséna. The other event nearly deprived the Emperor of the aid of Masséna himself in the coming battle. One day, as he and Napoleon were riding round the island, the marshal's horse put its foot in a hole and fell, injuring its rider's leg so that he could not keep his saddle. This was the more annoying that the battle was to take place on the same ground as that of Essling, which Masséna of course knew well. He showed, however, his determination by asserting that in spite of his pain he would be taken on to the field in a litter, like Marshal Saxe at Fontenoy. A litter was got ready; but it struck the marshal; upon a remark which I ventured to make, that this mode of transport was rather pretentious and not so safe as a light carriage, which, with four good horses, could get him about the ground more quickly than men. It was therefore arranged that he should go thus, accompanied by his surgeon, Dr. Brisset, who changed the compresses every hour with perfect coolness under fire during the two days which the battle of Wagram lasted, and in the subsequent fights.

Knowing that the enemy was expecting him to cross as before between Aspern and Essling, and that it was important to conceal his plan of turning their position by crossing opposite Enzersdorf, Napoleon had a careful watch kept over all who entered the island by the great bridges connecting it with Ebersdorf. Everyone on the island must have learnt the secret towards the end of the time; but as it seemed certain that none were on it but French soldiers or officers' servants, who were all guarded, no danger was apprehended from inquisitiveness on the enemy's part. This, as it turned out, was a mistake; for the Archduke had contrived to introduce a spy among us. Just when he was about to give information of the point which we were going to attack, an anonymous letter, written in Hungarian, was brought by a little girl to the Emperor's Mameluke, Roustan, with the warning that it was important and urgent. It was at first supposed to be a begging letter; but the interpreters soon translated it, and informed the Emperor. He came at once to the island, and on arriving, ordered all works to be suspended, and every soul—troops, staffs, commissaries, butchers, bakers, canteen men, even officers' servants—to be drawn up on parade. As soon as everyone was in the ranks, the Emperor announced that a spy had found his way into the island, hoping to escape notice among 30,000 men; and now that they were all in their places he ordered every man to look at his neighbour to right and left. The success of this plan was as instantaneous. In the midst of the dead silence, two soldiers were heard to cry, 'Here is a man we don't know.' He was arrested and examined, and admitted that he had disguised himself in a French uniform taken from men killed at Essling. This wretch had been born at Paris, and appeared very well educated. Having ruined himself at play, he had fled to Austria to escape his creditors, and there had offered himself as spy to the Austrian staff. A small boat used to take him across the Danube at night, landing him a league below Ebersdorf, and fetch him back the next night on a given signal. He had already been frequently on the island, and had accompanied detachments of our troops going to fetch provisions or materials from Ebersdorf. In order to avoid notice, he always went to places where there was a crowd, and worked with the soldiers at the entrenchments. He got his meals at the canteen, passed the night near the camps, and in the morning, armed with a spade as though on his way to join a working party, he would go all over the island and examine the works, lying down among the osiers to make hurried sketches of them. The next night he would go and make his report to the Austrians, and come back to continue his observations. He was brought before a court-martial and condemned to death; but the bitter regret which he expressed for having served the enemies of France disposed the Emperor to commute the penalty. When, however, the spy proposed to deceive the Archduke by going to make a false report on what he had seen, and coming back to tell the French what the Austrians were doing, the Emperor, disgusted at this new piece of infamy, abandoned him to his fate, and let him be shot.

Meanwhile the day of the great battle was drawing on. Napoleon had assembled round Ebersdorf the Army of Italy, the corps of Davout and Bernadotte with the guard, and transformed the island of Lobau into a vast fortress. Three strong bridges secured the passage of the large arm of the Danube, and everything was ready for throwing several across the small arm. To confirm the Archduke in the belief that he intended to cross again between Essling and Aspern, Napoleon had the small bridge by which we had retreated after the battle of Essling reconstructed after the night of July 1, and sent across two divisions whose skirmishers might attract the attention of the enemy while all was making ready for our attack on Enzersdorf. It is hard to understand how the Archduke could have supposed that Napoleon would make a front attack upon the huge fortifications with which he had surrounded Essling and Aspern; this would indeed have been taking the bull by the horns.

The second and third were passed by both sides in preparation. The French army, to the number of 150,000 men was massed on the isle of Lobau; the Archduke assembled an equal force on the left bank, where his troops, posted in two lines, formed an immense arc, overlapping those parts of the island which were opposite to them. The right-hand end of this arc rested on the Danube at Floridsdorf; their centre occupied the villages of Essling and Aspern, which were strongly entrenched, and connected by works armed with many guns. Finally, the left of the arc was at Gross-Enzersdorf, with a strong detachment at Mühlleiten. The Archduke, therefore, was watching all the points of the island by which we could emerge; but as, for some unexplained reason he had made up his mind that Napoleon would attack his centre, crossing the little arm of the Danube where he had done in May, the Austrian commander had concentrated his whole force in the wide plains which extend from those villages as far as Deutsch-Wagram and Markgrafen-Neusiedel, a large village on the Russbach stream, the steep banks of which, commanded by high ground, offer an excellent defensive position. His right was weak, and his left still weaker, because, though he had ordered his brother the Archduke John, commanding the Army of Hungary, with his 35,000 men, to be by the morning of July 5 at Unter-Siebenbrunn and in touch on the left with the second line of the main army, this order was not carried out.

In pursuance of the Emperor's instructions, the French army began its attack at 9 p.m. on July 5. Just then a tremendous storm burst; the night was of the darkest, the rain fell in torrents and the noise of the thunder mingled with that of our artillery, which, sheltered from the enemy shot by an epaulement, aimed all its fire at Essling and Aspern. Thus confirmed in the belief that we were going to land at that point, the Archduke turned all his attention thither, without troubling himself about Enzersdorf, upon which the bulk of our force was marching. As soon as the first shots were heard Marshal Masséna, though still in much pain, was placed in a small open carriage and, surrounded by his aides-de-camp, was driven towards the point where the first attack was to be made. The Emperor soon joined us. He was in good spirits and said to the marshal: 'I am delighted at this storm. What a fine night for us! The Austrians cannot see our preparations to cross opposite Enzersdorf, and they will know nothing of them till we have carried that important position, by which time our bridges will be placed and part of my army formed on the bank which they think we are defending.'

In fact Colonel Sainte-Croix, after having landed his 2,500 grenadiers in silence, took up his ground on the enemy's flank in front of Enzersdorf. A regiment of Croats was bivouacking at this point. Attacked unawares, they defended themselves obstinately with the bayonet; but our grenadiers, inspirited by the voice of Sainte-Croix, who had thrown himself into the hottest of the scuffle, drove back the enemy, who retreated in disorder upon Enzersdorf. That large village, surrounded by a loopholed wall, having in front of it a dyke cut in the form of a parapet, was full of infantry, while all the entrances were covered by small earthworks. To carry the village was all the more difficult, because the houses had been burnt down and the garrison might any moment be supported by General Nordmann's brigade posted a little in rear between this village and that of Mühlleiten. But no obstacle checked Sainte-Croix, who at the head of his grenadiers carried the outer works, pursued the enemy at the sword's point, and entered pell-mell with them into the redan which covered the south gate. The gate was closed, Sainte-Croix drove it in under a hail of bullets from the loopholed walls. Once masters of this passage, the colonel and his soldiers dashed into the village, while the garrison, weakened by its enormous losses, took refuge in the castle. But at sight of the scaling ladders which Sainte-Croix ordered up, the Austrian commander capitulated. Thus Sainte-Croix, to whom this fine feat of arms did the greatest honour, remained master of Enzersdorf, to the great satisfaction of the Emperor, whose plans were admirably served by its capture. He ordered eight bridges to be at once thrown over the small arm between the island and Enzersdorf. The first of these bridges was an invention of the Emperor's own. It was made in four sections, connected by hinges so as to allow it to turn and follow the windings of the bank; one end was fixed to the trees on the island, while the other was guided towards the opposite bank by the help of a cable carried by a boat. Swinging to the current, this new style of bridge turned on itself, made a complete wheel to the right and was ready for use in a moment. In a quarter of an hour the other seven were fixed, enabling Napoleon rapidly to bring over to the left bank the corps of Masséna, Oudinot, Bernadotte, Davout, and Marmont, Prince Eugène's army, the artillery reserve, all the cavalry, and finally the guard.

While the Emperor was thus profiting by the capture of Enzersdorf, the Archduke, still convinced that his enemy intended to debouch between Essling and Aspern, was wasting his time and his ammunition in hurling shot and shell on to the part of the island which faced those villages, under the impression that he was causing great loss to the French troops. As, however, we had at that point only a few scouts well protected by earthworks, the projectiles did no damage, and meanwhile the bulk of our troops were traversing the small arm of the river, and forming on the left bank. The Austrian general was astounded when, marching towards the old battle-field on the morning of July 5, with the intention of taking us at a disadvantage the moment we landed, he perceived that his left wing had been turned by the left army, which was marching upon Sachsengang, and shortly occupied that place. Thus surprised, and his rear threatened, the Archduke was obliged, in older to face us, to execute a retrograde movement on a vast scale towards the Russbach, always retreating before Napoleon, while our various corps were taking up their order of battle in the great plain which spread before them.

The Emperor sent three strong divisions of cavalry, with several battalions, supported by light artillery, to watch for the Archduke John at Siebenbrunn, these troops being regarded as outside the fighting line, and intended merely to prevent a surprise. Of the main army, Davout's corps, resting on the Russbach, formed the right; the center was composed of Bavarians, Wurtembergers, the corps of Oudinot and Bernadotte, and the Army of Italy. The left, under Masséna, moved along the small arm of the Danube, in the direction of Essling and Aspern. Each of these corps, as it advanced, was to carry the villages on its road. The reserve consisted of Marmont's corps, three divisions of cuirassiers, numerous artillery, and all the imperial guard. Finally, General Reynier, with one division and guns, remained to guard the island of Lobau, the old bridge which we had used at the time of the former battle having been replaced. A splendid day had succeeded the most horrible night. The French army in review order advanced majestically, preceded by an immense force of artillery, which crushed all opposition on the part of the enemy. The regiments composing the Austrian left, with General Nordmann in advance, were the first with whom he came in contact. Driven from Enzersdorf and Mühlleiten, they attempted to defend Raschdorf, but were pushed back, and General Nordmann was killed in the fight. This officer was from Alsace, formerly colonel of the Bercheny Hussars. He deserted to the enemy in 1793 with part of his regiment, at the same time as Dumouriez, and entered the Austrian service. Our march at first meeting no serious resistance, we occupied successively Essling, Aspern, Breitenlee, Raschdorf, and Süssenbrunn. So far Napoleon's plan had succeeded, the troops having crossed the Danube, and occupied the plain on the left bank. But nothing could be considered as decided until we had beaten and thoroughly broken up the enemy. He now made the serious mistake, instead of uniting his whole force on the Russbach, of dividing it, by retreating on two very divergent lines; one upon Markgraf and Neusiedel, behind the Russbach; the other upon the heights of Stamersdorf, where his right wing was obviously too far from the field of battle. The position on the bank of the Russbach is strong, commanding the plain and covered by the brook, which, though not large, forms a very good obstacle, its banks being too steep for infantry to cross, except with difficulty, while the only way for cavalry and artillery is over the bridges in the villages which the Austrians held. As, however, the Russbach was the key of the position, Napoleon resolved to seize it. He therefore ordered Davout to attack Neusiedel; Oudinot and Bernadotte, Baumersdorf and Wagram respectively; while Prince Eugène, supported by Macdonald and Lamarque, crossed the stream between the two latter villages. The light artillery of the guard crushed the Austrian masses with its fire, but Marshal Bernadotte, commanding the Saxons, attacked Wagram so feebly that he did not succeed. Macdonald and Lamarque crossing the Russbach, placed the enemy's centre for a moment in danger; but the Archduke, flinging himself upon that point with his reserves, forced our troops back again across the brook. This movement was at first executed in perfect order, but as night had approached, our infantry, who had just resisted a front attack of the Austrian light horse, seeing in their rear a brigade of French cavalry which General Salme was bringing up to their support, thought they were cut off and some disorder ensued, aggravated by the blunder of some Saxon battalions firing on Lamarque's division. This confusion, however, was quickly repaired. Oudinot's attack on Baumersdorf, being made with a lack of cohesion, was also repulsed; Davout alone had any success; having forced the Russbach and turned Neusiedel, he was on the point of capturing that village, in spite of an obstinate defence, when night compelled him to suspend the attack, and shortly after the Emperor ordered him to retire, so as not to leave him exposed by being isolated on the further side of the stream.

Chapter 17
Wagram (2)

July 5, the chief events of which I have recorded, served only as preparation for the decisive battle of the morrow. The night passed quietly; our army, with its three cavalry divisions detached towards Leopoldsdorf, had its true right near Grosshofen; our centre was at Aderklaa; our left somewhat withheld at Breitenlee, giving our line the form of an angle, of which Wagram was the apex. The tents of the Emperor and his guard were a little in advance of Raschdorf. A glance at the plan of the battle of Wagram will show that the enemy's right, starting from the environs of Rampendorf and passing along the left bank of the Russbach to Helmhof, whence it reached by Sauring to Stamersdorf, formed thus a re-entering angle, of which the apex was equally at Wagram. This, therefore, was the essential point of which each side wished to get possession. To succeed in this, the object of either was to turn his enemy's left flank; but the Archduke, having extended his army too much, was obliged to send his orders in writing, and these were either misunderstood or ill-executed; while the Emperor, having his reserves under his hand, could see and superintend the carry-out of his instructions.

At daybreak on the 6th the battle was renewed with more vigour than on the previous day. Much to Napoleon's surprise, the Archduke, who had till then confined himself to the defensive, began to attack, and took Aderklaa from us. Soon the artillery fire extended over the whole line; never in the memory of man had the like been seen, for the number of pieces brought into action by the two armies amounted to 1,200. The Austrian left wing, under the Archduke in person, crossed the Russbach, and debouched by those columns towards Leopoldsdorf, Glinzendorf, and Grosshofen, but was stoutly resisted, and even checked, by Davout and Grouchy's cavalry by the time that Napoleon came up at the head of an enormous reserve. Seeing the extreme right of his line engaged, he had supposed for a moment that the Archduke John had joined the enemy's main army. So far was this, however, from being the case, that, as we afterwards learnt, he was at that moment at Pressburg, eight leagues from the field of battle. Deprived of the support from him which they had hoped for, the Austrian left soon repented having attacked us. Overwhelmed by superior forces, more especially of artillery, it was driven back across the Russbach, with heavy loss, by Davout, who then sent a portion of his troops across, and marched by both banks on Neusiedel. His right thus secured, the Emperor returned with his guard to the centre, and while Bernadotte attacked Wagram and Oudinot marched on Baumersdorf, he ordered Masséna to retake Aderklaa. Taken and re-taken, this village finally remained in the hands of the Austrian grenadiers, whom the Archduke led to a renewed attack, while at the same time he launched a strong column of cavalry against the Saxons under Bernadotte, routing them completely, and flinging them on Masséna's troops, who were thrown into momentary disorder. The marshal was in his carriage, and the enemy noticing it with its four white horses in the middle of the line, guessed that its occupant must be a person of importance and poured a storm of shot upon it. The marshal and those about him were in great danger; we were surrounded with dead and dying. Captain Barain, an aide-de-camp, lost an arm, and Colonel Sainte-Croix was wounded.

The Emperor, galloping up, became aware that the Archduke, in order to turn or even surround his left, was bringing forward his own right wing, which already occupied Süssenbrunn, Leopoldau, and Stadlau, and was marching on Aspern, thus threatening the column of Lobau. In order to be better seen by the troops, he got for a moment into the carriage, beside Masséna, and at sight of him order was restored. He bade Masséna change front to the rear, in order to bring his left to Aspern and front towards Hirschstetten, causing Macdonald, with three divisions, to take up the ground which Masséna left. These movements were carried out in good order, under an artillery fire from the enemy. Thus Napoleon, profiting by the concentration of his principal forces, brought up to support Macdonald, not only strong reserves of all arms, but finally the imperial guard, which took up its position in three lines in rear of the other troops.

At this moment the positions of the two armies were very curious, the opposed lines having almost the shape of two letters Z placed side by side. The Austrian left, posted at Neusiedel, was giving way before our right, while the two centres were holding their respective places, and our left wing was retreating along the Danube before the enemy's right. The chances of either side thus seemed to be about equal. Really, however, they were all in favour of Napoleon—in the first place, because it was unlikely that the village of Neusiedel, where the only means of resistance was afforded by an old fortified tower, would hold out long against the attack which Davout was delivering with his usual vigour; and it was easy to see that when this was taken, the Austrian left, being outflanked and without support, would retreat indefinitely and get separated from the centre, while our left wing, though beaten at the moment, was in its retreat coming nearer to the island of Lobau, the powerful artillery on which would check the Austrians, and prevent them from following up their success. Secondly, Napoleon, acting on inner lines, could hold a great part of his troops in reserve, and yet show a front in different directions; while the Archduke, being obliged to extend his army, in order to execute his great movement on an outer line with the view of surrounding us, was not in force at any point. The Emperor, observing this mistake, was perfectly calm, though he could read in the faces of his staff the anxiety caused by the conquering march of the enemy's right, which, always driving Masséna's corps before it, had already reached the battle-field of May 22, and after crushing Boudet's division by a formidable charge of cavalry, was threatening our rear. But the success of the Austrians was short-lived. The hundred heavy guns with which Napoleon's foresight had armed the island of Lobau opened a scathing fire upon the enemy's right, and it was compelled, under pain of annihilation, to halt in its triumphant course, and retire in its turn. Masséna was then able to reform his divisions, which had lost heavily. We thought that Napoleon would profit by the disorder into which the cannonade had thrown the enemy's right wing to attack with his reserves; Marshal Masséna, indeed, sent me to ask for instructions on this point. But the Emperor remained impassive, his eyes ever fixed on the extreme right, towards Neusiedel (which lies high and is surmounted by a tall tower, visible from all parts of the field), waiting to hurl himself upon the enemy's centre and right until Davout had beaten the left and flung it back beyond that village. A valiant defence was being maintained by the Prince of Hesse-Hommburg, who was there wounded; but at last we suddenly saw the smoke of Davout's guns beyond the tower. Beyond a doubt the enemy's left was beaten. Then, turning to me, the Emperor said: 'Quick! tell Masséna to fall upon whatever is in front of him, and the battle is won.' At the same time the aides-de-camp from all the other corps were sent off to their chiefs with an order for a simultaneous attack. At this supreme moment Napoleon said to General Lauriston, 'Take a hundred guns, sixty from my guard, and crush the enemy's column.' As soon as their fire had shaken the Austrians, Marshal Bessières charged them with six regiments of heavy cavalry, supported by part of the cavalry of the guard. In vain did the Archduke form squares, they were broken, with the loss of their guns and a great number of men. Our centre advanced in its turn, under Macdonald, and Süssenbrunn, Breitenlee, and Aderklaa were carried after a smart resistance. Meanwhile Masséna had recovered the ground lost on our left, and was pressing the enemy hard, forcing him back beyond Stadlau and Kagran; and Davout, calling Oudinot to his support, occupied the heights beyond the Russbach and captured Wagram. This decided the defeat of the Austrians: they retreated all along the line, retiring in very good order along the road to Moravia.

The Emperor has been blamed for not pursuing the defeated army with his usual vigour; but the criticism is baseless. Napoleon was hindered by many weighty reasons from launching his troops too promptly on the enemy's track. In the first place, the high road to Moravia would bring them into a rough country, divided by wooded hills, ravines, and gorges, commanded by the mountains and forests of Bisamberg, which would offer excellent defensive positions, all the more difficult to carry that the Archduke could occupy them with a large force, much of which had not been engaged, while his rear-guard was protected by powerful artillery. We might therefore expect a stubborn resistance, which, if prolonged, would lead to a night battle. Of these the chances are always uncertain, and the Emperor's victory might well be compromised.

In the second place, to ensure the assembling of the French army in the isle of Lobau by the 4th, it had been necessary to put some of the corps in movement as early as the 1st. These, in order to reach the meeting-place, had had to make forced marches, succeeded without any rest between by a battle extending over two days of very hot weather. Our troops were therefore worn out; while the Austrians, who had been for more than a month in camp, had had only the fatigues of the battle to endure. Thus, if we had attacked the Archduke in the strong position which he had taken up, every advantage would have been on his side.

But a third and still more powerful argument checked Napoleon's ardour and decided him to allow his troops time to rest on the field of battle. He had just been warned by the generals of his light cavalry placed by him to look out beyond his extreme right that an enemy's force of 35,000 to 40,000, under the command of the Archduke John, had been seen debouching at Unter Siebenbrunn, that is to say, upon what, since our change of front, had become our actual rear. The reserve provided by the Emperor would doubtless have been enough to repulse the Archduke; but one must admit that prudence would lead Napoleon not to engage his troops in the attack of the strong positions which the Archduke Charles appeared determined to defend obstinately, so long as he himself was open to an attack in rear from the Archduke John at the head of a strong and perfectly fresh force. The Emperor therefore ordered the pursuit to cease, and made his army bivouac in such a way that one part fronted to the side where the Archduke John was, and was ready to receive him if he ventured into the plain. Fearing, however, to come into contact with our victorious troops, he retreated hastily towards Hungary. If Napoleon had pursued with his usual vigour, the trophies from Wagram would probably have been more numerous, but on considering the motives which decided him to halt one cannot but praise his caution. If he had always acted with as much prudence he would have spared both France and himself great calamities.

In order to rest for a few hours after its victory, our army took up its position with its left at Floridsdorf, its centre in front of Gerpardsdorf, and its right beyond the Russbach. The Emperor's tents were pitched between Aderklaa and Raschdorf, and Masséna's headquarters were at Leopoldau. The replacement of the old Spitz bridge put the army in direct communication with Vienna, which favoured the transport of the wounded to the hospitals, and of food and ammunition to the army.

The Austrians have, not without reason, blamed the Archduke John for the delays in his march and his carelessness in carrying out the Archduke's Charles' orders. Indeed, on the evening of the 4th Charles wrote to his brother to leave Pressburg at once, and form a junction with the Austrian left at Siebenbrunn; but although John received the order by 4 A.M. on the 5th he did not march till eleven in the evening, and moved so slowly that, although he had only eight leagues to do, he took twenty hours to reach Siebenbrunn, not coming up till seven o'clock on the 6th, by which time the battle was lost and the Austrians were in full retreat. The Archduke Charles never forgave his brother for not carrying out his orders; John lost his command and was banished to Styria.

In the absence of pursuit, the Austrian losses were much less considerable than they might have been. Still, they admitted 24,000 killed and wounded, among the former three of their generals. One of them, Wukassowitz, had distinguished himself against Bonaparte in Italy; the other two, Nordmann and D'Aspre, were Frenchmen in arms against their country. According to the bulletins we made 20,000 prisoners and captured 30 guns; but I believe this estimate was much exaggerated. We only took a few colours. Our loss was nearly equal to that of the enemy; Generals Lacour, Gauthier, and Lasalle, and seven colonels were killed. The enemy had ten generals, including the Archduke, wounded; the number of ours was twenty-one, among them, Marshal Bessières. Among the twelve colonels wounded three were special favourites with the Emperor—Dumesnil, Corbineau, and Sainte-Croix: the two first, who belonged to the chasseurs a cheval of the guard, lost a leg apiece; the Emperor rewarded them richly. As for Sainte-Croix, who had his skin grazed by a cannon-ball, his wound was not dangerous, at which his friends rejoiced. However, if he had lost a leg he might perhaps have been living now, as well as his brother Robert, one of whose legs remains on the battlefield of Moskwa. Although Sainte-Croix had been only two months colonel, and was not yet twenty-seven, the Emperor made him major-general, Count with 25,000 francs pension, Grand Cross of the Order of Hesse, and Commander of that of Baden. On the evening of the battle the Emperor rewarded the services of Macdonald, Oudinot, and Marmont by giving each of them his marshal's bâton. It was not, however, in his power to give them the talents required to command an army, brave and good divisional generals as they were when in the Emperor's hands, they showed themselves clumsy when they were away from him, either in devising a plan of campaign, or in executing it, or modifying it according to circumstances. It was held in the army that the Emperor, not being able to replace Lannes, wanted to get the small change for him: a severe judgment, but we must remember that these three marshals played an unlucky part in the campaigns which ended in the fall of Napoleon and the ruin of the country.

Chapter 18
After the Battle

At the close of the battle of Wagram, Lasalle's Light Cavalry division had not been engaged. He came and begged Masséna to let him pursue, and the marshal assented, on condition that he would act with prudence. Hardly had Lasalle started, when he saw a brigade of enemy's infantry, which was hastening, closely pressed, to reach the village of Leopoldau, in order to obtain a regular capitulation and escape the fury of the victors in the open. Lasalle guessed what the Austrian general was after, and, pointing to the setting sun, addressed his men, 'The battle is ending, and we alone have not contributed to the victory. Come on!' He dashed forward, sword in hand, followed by his squadrons, and, in order to prevent the enemy from entering the village, made for the narrow space now left between the head of the column and Leopoldau. The others, seeing themselves cut off from the hoped-for shelter, halted and opened a brisk file-fire. A bullet struck Lasalle in the head, killing him on the spot. His division lost a hundred troopers, besides many wounded. The Austrians opened their way to the village, and when our infantry divisions came up, capitulated, the officers declaring that that had been their intention in making for Leopoldau. Thus, Lasalle's charge was useless, and he paid dear for a mention in a bulletin.

His death left a great gap in our light cavalry, which he had trained to a high degree of perfection. In other respects, however, he had done it much harm. The eccentricities of a popular and successful leader are always imitated, and his example was long mischievous to the light cavalry. A man did not think himself a chasseur, still less a hussar, if he did not model himself on Lasalle, and become, like him, a reckless, drinking, swearing rowdy. Many officers copied the fault of this famous outpost leader, but none of them attained to the merits which in him atoned for the faults.

When a battle is fought in summer, it often happens that the ripe corn is set on fire by shells and gun-wadding; but in no battle of the Empire did this occur on such a scale as at Wagram. The season was early, and the weather hot; the battle-field was completely covered with crops ready for harvest, which caught quickly and carried the fire with terrific rapidity. The movements of both armies were hampered by the necessity of avoiding it; for if once troops were overtaken by it, pouches and wagons exploded, carrying destruction through the ranks. Whole regiments might be seen hastening out of the way of the fire, and taking up their position where the corn had been burnt already; but this means of escape was only open to the able-bodied. Of the soldiers who were severely wounded great numbers perished in the flames; and of those whom the fire did not reach, many lay for days hidden by the tall corn, living during that time on the ears. The Emperor had the plain searched by bands of cavalry, and vehicles were brought from Vienna to remove the wounded, friends and foes alike. But few of those even whom the fire had passed recovered, and the soldiers had a saying that straw-fire had killed nearly as many as gun-fire.

The two days of the battle were an anxious time for the Viennese, who, from their roofs and towers, could enjoy a full view of all that took place, and who swayed from hope to fear with the progress of the fight. The famous and witty field-marshal Prince de Ligne, now well advanced in years, had assembled the best society in Vienna in his country house, in the highest of the neighbouring hills, whence the eye could take in the whole field of battle. With his experience of war and his keen intelligence, he quickly seized Napoleon's design and the Archduke's blunders, and foretold the defeat of the latter. When the Viennese saw the right of their army, on the 6th, rolling back our left, they broke into a frenzy of joy, and through our glasses we could see thousands of men and women waving hats and handkerchiefs to kindle still further the courage of their troops, who were winning at that point, but there only. The Prince de Ligne did not share the joy of the Viennese, and I have it from one who was close by the old soldier that he said to his guests, 'Do not rejoice just yet; in less than a quarter of an hour the Archduke will be beaten. He has no reserves, and you see the plain is crowded with the masses of Napoleon's!' His prediction was justified. As, however, one must do justice even to an enemy, I may say, after criticising the Archduke's tactics that his blunders are vastly excused by the hope, which he was justified in having, of the arrival of his brother with 35,000 or 40,000 men to fall on our right or rear. Moreover, it must be allowed that, having formed his plan, he carried it out with much vigour, showing great personal courage, with a remarkable gift of keeping up the spirit of his troops. Of this I will cite a striking instance.

As is well known, every regiment has, besides its colonel commanding, a proprietary colonel, whose name it bears; usually some prince or general. At his death the regiment passes to another, so that a corps may often have to abandon a name illustrated on a score of fields, and take some new and unknown designation. In this way Latour's dragoons, so famous throughout Europe in the days of the early Revolution wars, when General Latour died took the name of General Vincent, whereby a fine tradition was destroyed, the self-esteem of the regiment injured, and their zeal materially weakened. Now it happened on the first day of Wagram that the Archduke, seeing that his centre was on the point of being broken by Oudinot's corps, decided to attack this with cavalry, and ordered Vincent's dragoons, who were at hand, to charge. They did so, but without vigour; they were a beaten off, and the French advance continued. Again the Archduke sent the regiment at them, and again it recoiled before our battalions. The Austrian line was pierced. In this emergency the Archduke, hastening to meet the regiment, stopped it in its flight, and, to shame it for its lack of vigour, said in a loud voice, 'Vincent's Dragoons, it is easy to see that you are no longer Latour's Dragoons!' Humiliated by this cutting but deserved reproach, they replied, 'Yes, yes, we are!' 'Well, then,' cried the Archduke, drawing his sword, 'show yourselves worthy of your old fame, and follow me!' A bullet struck him, but he flew upon the French. Vincent's regiment followed him with ardour; their charge was terrible, and Oudinot's grenadiers fell back with heavy loss. This is how an able and energetic general contrives to turn everything to account which can restore the shaken courage of his men. The Archduke's address kindled the dragoons to such a degree that after stopping Oudinot's grenadiers, they charged Lamarque's division, and recaptured 2,000 prisoners and five stand of colors which it had just taken. In complimenting the dragoons the Archduke said, 'Now you can be proud to bear the name of Vincent, which you have just made no less illustrious than that of Latour.' This regiment was one of those which on the following day contributed most to the rout of Boudet's division of infantry.

Among the multitude of episodes to which the battle of Wagram gave rise, the most important, and one which produced very strong feeling in the army, has not been related by any author. I mean the disgrace of General Bernadotte, who was ordered off the field by the Emperor. Between these two eminent persons no love was ever lost; and since the conspiracy of Rennes, got up by Bernadotte against the Consular Government, they had been on very bad terms. This notwithstanding, Napoleon had included Bernadotte in the first creation of marshals, and made him Prince of Ponte Corvo at the request of Joseph Bonaparte, whose sister-in-law Bernadotte had married. Nothing, however, could appease Bernadotte's hatred and envy of Napoleon. He flattered him to his face, and afterwards, as the Emperor well knew, criticised and found fault. The ability and courage which he had shown at Austerlitz would have induced the Emperor to overlook his misdeeds had he not aggravated them by his conduct at Jena. In spite of the requests of his generals, he let his three divisions remain wholly inactive, refusing to support Davout, who a league away, at Auerstadt, was withstanding half the Prussian army under the King in person, and ultimately beat them. The army and all France were indignant with Bernadotte, but the Emperor did no more than reprimand him severely. Stimulated by this, the marshal did well at Hall and Lubeck, but soon fell back into his customary laziness, ill-will possibly, and, in spite of orders, was two days late for the battle of Eylau. This lukewarm conduct roused afresh the Emperor's dissatisfaction, which grew more and more during the campaign in Austria. Bernadotte, in command of a corps of Saxons, always came up late, acted without energy, and criticised not only the Emperor's tactics, but the way in which the other marshals handled their troops. The Emperor, however, restrained his irritation until on the first day of the battle of Wagram Bernadotte's lack of vigour and false tactics allowed the Austrians to retake the important position of Deutsch-Wagram. It seems that after this repulse Bernadotte said to some officers that the crossing of the Danube and subsequent action had been mismanaged, and that if he had been in command he could by a scientific manœuvre have compelled the Archduke to surrender almost without a blow. This remark was reported the same evening to the Emperor, who was naturally angry. Such were the terms on which Napoleon and Bernadotte stood when the undecided action was resumed on the 6th.

We have seen that when the battle was at its height, the Saxons, badly handled by Bernadotte, were repulsed and charged by the enemy's cavalry, being flung in disorder upon Masséna's corps, which they nearly carried with them. The Saxons are brave, but the best of troops are sometimes routed; and in such cases it is of no use for the officers to try to rally the men who are within reach of the enemy's sabres and bayonets. Generals and colonels should get as quickly as possible to the head of the flying mass, then face about, and by their presence and their words arrest the movement of retreat, and re-form the battalions. In conformity with this rule, Bernadotte, whose personal bravery was unquestioned, galloped off into the plain at the head of his staff, to get in front of the fugitives and stop them. Hardly was he clear of the throng, when he found himself face to face with the Emperor, who observed, ironically, 'Is that the scientific manœuvre by which you are going to make the Archduke lay down his arms?' Bernadotte's vexation at the rout of his army was heightened by learning that the Emperor knew of his inconsiderate remark of the previous day, and he remained speechless. Presently recovering himself, he tried to mutter some words of explanation; but the Emperor in a severe and haughty tone, said: 'I remove you, sir, from the command of the army corps, which you handle so badly. Withdraw at once, and leave the Grand Army within twenty-four hours; a bungler like you is no good to me.' Therewith he turned his back on the marshal, and taking command for the moment of the Saxons, restored order in their ranks, and led them again to meet the enemy.

Under any circumstances, Bernadotte would have been in despair at such an outburst; but as he had been ordered to leave the field at the moment when he was galloping ahead of the fugitives, which might give an opening for slanderous tongues to reflect on his courage, though the object of his retreat was to check that of his soldiers, he understood how much worse it made his position, and it is asserted that in his despair he wished to throw himself on the enemy's bayonets. His aides-de-camp, however, held him back, and took him away from the Saxon troops. All day long he strayed about the battle-field, and stayed towards evening behind our left wing at the village of Leopoldau, where his officers persuaded him to pass the night in the pretty little château belonging to that place. Hardly, however, was he established, when Masséna, who had ordered his headquarters to be fixed at Leopoldau, came to take possession of the same house. As it is customary for generals to be quartered in the midst of their troops, and not to lodge in villages where their colleague's regiments are, Bernadotte wished to give way to Masséna; the latter, however, not yet knowing of his colleague's mishap, begged him to stay and share the quarters with him, to which Bernadotte agreed. While arrangements were being made for their lodging, an officer who had witnessed the scene between the Emperor and Bernadotte came and told Masséna of it, whereupon he changed his mind, and discovered that the house was not roomy enough for two marshals and their staffs. Wishing, however, to keep up an appearance of generosity, he said to his aides-de-camp, 'This lodging was mine by rights, but as poor Bernadotte is in trouble I must give it up to him; find me another place—a barn, or anywhere.' Then he got into his carriage and went off without a word to Bernadotte, who felt this desertion deeply. In his exasperation he committed another and very serious mistake; for though no longer in command of the Saxon troops, he addressed them in a general order, in which he made the most of their exploits, and consequently of his own, without waiting for the usual assignment of credit on the part of the commander-in-chief. This infringement of regulations increased the Emperor's anger, and Bernadotte was obliged to withdraw from the army and return to France.

Among the remarkable incidents of the battle of Wagram, I may mention the combat between two cavalry regiments, which, though serving in hostile armies, belonged to the same proprietary colonel, Prince Albert of Sachs-Teschen. He had married the celebrated Archduchess Christina of Austria, governor of the Low Countries, and, having the title of prince in both states, he possessed a regiment of hussars in Saxony and of cuirassiers in Austria. Both one and the other bore his name, and, as was the custom of both states, he appointed all the officers in each. Austria and Saxony having been at peace for many years, whenever he had an officer to place he would put him indifferently in whichever regiment had a vacancy, so that out of one family there could be found some members in the Saxon hussars, and others in the Austrian cuirassiers. Now, by an accident at once deplorable and extraordinary, these two regiments met on the battle-field of Wagram, and, impelled by duty and by the point of honour, they charged each other. Strange to say, the cuirassiers were broken by the hussars, who, in their desire to retrieve under the eyes of Napoleon the repulse of the Saxon infantry, fought with the greatest vigour. Indeed, the Saxon infantry, though it has often shown its courage, is far from being either as solidly organised or as well trained as the cavalry, which is rightly held to be one of the best in Europe.

Chapter 19
My Own Adventures at Wagram

You will probably now like to hear my own adventures in this terrible battle. Though frequently much exposed, especially on the second day, when the enemy's artillery converged its fire on Marshal Masséna's carriage, and we were literally under a hail of cannon-balls, which struck down a good many around me, I was lucky enough not to be wounded. I was also in considerable danger when the Austrian cavalry had broken and routed Boudet's division, and the marshal sent me to that general in the middle of 10,000 flying soldiers, who were being hewn down by the cavalry. Again I was more than once in danger when, in carrying orders, I had to pass near some of the many spots where the corn was blazing. By frequent detours I managed to escape the flames, but it was impossible to avoid crossing the fields where the ashes of the burnt straw were still hot enough to scorch the horses' feet. Two of mine were rendered useless for some time by the injuries they thus received, and a third was in such pain that he was within an ace of rolling me over in the half-extinguished straw. However, I got through without any serious accident; but though I escaped personal damage, a disagreeable thing befell me, which had very injurious results. On the second day of the battle I got into almost hopeless trouble with Masséna. The way of it was this. The marshal sent me with a message to the Emperor; I had the very greatest difficulty in reaching him, and was coming back after having galloped more than three leagues over the yet burning ashes of the corn. My horse, dead beat, and with his legs half burnt, could go no further when I got back to Masséna, and found him in a great difficulty. His corps was retreating before the enemy's right along the Danube, and the infantry of Boudet's division, broken by the Austrian cavalry, which was sabring them mercilessly, were flying pell-mell across the plain. It was the most critical moment of the battle. From his carriage the marshal could see the imminent danger, and was calmly making his dispositions to maintain order in the three infantry divisions which as yet were unbroken. For this purpose he had been obliged to send so many aides-de-camp to his generals that he had none with him except his son, Prosper Masséna, a young lieutenant. At that moment he saw that the fugitives from Boudet's division were making for the three divisions which were still fighting, and were on the point of flinging themselves upon their ranks, and drawing them along in a general rout. To stop this catastrophe the marshal wished to tell the generals and officers to direct the torrent of fliers towards the island of Lobau, where the disordered troops would find a secure shelter behind the powerful artillery. It was a dangerous mission, as there was every probability that the aide-de-camp who went into that disorderly rabble would be attacked by some of the enemy's troopers. The marshal could not make up his mind to expose his son to this danger, but he had no other officer near him, and it was clear that the order must be carried.

I came up just at the right moment to extricate Masséna from this cruel dilemma, so, without giving me time to take breath, he ordered me to throw myself into the danger which he dreaded for his son; but observing that my horse could hardly stand, he lent me one of his, which an orderly was leading. I was too well acquainted with military duty not to be aware that a general cannot bind himself to follow the arrangement which his aides-de-camp have made amongst themselves for taking their turn of duty, however great the peril may be; the chief must be free in a given case to employ whichever officer he thinks best suited to get his orders executed. Thus, although Prosper had not carried a single order all day, and it was his turn to go, I made no remark. I will even say that my self-esteem hindered me from divining the marshal's real motive in sending me on a duty both difficult and dangerous when it ought to have fallen to another, and I was proud of his confidence in me. But Masséna soon destroyed my illusion by saying, in a wheedling tone, 'You understand, my friend, why I do not send my son although it's his turn; I am afraid of getting him killed. You understand? you understand?' I should have held my tongue, but, disgusted with such ill-disguised selfishness, I could not refrain from answering, and that in the presence of several generals: 'Marshal, I was going under the impression that I was about to fulfil a duty; I am sorry that you have corrected my mistake, for now I understand perfectly that, being obliged to send one of your aides-de-camp to almost certain death, you would rather it should be I than your son, but I think you might have spared me this cruel plain speaking.' And without awaiting a reply I went off at full gallop towards Boudet's division, which the enemy's troopers were pitilessly slaughtering. As I left the carriage I heard a discussion begin between the marshal and his son, but the uproar of the battle and the speed at which I was going prevented me from catching their words. Their sense, however, was shortly explained, for hardly had I reached Boudet's division and begun doing my utmost to direct the terrified crowd towards the island of Lobau, when I beheld Prosper Masséna at my side. The brave lad, indignant at the way in which his father had sent me into danger and wished to reduce him to inactivity, had escaped unawares to follow me; 'I wish,' said he, 'at least to share the danger from which I ought to have saved you if my father's blind affection had not made him unjust to you when it was my turn to go.' The young man's noble straightforwardness pleased me; in his place I should have wished to do the same. Still, I had rather he had been further off at this critical moment, for no one who has not seen it can form an idea of a mass of infantry which has been broken and is being actively pursued by cavalry. Sabres and lances were working terrible execution among this rabble of terrified men, who were flying in disorder instead instead of taking the equally easy and much safer course of forming themselves into groups and defending themselves with the bayonet. Prosper Masséna was very brave, and in no way dazed by the danger, although we found ourselves every moment in this chaos face to face with the enemy's troopers. My position then became very critical, since I had a threefold task to fulfil. First, to parry the blows aimed at young Masséna, who had never learnt the sword exercise and used his weapon clumsily; secondly, to defend myself, and lastly, to speak to our demoralised soldiers to make them understand that they were to go towards the island of Lobau and not towards the divisions which were still in line. Neither of us received any wound, for when the Austrian troopers perceived that we were determined to defend ourselves vigorously, they left us, and turned their attention to the unresisting foot-soldiers.

When troops are in disorder, the soldiers fling themselves like sheep in the direction where they see their comrades running, and thus, as soon as I had imparted the marshal's orders to a certain number of officers, and they had shouted to their people to run towards the island, the stream of fugitives made in that direction. I found General Boudet at last, and he succeeded under the fire of our guns in rallying his troops. My task was thus at an end, and I returned with Prosper towards the marshal. But in my desire to take the shortest road, I imprudently passed near a clump of trees, behind which some hundred Austrian uhlans were posted. They charged upon us unawares, we meanwhile making at full speed for a line of French cavalry which was coming our way. We were none too soon, for the enemy's squadron was on the point of reaching us, and was pressing us so close that I thought for a moment that we were going to be killed or taken prisoners. But at the approach of our men the uhlans wheeled about, all but one officer, who, being admirably mounted, would not leave us without having a shot at us. One bullet pierced the neck of Prosper's horse, and the animal, throwing up his head violently, covered young Masséna's face with blood. I thought he was wounded, and was getting ready to defend him against the uhlan officer, when we were met by the advanced files of the French regiment. These, firing their carbines at the Austrian officer, laid him dead on the spot, just as he was turning to gallop off.

Prosper and I then returned to the marshal, who uttered a cry of grief on seeing his son covered with blood. But on finding that he was not wounded he gave free vent to his anger, and in the presence of several generals, his own aides-de-camp, and two orderly officers of the Emperor's, he scolded his son roundly, and ended his lecture with the words, 'Who ordered you to go and stick your head into that row, you young idiot?' Prosper's answer was really sublime. 'Who ordered me? My honour! This is my first campaign. I am already lieutenant and member of the Legion of Honour; I have received several foreign decorations, and so far I have done nothing for them. I wished to show my comrades, the army, and France that if I am not destined to have the military talent of my illustrious father, I am at least worthy by my courage to bear the name of Masséna.' Seeing that his son's noble sentiments met with the approbation of all the bystanders, the marshal made no answer; but his anger fell chiefly on me, whom he accused of having carried his son away, when, on the contrary, his presence was a great hindrance to me. The two orderly officers having reported at headquarters the scene between the marshal and his son, Napoleon heard of it, and happening to come that evening to Leopoldau, sent for Prosper, and said to him, taking him in a friendly way by the ear: 'Good, very good, my dear boy; that is how young people like you ought to start on their career.' Then, turning to the marshal, he said in a low tone, but loud enough to be heard by General Bertrand, from whom I have the story, I love my brother Louis no less than you your son; but when he was my aide-de-camp in Italy he did his turn of duty like the others, and I should have been afraid of bringing him into discredit if I had sent one of his comrades into the danger instead of him.' This reproof from the Emperor, in addition to the answer which I had been foolish enough to make to Masséna, naturally set him still more against me. From that day forward he never addressed me with 'tu', and although outwardly he treated me well, I knew that the grudge would remain, and as you will see I was not mistaken.

Never again did the Austrians fight with so much vigour as at Wagram; their retreat was admirable for its coolness and good order. They had, no doubt, the advantage, for the reasons I have stated, of leaving the field without being pursued; but I am not able to explain the reasons for Napoleon's delay in following them up on the ensuing morning. It has been said that as the roads both to Bohemia and to Moravia were in front of him, the Emperor was awaiting the result of reconnaissances in order to know what force the Archduke had on each of these roads. Reconnaissances, however, can only give very incomplete information, since the enemy's rear-guard very soon brings them to a halt, and they can see nothing beyond. Precious time was therefore lost uselessly; we had seen the enemy's columns marching off on both the roads, and should have pursued them at daybreak on the 7th by one or the other. However that may be, the Emperor did not commence the pursuit till 2 p.m., and went himself no more than three leagues, staying the night at the château of Volkersdorf, from which the Emperor of Austria had on the two previous days watched the battle. General Vandamme was left in command at Vienna, General Reynier in the island of Lobau, Oudinot at Wagram, and Macdonald at Floridsdorf. His rear thus secured, Napoleon sent Marmont and Davout in pursuit on the road to Moravia, and Masséna on that to Bohemia. The Army of Italy and the guard marched between the two high roads, ready to give support where it was wanted.

The stronger portion of the Austrian army was on the road to Bohemia. The Archduke had made good use of the night of the 6th, and so much of the 7th as Napoleon had allowed him, and his baggage wagons and artillery were well out of our reach. On leaving the field of battle we fell in with the scouts of the enemy's rear-guard in the defile of Langen-Enzersdorf, a long and narrow passage which would have been fatal to the Archduke if, on the previous day, we had been able to push him back to it. Passing this we entered a wide plain, in the middle of which stands Korn-Neuburg, a small walled town. Here the rear-guard, composed of nine battalions of Croats and Tyrolese Jägers, with a strong body of cavalry and plenty of guns, awaited us in impressive tranquillity. No doubt it is right in war to be enterprising, especially in presence of an already beaten foe; but this rule must not be followed beyond the limits of prudence. French cavalry generals are often too venturesome. Here they repeated the fault which Montbrun had committed before Raab in the previous June, when he would not wait for the infantry, and, leading his squadrons too near the fortress, suffered heavily from its artillery. In spite of that severe lesson, General Bruyère, who had succeeded Lasalle in the command of the light cavalry of Masséna's corps, having the lead when we emerged from the defile, would not wait for the infantry to pass him and form in the plain. Deploying his squadrons, he advanced towards the enemy, who, remaining quite still, let him come within cannon-range, then opened a heavy fire, under which he lost heavily. At sight of this Masséna got very angry, and sent me to Bruyère to express his dissatisfaction. I found the general at the head of his division, under a storm of balls, brave enough, but much vexed at having run into this risk, and much perplexed as to his best course. If he charged the Austrian cavalry, of twice his own numbers, he would have his division cut up. On the other hand, if he retreated to get out of range, and await the infantry, it was certain that the enemy's cavalry would be on him as soon as he had faced about, and would drive him back on our battalions, as they issued from the defile. The only other thing was to stay where he was, and wait for the infantry; and this seemed the least of evils, as I permitted myself to tell General Bruyère, when he did me the honour to ask my advice. When I repeated it to the marshal, he approved but was still in a high rage with the general, exclaiming every moment: 'Can you conceive anyone getting his people killed like that for no good?' Meanwhile, he hurried up Legrand's division, and, as soon as it was formed, sent the 26th to attack Korn-Neuburg. The place was taken, and the enemy's cavalry driven back by Bruyère's squadrons, who much preferred the danger of a charge to being pounded, as they had been for half-an-hour, by the artillery. The general behaved like a hero in the hand-to-hand fighting, which did not save him from being sharply reprimanded by the marshal.

On the 8th Masséna continued the pursuit, but we only had a slight engagement. We occupied the town of Stockerau, taking large stores of provisions, especially wine, which delighted the soldiers. Continuing on the 9th, the army was stopped by a strong force, before Hollabrunn. A brisk fight ensued, in which General Bruyère, remembering his mistake, handled his division more prudently, but exposed himself freely, and got severely wounded. The unlucky town of Hollabrunn, hardly rebuilt after the fire in 1805, was again reduced to ashes, and again many wounded men were buried in the ruins. The enemy withdrew with loss.

During the night of the 9th the marshal sent me to the Emperor with a report of the action. After a long march, and frequently losing my way in country roads, I reached Napoleon, still at the château of Volkersdorf. His Majesty had just learned that a great part of the Austrian army, leaving the road to Moravia, was marching towards Laa, to cross the Taya, and rejoin the Archduke at Znaym, and had sent Marmont in haste to follow them. He took the same direction himself on the 10th, while Davout pushed on to Nikolsburg, and took it. I was sent back to Masséna with orders to march quickly on Znaym, where the enemy appeared to be concentrating, with the view of again giving battle. All through the 10th the enemy's rear-guard retreated steadily before Masséna's corps. After its losses at Hollabrunn, some disorder began to show itself, and we made a great many prisoners. The same day, Prince Liechtenstein appeared at our outposts with a flag of truce, to ask for an armistice on the part of the Austrian commander-in-chief. Masséna sent him on to Napoleon with one of his officers, but by the time they reached Volkersdorf the Emperor had set out for Laa, and the flag of truce only reached him the next evening at Znaym, a delay which cost a good many lives. The Austrian rear-guard, after retreating all day without fighting, in the evening disputed our entrance into the village of Guntersdorf. There was a brisk artillery engagement in the course of which a ball struck Masséna's carriage, and another killed one of the horses. Luckily, the marshal had got out five minutes before. We repulsed the enemy at length, and passed the night at Guntersdorf.

Chapter 20
I Announce the Armistice

On July 11, an ill-omened day for me, Masséna's corps appeared before Znaym about 10 A.M., and half a league to our right we could see Marmont's divisions on the plateau of Teswitz, which they had reached by the road from Laa to Brunn. By mid-day the Emperor and his guard were at Zuckerhandel, and the Army of Italy not far away: The town of Znaym is surrounded by a solid wall, and stands on a vine-clad hill, at the foot of which runs the river Taya and a large brook named Lischen, which joins the Taya below Teswitz. Thus the hill of Znaym forms a position entrenched by nature, for the banks at most points bristle with steep rocks difficult of access. The ground falls towards the village of Oblass, through which runs the Vienna road, by which we arrived.

Having had no answer to his proposal of an armistice, the Archduke resolved to profit by the good position which he occupied, and risk the chance of another battle. Accordingly he formed his army in two lines, the first having its right on the Taya near Klosterbruck, its centre opposite Teswitz, and its left reaching to Kukrowitz. The second line occupied Znaym, the Galgenberg, and Brenditz, with the reserves in rear; while a swarm of skirmishers defended the vineyards between Znaym and the two streams.

On arriving before Oblass Masséna occupied that village and the double bridge which crosses the river at the so-called 'Pheasants' Island.' Legrand's division, after capturing it, went on towards Alt-Schallersdorf and Klosterbruck, a large convent turned into a tobacco factory. Here our troops met with a brisk resistance, and as our artillery were unable to pass through the vines, and had consequently to fire uphill from the bank of the river, it was unable to afford them any support. The marshal regretted that his inability to mount his horse prevented him from going to see for himself what could be done to remedy this state of things; whereupon I ventured to say that having explored the ground before the attack, I thought that a battery going from Oblass along the right bank of the river, and taking up its position above the village of Edelspitz, might do good service. Masséna, thanking me for the suggestion, ordered me to guide six guns to the spot named; and these, taking in rear the troops defending Klosterbruck and Alt-Schallersdorf, did so much execution among them that they quickly abandoned those two positions to our troops. As the marshal was congratulating himself on the effect produced by this battery, I went up and suggested taking another to the Kuhberg, the highest ground on the left bank, which could be reached by strengthening the teams. He agreed; and after some trouble I got eight guns on to the Kuhberg, whence they could play full on the Austrians massed in front of Znaym; so that I have no doubt but that, if the battle had continued, our battery on the Kuhberg would have been of great use by forcing the enemy to retire within the place. It is the best point from which to reduce the fortress of Znaym with artillery.

While this brisk cannonade was going on, a fearful storm burst over the district. In a moment everything was under water; the Taya overflowed; not a gun or musket could be fired. General Legrand's troops took shelter in Klosterbruck and Schallersdorf, and most of all in the cellars hollowed out among the vineyards. But while our soldiers, unheeding the enemy, whom they supposed to be under shelter in Znaym, were emptying the casks, the Archduke, informed doubtless of this carelessness, and wishing to cut off the retreat of Legrand's division, sent a column of a thousand men from the town. Marching at the double down the high road, they went through Alt-Schallersdorf, and reached the first bridge at Oblass just as I was coming down from the Kuhberg. I had gone up by way of Neu-Schallersdorf, having brought my guns from Oblass; but when I went back alone it seemed useless to go so far round, as I knew that all the ground between Znaym and the Taya was occupied by our infantry. So, as soon as I reached the little bridge between Edelspitz and Pheasants' Island, I crossed the Taya to reach the large bridges on the high road opposite Oblass, where I had left the marshal. Just as I had got on to the causeway connecting these two bridges, I heard behind me, in spite of the storm, the sound of many feet marching in time. Turning my head I beheld a column of Austrian grenadiers not twenty-five paces away. My first impulse was to go off at full speed to warn the marshal and his troops; but to my great surprise I found the bridge nearest to Oblass occupied by a brigade of French cuirassiers. General Guiton, who commanded it, knowing that Legrand was on the other side of the river, and having received an indistinct order, was quietly advancing at a walk. I had hardly time to say, 'There is the enemy,' when the general saw them, drew his sword, and shouting 'Gallop!' flew at the Austrian grenadiers. Having come to attack us unawares, they were so astounded at being thus unexpectedly attacked themselves that the foremost ranks had hardly time to bring their bayonets down. In a moment the three battalions were literally rolled over under the hoofs of the cuirassiers' horses, not one remaining on his legs. One only was killed; we took all the rest prisoners, with three guns which they had brought to fortify the Pheasants' Island.

Their return to the offensive would have had awkward results for us, if the Archduke had carried it out with more troops, and at the same time attacked Legrand's division in the vineyards. Unable to retreat by the bridges, our men would have undergone a severe reverse. But the Austrian general miscalculated when he flattered himself that a thousand of his men on the Pheasants' Island could have held it against three of our divisions, while Legrand's division, when attacked itself, would certainly have tried to force a passage. Thus caught between two fires, the thousand grenadiers would equally have had to surrender, though General Guiton's unexpected attack doubtless saved much loss of life. Emboldened by their success, though not knowing the ground, the cuirassiers charged right up to the gates of Znaym, General Legrand's infantry hurrying up to their support, and the town was nearly carried. But superior forces, backed by powerful artillery, forced the French back to Alt-Schallersdorf, and Klosterbruck, when Masséna sent Carra-Saint Cyr's infantry division to their support.

At this moment, the Emperor, posted on the heights of Zuckerhandel, ordered Marshal Marmont to debouch from Teswitz and get in touch with Masséna's right. The battle was spreading gradually, and in order to get nearer to it, Napoleon came to Teswitz. Masséna sent me to his Majesty to report, and I came back with orders to carry the town at any cost. Our battery on the Kuhberg was hammering it, and Marmont was about to assault by the valley of the Leska. As they beat the charge on all sides, the sound of the drums, muffled by the rain, mingled with the thunder. Our troops, in good spirits, advanced bravely against the battalions which were stoutly awaiting them in their position before Znaym; only an occasional shot came from the houses. Everything foretold a bloody bayonet fight, when an officer from the Emperor galloped up with an order for Masséna to cease fighting, as an armistice had just been concluded. The marshal at once sent officers with the news to the different points of the line, and appointed me by name to go towards that one of our brigades which was nearest to the town and had the smallest distance to cross in order to reach the enemy. Coming up in the rear of these regiments, I vainly tried to speak; my voice was drowned by cries of 'Vive l'Empereur!' which always preceded a fight, and the bayonets were already crossing. A moment longer, one of those terrible infantry tussles would take place, which, once started, cannot be checked. I hesitated no longer, and passing through the files, I got between the two lines, which were on the point of meeting. As I was shouting, 'Peace! peace!' and with my left hand giving the sign for a halt, suddenly a bullet from the outskirts of the town struck me on the wrist. Some of our officers, understanding at length that I brought the order to suspend hostilities, halted their companies; others, seeing the Austrian battalions within a hundred paces, were doubtful. At the same moment, an aide-de-camp from the Archduke came between the two lines, with a view of preventing attack and got a bullet through his shoulder, from the same quarter. I hastened towards him, and to make both sides see for what purpose we had been sent, we testified it by embracing each other. At sight of this, the officers on both sides had no more hesitation about ordering a halt. Flocking round us, they learnt that an armistice had been agreed on. There were mutual congratulations; the Austrians returned to Znaym, and our troops to their former position.

The blow which I received had been so sharp that I thought my wrist was broken; luckily, it was nothing of the kind, but the bullet had injured the tendon. None of my many wounds have caused me so much pain; I had to carry my arm in a sling for six months. My wound, however, was far less severe than that of the Austrian aide-de-camp. He was quite a young man, full of pluck, and in spite of what had happened would come with me to Masséna, quite as much to see the famous old warrior as to carry a message which the Archduke had sent by him. As we were going together to Klosterbruck, the Austrian officer, who was losing blood freely, nearly fainted, and I proposed to take him back to Znaym. But he persisted in coming with me to be treated by the French surgeons, who, he said, were much better than those of his own army. His name was Count d'Aspre, and he was the nephew of the general of that name who was killed at Wagram. Masséna received him kindly, and took every sort of care of him. As for me, the marshal seeing me wounded again, felt bound to agree with all the officers, and even the soldiers of the brigade, who praised my devotion in going between the two armies to prevent bloodshed. Napoleon came round the bivouacs in the evening, and expressed his satisfaction with me in lively terms, adding, 'You get wounded very often, but I will reward your zeal.' He had formed a plan of creating a military order of the Three Fleeces, the knights of which were bound to have had at least six wounds, and I learnt afterwards that his Majesty had entered me on the list of officers to receive this decoration, of which I shall have to speak hereafter. He asked to see M. d'Aspre, who had devoted himself as I had, and gave him many complimentary messages for the Archduke.

While deeming it fortunate that the cuirassiers had reached the bridges just at the moment when the Austrian grenadiers were going to take possession of them, Napoleon was surprised that heavy cavalry should have been sent across the river on to a hill-side, where the only passage was a high road with steep sides along vineyards. No one, therefore, admitted having given the order; it came neither from the marshal nor from his chief of staff, and as the general of cuirassiers could not point out the officer who had brought it, the author of this lucky blunder remained unknown.

In the few minutes during which the grenadiers occupied Pheasants' Island, they captured three of our generals, Fririon, Masséna's chief of staff, Lasouski, and Stabenrath, and relieved them in a trice of their purses and silver spurs. The generals, who had been set free the next moment by our cuirassiers, treated their short captivity as a good joke.

I have mentioned that before I received my wound, immediately after the brilliant charge of the cuirassiers, the marshal had ordered me to report it to the Emperor at Zuckerhandel. As the storm had made it impossible to ford the Taya, I had to cross it in front of Oblass, by the Pheasants' Island bridges, just as Marshal Marmont's troops were debouching from Teswitz. The enemy's artillery had opened a terrible fire upon them, so that the ground near the river was ploughed up by the balls. But as there was no means of taking another road without going a long way round, I took that line. I had left Oblass with Major de Talleyrand Périgord, who was on the imperial staff, and was returning after bringing an order to Masséna. He had already been that way, and offered to guide me. As he was going in front of me along the narrow path beside the right bank of the Taya, the enemy's fire increased and we quickened our pace. All of a sudden a confounded soldier of the transport corps, his horse ladened with plundered chickens and ducks, came out from the willows on the river bank, a few paces from M. de Talleyrand, and went off along the path at full gallop. But his horse being knocked over by a cannon-ball, that of M. de Talleyrand, who was just behind him, tumbled over its body, and came down with a crash. Seeing my companion fall, I dismounted to help him up, a difficult job, for one of his feet was entangled in the stirrup under the horse's body. The transport man, instead of helping us, ran and hid among the trees, and I was left alone to perform a task which was made all the more troublesome by the cannon-balls pitching all round us, and by the fact that the enemy's skirmishers were pushing ours back, and might come upon us. I could not, however, leave a comrade in this awkward position, so I set to work, and after incredible efforts I was lucky enough to get the horse up, and put M. de Talleyrand back in his saddle, and we resumed our course. I felt all the more deserving because I had never met my companion before; he expressed his gratitude in the warmest terms, and when we had got to Zuckerhandel, and I had delivered my message to the Emperor I was congratulated by all the officers of the headquarters staff. M. de Talleyrand had told them what I had done, and kept repeating, 'That's what you may call a first-rate comrade.' Some years afterwards, on my return from the exile to which I was condemned at the Restoration, M. de Talleyrand, then General of the Royal Guard, received me pretty coldly. However, when I met him twenty years later at Milan, whither I accompanied the Duke of Orleans, I bore him no grudge, and we shook hands. It was on the same journey that I met M. d'Aspre at Cremona; he was then a general in the Austrian service, having been till 1836 in that of Spain. Later on, he was second in command of the Army of Italy, under the famous Marshal Radetzky.

But to return to Znaym. The Austrians evacuated the town, and Masséna fixed his headquarters there, his army corps encamping in the neighbourhood. By the armistice a third of the Austrian monarchy with eight million inhabitants had been provisionally given up to Napoleon--a powerful guarantee of peace.

M. d'Aspre, being too badly hurt to rejoin his own army, stayed at Znaym. I saw much of him; he was a quick-witted man, but rather excitable. I too had a good deal of pain from my wound, and could not ride; therefore, Masséna sent me with despatches for the Emperor, bidding me post to Vienna, where he and the staff soon came. Our people and horses remained at Znaym. Peace took a long time to conclude, Napoleon wishing to crush Austria, while the Austrians were encouraged to hold out for better terms by the news that the English had landed in Holland and taken Flushing. Cambacérès, who governed France during the Emperor's absence, sent all available troops to the Scheldt, putting (much to Napoleon's displeasure) Bernadotte in command. The English withdrew before long. The conferences were resumed, and went on no faster. We continued to occupy the country, and Masséna's headquarters remained at Vienna till November 10. My wound prevented me from taking any part in the amusements of the place, but I was kindly treated by the Countess Stibar, on whom I was quartered. At Vienna I found my friend, General Sainte-Croix, who was kept some months in bed by his wound. He was quartered in the Lobkowitz palace, where Masséna was. I passed much time with him every day, and told him about the dislike which the marshal seemed to have conceived for me since the incident at Wagram. As he had great influence with Masséna, he used it in my favour, and this, with my conduct at Znaym, restored me to a fairly good place in the marshal's esteem; but then by overplain speaking I destroyed the good result, and revived the marshal's ill-will towards me.

As I have told you, the injury to his leg caused by the fall from his horse at Lobau had compelled Masséna to use a carriage at the battle of Wagram and the subsequent actions. In the first instance, artillery horses were to be harnessed to the carriage, but it was found that they were too long for the pole and not easy enough in their action, so four horses from the marshal's stable were substituted. Two soldiers from the transport train were to drive, and they were just getting into the saddle on the evening of July 4, when the marshal's own coachman and postilion declared that as he was using his own horses it was their business to drive. No representation of the danger into which they were running could deter them from their purpose; the coachman got on the box and the postilion mounted just as if they were going for a drive in the Bois de Boulogne. The two brave servants were in constant danger for eight days, especially at Wagram, where many hundred men were killed close to the carriage, and at Guntersdorf, where the ball which struck the carriage went through the coachman's overcoat, and another ball killed the horse under the postilion. Nothing seemed to frighten these two faithful attendants, whose devotion was admired by the whole army. Even the Emperor complimented them, and observed once to Masséna: 'There are 300,000 combatants on the field; now do you know who are the two bravest? Your coachman and your postilion. For all the rest of us are here in pursuance of our duty, while these two men might have excused themselves from being exposed to death. Their merit is therefore greater than that of anyone else.' To the men themselves he called out: 'You are two brave fellows!' Napoleon would certainly have rewarded them, but he could only have given them money, and he probably thought that this might offend Masséna, in whose service the danger had been incurred, and indeed, it was the marshal's business, and all the more so that he had an enormous fortune; 200,000 francs as army leader, another 200,000 as Duke of Rivoli, and 500,000 as Prince of Essling. But for all that he allowed two months to pass without telling the men what he meant to do for them. One day when I and several of the aides-de-camp happened to be by Sainte-Croix's bedside, Masséna came into the room, and as we chatted over the events of the campaign, he said how fortunate it was that he had followed my advice and gone on to the field in a carriage, instead of being carried by grenadiers, and thence he naturally went on to speak of the plucky conduct of his coachman and postilion. He ended by saying that he wished to reward them well, and was going to give each of them 400 francs. Then, turning to me, he had the face to ask if the two men would not be pleased? I had better to have held my tongue, or merely suggested a rather higher sum; but I made the mistake of speaking too plainly and too mischievously into the bargain. I knew perfectly well that Masséna only intended to give them 400 francs only; but I answered that with a pension of 400 francs added to their savings, the coachman and postilion would be secured from want in their old age. The eyes of a tigress who sees her young attacked by the hunter are not more terrible than were Masséna's on hearing me speak thus. He leapt from his chair, exclaiming: 'Wretch! do you want to ruin me? What! an annuity of 400 francs? No, no, no: 400 francs once for all!' Most of my comrades prudently held their peace; but General Sainte-Croix and Major Ligniville declared plainly that the proposed reward was unworthy of the marshal, and that he ought to make it an annuity. At this Masséna could restrain himself no longer; he rushed about the room in a rage, upsetting everything in his way, even large furniture, and cried, 'You want to ruin me!' His last words as he left the room were, 'I would sooner see you all shot, and get a bullet through my arm, than bind myself to give an annuity of 400 francs to anyone. Go to the devil the lot of you!' Next day he came among us again, very calm outwardly, for no one could play a part better; but from that day forward General Sainte-Croix lost much of his esteem, and he bore a grudge against Ligniville which he let him see the next year in Portugal. As for me he was angry with me of all, because I was the first to mention the annuity. The story travelled from mouth to mouth till it reached the Emperor, and one day when Masséna was dining with him, Napoleon kept bantering him about his avarice, and said that he understood he had at any rate given a good pension to the two brave servants who drove his carriage at Wagram. Then the marshal answered that he was going to give each an annuity of 400 francs; so he did it without having to be shot through the arm. He was all the more angry with us, and often said to us with a sardonic laugh, 'Ah! My fine fellows, if I followed your good advice you would soon have me ruined.'

Seeing that the Austrian plenipotentiaries kept putting off the conclusion of the treaty of peace, the Emperor kept ready for war, bringing up numerous reinforcements, which he inspected daily at the parade held in the court of the palace of Schönbrunn. The recruits attracted many sightseers, who were allowed to approach too freely; thus one day a student named Frederick Stabs, son of a bookseller at Naumburg, and member of the secret society called the Tugendbund, or League of Virtue, took advantage of this lack of supervision to slip into the group which surrounded the Emperor. General Rapp had twice told him not to come so near, and on pushing him away for the third time he felt that the young man had arms concealed under his clothes. Being arrested, he confessed that he wished to deliver Germany from the Emperor's yoke by killing him. Napoleon would have spared his life and treated him as insane; but as the doctors declared that he was not mad, and the man himself persisted in saying that if he escaped he should try to accomplish what had been a longstanding purpose, he was tried by court-martial and shot.

The treaty of peace was signed on October 4; the Emperor left Austria on the 22nd, and it was ten days later before the troops had left the place. Then Masséna permitted his officers to return to France. I left Vienna November 10, driving as far as Strasburg with my comrade Ligniville. I had left my servant behind to bring one of my horses on to Paris. From Strasburg I was afraid to continue my journey alone, for my arm was much swelled, and I was in great pain. Fortunately, I found in my hotel the surgeon major of the 10th Chasseurs, who was kind enough to dress my wound and to share my carriage as far as Paris, taking care of me on the way. The doctor left the army, and settled at Chantilly, where I met him, twenty years later, at the table of the Duke of Orleans, as commandant of the national guard. I was still very poorly when I reached Paris, but rest and my mother's care soon made me well.

Thus ended the year 1809. Now, if you recollect that I began at Astorga, in Spain, during the campaign against the English, and then took part in the siege of Saragossa, where I got a bullet through my body; if you consider that I had next to cross part of Spain, and the whole of France and Germany; that I was present at the battle of Eckmühl; mounted the walls of Ratisbon; performed the risky passage of the Danube at Mölk; fought for two days at Essling, where I was wounded in the leg; then was engaged for sixty hours at the battle of Wagram; and, lastly, was wounded in the arm at the action at Znaym, you will agree that this year had been very eventful for me, and had seen me pretty frequently in danger.

Chapter 21
The 'Sheperdess' and the Three Fleeces

The year 1810 opened happily for me. I was at Paris with my mother, and my wounds being quite healed, I was able to go out in society. I became very intimate with M. and Mme Desbrières, whose daughter I married in the following year. Before that happy moment came, however, I had a laborious campaign and plenty of danger to go through. The Emperor had appointed Marshal Masséna to the command of a formidable army, which was to march in the spring upon Lisbon, then occupied by the English. We made our arrangements, therefore, to set out; but as the French was is to make amusement a prelude to fighting, Paris was unwontedly brilliant that winter. Everywhere, both at court and in private houses, were balls and parties, to which, as aide-de-camp of the Prince of Essling, I had instant invitations. The Emperor required that the great officials, to whom he gave enormous salaries, should encourage trade by luxurious entertainments, and they rivalled each other in earning their master's favour by doing their duty in this respect. Of them all the most conspicuous was Count Marescalchi, ambassador from Napoleon, King of Italy, to Napoleon, Emperor of the French. This diplomatist, who had a fine house in the Champs Elysées, at the corner of the present Avenue Montaigne, had devised a form amusement which, if not new, was brought to perfection by him; I mean the fancy-dress or masked ball. As etiquette prevented fancy-dress from being worn at Court or at high officials houses, M. Marescalchi had a monopoly on this kind of entertainment. All the best society went to them, and the Emperor (who had just been divorced from Josephine, but had not yet married Marie-Louise) never missed one; it was even said that he arranged them. Wearing a plain black domino and common mask, and with Duroc, similarly disguised, on his arm, Napoleon used to mix with the crowd and puzzle the ladies, who were rarely masked. The crowd, it is true, consisted of none but trustworthy persons, because M. Marescalchi always submitted his list to the minister of police; and also because the assistant-adjutant-general, Laborde, so well known for his talents in scenting a conspirator, was at the entrance of the rooms, and allowed no one to enter without showing his face and ticket, and giving his name. Agents in disguise went about, and a battalion of the guard furnished sentries to every exit. These precautions, however, were so well managed by Duroc, that once in the room, the guests were unconscious of any supervision.

I never missed one of these gatherings, and had much amusement at them. One night, however, my pleasure was disturbed by an awkward incident which is worth recording. My mother was some kind of relation to General Sahuguet d'Espagnac, whose father had been governor of the Invalides under Louis XV. General Sahuguet was appointed, under the Consulate, Governor of Tobago, and died there, leaving a widow, who came to live at Paris. She was a good woman, but of a sharpish temper; so my mother and I did not often visit her. Now, it happened that once in the course of this winter I met at her house a friend of hers, of whom I had often heard, but whom I did not know. Mme X—— was a lady of great stature, over fifty years of age. She was said to have been very handsome, but nothing remained of it save her splendid hair. Her voice and demeanour were those of a man; with her lofty air and vigorous language, she was the very 'dragoon'. Her late husband had held high office, but he had abused the confidence of the Government, and her pension had been commuted, on what she thought inadequate terms. Having come to Paris to protest against what she called a crying injustice, and finding her claims rejected by the ministry, she applied in vain to all the members of the Imperial family, and, finally, in despair, resolved to speak to the Emperor himself. Unable to obtain an audience, she pursued Napoleon everywhere, trying to get at him wherever he went. She had found out that he was going to M. Marescalchi's ball, and thinking that the diplomatist would not decline to receive the widow of a man once in a high position, she boldly wrote, asking for an invitation. The ambassador put her name on his list, where it escaped the notice of the police, and Mme X— had just received a ticket for a ball on the evening of the day when I met her at Mme Sahuguet's. In the course of conversation she found out that I was going, and said that she should be glad to meet me there, as she had few friends in Paris, and none of them went to Marescalchi's balls. I replied by some polite commonplace, little thinking that the result would be one of the most awkward situations I ever was in.

Night came, and I went to the Embassy. The ball was on the ground floor, card-tables being on that above. When I entered quadrilles were going on, and a crowd was gazing at the magnificent costumes. Suddenly, in the midst of silk, velvet, feathers, and embroideries appeared a colossal female figure, clad in plain white calico, with red corset, and bedizened with coloured ribbons in the worst taste. This was Mme X——, who had found no better way of displaying her magnificent hair than dressing as a shepherdess, with a little straw hat over one ear, and two large tresses down to her heels, Her curious get-up, and the strange simplicity of the dress in which she appeared in the brilliant assembly, drew all eyes towards her. I had the curiosity to look that way, having unluckily taken off my mask. Mme X——, feeling awkward in the crowd of strangers, came to me, and; took my arm without more ado, saying aloud, 'Now I shall have a partner.' I should have willingly seen this strange shepherdess as the devil, all the more so that from her indiscreet confidences I feared a scene with the Emperor, which would have seriously compromised me. I was looking for an opportunity of getting rid of her, when a pretext spontaneously presented itself. As I have said, most of the ladies unmasked on coming in, which made the gathering more pleasant. Some men did the same for coolness, and so long as they were few in number it was allowed. If, however, all had uncovered their faces, the only two masked men would have been the Emperor and Duroc, and the occasion would have lost all its attraction for Napoleon, who liked to go about incognito and hear what people said. Now, just when I was wishing most ardently to get away from Mme X——, many men beside myself had their masks off, and M. Marescalchi's secretaries were beginning to go round the rooms, requesting us to resume them. Mine was in my pocket, but I pretended to have left it in the next room, and, promising to return quickly, I left the shepherdess under the plea of going to fetch it.

Rid at length of this dreadful incubus, I hastened up to the first floor, where, going through the quiet card-rooms, I went and established myself in a room at the further end, dimly lighted by a shaded lamp. No one being there, I took off my mask, and was resting and consuming an excellent ice, rejoicing in my escape, when two masked men, short and stoat, in black dominoes, entered the little room. 'Here we shall be out of the crowd,' said one; then, calling me by my name without prefix, he beckoned me to him. I could not see his face, but as I knew all the great dignitaries of the Empire were in the house, I felt sure that a man who could so imperatively summon an officer of my rank must be an important personage. I came forward, and the unknown said in a whisper, 'I am Duroc; the Emperor is with me. He is overcome by the heat and wishes to rest in this out-of-the-way room; stay with us, to obviate any suspicion on the part of chance enterers. The Emperor sat down in an arm-chair looking towards a corner of the room. The general and I placed ours back to back with his, so as to cover him, facing the door, and began to chat, by the general's wish, as if he were one of my comrades. The Emperor, taking off his mask, asked the general for two handkerchiefs, with which he wiped his face and neck; then, tapping me lightly on the shoulder, he begged me (that was his term) to get him a large glass of cold water, and bring it myself. I went at once to the nearest buffet, and filled a glass with iced water; but as I was about to carry it to the room where Napoleon was, I was accosted by two tall men in Scotch costume, one of whom said in my ear, 'Can Major Marbot answer for the wholesomeness of that water?' I thought I could, for I had taken at it at random from one of the many decanters standing there for the use of all comers. Doubtless, these two persons were some of the police agents who were distributed about the house under various disguises to look after the Emperor without worrying him by too ostentatious attention, and moved about at a respectful distance, ready to fly to his help if they were wanted. Napoleon received the water which I brought him with so much satisfaction that I thought he must be parched with thirst; to my surprise, however, he swallowed only a small mouthful, then, dipping the two handkerchiefs in the iced water, he told me to put one on the nape of his neck while he held the other to his face, repeating 'Ah! that's good, that's good!' Duroc then resumed his chat with me, chiefly about the recent campaign in Austria. The Emperor said, 'You behaved very well, especially at the assault of Ratisbon and your crossing of the Danube; I shall never forget it, and before long I will give you a notable proof of my satisfaction.' I could not imagine what this new reward was to consist of, but my heart leapt for joy. Then, oh, woe! The terrible shepherdess appeared at the end of the little room. 'Oh! there you are, sir! I shall complain to your cousin of your rudeness,' she exclaimed. 'Since you deserted me I have been all but smothered ten times over. I had to leave the ball-room, the heat is stifling. It seems comfortable here; I will rest here. So saying, she sat down beside me.

General Duroc said nothing, and the Emperor, keeping his back turned and his face in the wet handkerchief, remained motionless; more and more so as the shepherdess, giving free play to her reckless tongue, and taking no notice of our neighbors, told me how she thought she had more than once recognised the personage whom she sought in the crowd, but had not been able to get at him. 'But I must speak to him', she said, 'he absolutely must double my pension. I know that people have tried to injure me by saying that I was free in my youth. Good heavens! go and listen for a moment to the talk down there, between the windows. Besides, what about his sisters? What about himself? What does he come here for, if not to be able to talk as he likes to pretty women? They say my husband stole; poor devil! he took to it late, and was pretty clumsy at it! Besides, have not his accusers stolen, too? Did they inherit their town houses and their fine estates? Didn't he steal in Italy, Egypt, everywhere?' 'But, madam,' said I, 'allow me to remark that what you say is very unseemly, and I am all the more surprised you should say it to me, that I never saw you till this morning.' 'Oh! I speak the truth before anyone. And if he does not give me a good pension, I will tell him, or write to him, what I think of him pretty plainly. Oh! I am not afraid of anything.' I was on tenterhooks, and would willingly have exchanged my situation for a cavalry charge or a storming-party. However, my agony was alleviated by feeling that Mme X——'s chatter would clear my character with my two neighbours when they heard that I had never seen her till that morning, had not brought her to the ball, and had got away from her as soon as I could.

Nevertheless I was rather anxious about the way in which this scene would end, when Duroc, leaning towards me, said: 'Don't let this woman follow us.' He rose; the Emperor had replaced his mask while Mme X— was raving at him, and as he passed in front of her he said to me, 'Marbot, people who take an interest in you are pleased to know that you never met this charming shepherdess till to-day, and you would do well to send her off to feed her sheep.' So saying, Napoleon took Duroc's arm and went out. Mme X—, astounded and thinking she recognised them, wanted to dart after them. I knew that, strong as I was, I could not hold this giantess by the arm, but I seized her by the skirt, which tore at the waist with a loud crack. At the sound the shepherdess, feeling that if she pulled she would presently find herself in her shift, stopped short, saying, 'It's he! it's he!' and reproaching me bitterly for having hindered her from following. This I endured patiently until I saw in the distance the Emperor and Duroc with the two Scotchmen following a little way off come to the end of the long suite of rooms and reach the staircase. Judging, then, that Mme X— would not be able to find them in the crowd, I made her a low bow without a word, and went off as quick as could be. She was ready to choke with rage, but feeling that the lower part of her garment was about to desert her, she said to me, 'At least, try to get me some pins, for my dress is falling off.' But I was so angry at her that I left her in the lurch, and I will even admit that I was mischievous enough to rejoice at her awkward position. I quickly left the house and returned home. I passed a disturbed night, seeing myself in my dreams pursued by the shepherdess, who, in spite of my remonstrances, kept insulting the Emperor horribly. Next day I went to cousin Sahuguet to tell her the extraordinary conduct of her dangerous friend: she was disgusted, and forbad her house to Mme X—, who a few days after received orders to leave Paris, nor do I know what became of her.

The Emperor, as is well known, attended a state Mass every Sunday, after which there was a grand reception at the Tuileries, open to everyone who had reached a certain rank in the civil or judicial service, and to officers in the army. As such I had the entrée, of which I only availed myself once a month. The Sunday following the day on which the scene I have related took place I was in a perplexity. Ought I to show myself to the Emperor so quickly, or would it be better to let some weeks pass? I consulted my mother, and her opinion was that as I was in no way to blame in the affair, I had better go to the Tuileries, showing no signs of embarrassment, which advice I followed. The people who came to court formed a rank on each side of the way to the chapel. The Emperor passed in silence between them, returning their salutes. He replied to mine by a good-natured smile, which seemed to me of good omen and completely reassured me. After the Mass, as Napoleon went through the rooms again and, according to his custom, addressed a few words to the people who were there, he stopped in front of me, and being unable to express himself freely in presence of so many hearers he said to me, sure that I should take his meaning: 'I am told that you were at Marescalchi's last ball; did you enjoy yourself very much?' 'Not the least bit, sir.' 'Ah!' replied the Emperor, 'if masked balls sometimes offer agreeable adventures, they are apt also to cause very awkward ones. The great thing is to get well out of them, and no doubt that is what you did.' As soon as the Emperor had passed on, General Duroc, who was behind me, said in my ear, 'Confess that there was a moment when you were in a considerable fix. I was so no less, for I am responsible for all the invitations; but it won't happen again. Our impudent shepherdess is far away from Paris, and will never come back.' The cloud which had a moment disturbed my tranquillity was dissolved, and I recovered my habitual gaiety. Very soon I had cause to be well satisfied, for at the following reception the Emperor was good enough to tell me in public that he had included me in the number of officers who were to receive the order of the Three Fleeces.

You will doubtless like to know something about this new order, the creation of which, though announced in the 'Moniteur,' was never carried into effect. As you know, Philip the Good, Duke of Burgundy, founded in the fifteenth century the famous order of the Golden Fleece. By the marriage of the daughter of Charles the Bold to the heir of the house of Austria, the Duchy of Burgundy, and with it the right of conferring the Golden Fleece, passed to that house, and the Emperor Charles V., after uniting the crown of Austria to that of Spain, continued to enjoy the privilege. When Spain and Germany were separated after his death, the princes of the house of Austria, though no longer possessing the Duchy of Burgundy, preserved the grand mastery of the Golden Fleece uncontested. But when, on the extinction of the Austrian branch in Spain, a French prince mounted that throne, the Kings of Spain, as well as the house of Austria, claimed the right of conferring the order. Some people considered that neither the one nor the other had the right; but that since Burgundy now formed part of France it was proper that a Burgundian order should be given by our kings. They never did give it, however, but the sovereigns of Austria and Spain each continued to do so, so that there was both a Spanish and an Austrian Golden Fleece. Finding things in this state at his accession, the Emperor Napoleon resolved, as being actually in possession of the old Burgundy, to throw the two rival orders into the shade by creating that of the Three Fleeces, restricting the members to a small number in order to make it more illustrious, and admitting them only on condition of distinguished service, the first requirement being that the receiver should have been wounded at least four times. Great privileges and a considerable pension were to be attached to the decoration.

By a sentiment which one can easily understand, Napoleon chose to date the decree founding the new order from Schönbrunn, the palace of the Emperor of Austria, at a moment when the French armies, having just conquered half of his dominions, were occupying Spain. The King of Spain, probably, did not feel this fresh outrage, which was a small matter after the loss of his crown, but it was otherwise with the Emperor of Austria. He, it is said, was much hurt on learning that Napoleon intended to tarnish the splendour of an order founded by one of his ancestors, and highly valued by the princes of his house.

In spite of the numerous congratulations which I received, and the joy which I felt, I could not help inwardly blaming the creation of the order. I thought that the splendour which the Emperor wished to give it must lower that of the Legion of Honour, the institution of which had already produced such great results. Still, I congratulated myself on having been thought worthy to receive the new order. But whether Napoleon feared to lower the value of the Legion of Honour, or wished to please his future father-in-law, he renounced his purpose, and, after his marriage with the Archduchess Marie-Louise, no more was heard of the order of the Three Fleeces.

The civil marriage was celebrated at Saint-Cloud, April 1, and the religious ceremony took place the next day in the chapel of the Louvre. I was present both at this and at the many festivities and rejoicings in honour of this event, which, as they said, was going to secure the crown on Napoleon's head, and which, on the contrary, actually contributed so much to his fall.

Chapter 22
To Spain Again

The time was drawing near when Marshal Masséna was to go to Portugal, and the troops which were to compose his army were already assembled in great numbers in the south-west of Spain. As I was the only one of his aides-de-camp who had ever been in the Peninsula, he decided that I should go on in front to establish his headquarters at Valladolid. I left Paris on April 15 with a sad presentiment that I was going to make a disagreeable campaign in all ways. This seemed to be justified at the outset, for one of the wheels of the post-chaise in which I was travelling with my servant Woirland broke when we were a few leagues from Paris, and we had to walk on to the post at Longjumeau. It was a holiday, and we lost more than twelve hours. Wishing to make them up by travelling night and day, I was rather tired when I got to Bayonne. Beyond that town one could not travel in a carriage; we had therefore to ride post; and, to complete our troubles, the weather, which was magnificent when I left France, suddenly turned to rain, and the Pyrenees were covered with snow. I was very soon wet through and worn out, but there was nothing to do but to go on.

I am not superstitious; but at the moment when I left French soil, and was crossing the Bidassoa to enter Spain an incident happened which struck me as an evil omen. A huge hideous black jackass, with rough and shaggy coat, was standing in the middle of the bridge, apparently disputing our passage. The outrider, who was a little in front of us, administered a sharp cut with his whip to make it get out the way, when the animal in a fury threw itself upon the man's horse and bit it savagely, lashing out all the time at Woirland and myself, who had come up to the rescue. The blows which we all three dealt to the infernal beast, so far from making him let go, seemed to excite him still further; and I really do not know how the ridiculous fight would have ended but for the help of the custom-house officers, who pricked the donkey's rump with their spiked sticks. My melancholy anticipations were certainly justified by the event, for my two campaigns in the Peninsula were exceedingly laborious. I was twice wounded without obtaining any reward, and scarcely any mark of kindness from Masséna.

After crossing the Bidassoa and reaching Irun there was no more security. Officers bearing despatches had to be escorted by a picket of the so-called Burgos gendarmerie, which had been formed of picked men in the town of that name, and had the special duty of protecting the communications. To this end there was at every posting-station a detachment in an entrenched blockhouse. The gendarmes, men in the prime of life, had very severe service for five years, and lost heavily, since it was war to the death between them and the Spanish insurgents. It was raining hard as I left Irun. After some hours' march through the mountains, as I was reaching the little town of Montdragon, I heard a brisk musketry fire about half a league ahead. I stopped to consider. If I went forward it might be to fall into the hands of the bandits, with whom the country was swarming. On the other hand, if an officer bearing despatches turned back every time he heard a musket-shot it would take him several months to go the shortest journey. So I went on, and soon came upon the corpse of a French officer. The poor man, on his way from Madrid to Paris with letters from King Joseph to the Emperor, had just changed horses at Montdragon. He was not two cannon-shots from the station when he and his escort received an almost point-blank discharge from a group of bandits hidden behind a rock. The officer had several bullets through his body, and two of the gendarmes in his escort were wounded. If he had started a quarter of an hour later from Montdragon, I should undoubtedly have been the one to fall into the ambush. This looked promising, and I had still more than one hundred leagues to traverse through provinces all up in arms against us. The attack at the very gates of Montdragon had put the little garrison of the town on the alert, and they had started in pursuit of the brigands. These, delayed in their march by their wish to carry off three of their men, who had been wounded by the gendarmes, were quickly overtaken and forced to escape into the mountains leaving their wounded behind. These last were shot.

My experience in the former Spanish campaign had taught me

that the most favourable moment for an officer who has a difficult country to traverse is just after one of these attacks, when the brigands, in their fear of being pursued, are in a hurry to get out of the way. I was therefore getting ready to proceed, but the officer in command of the place objected—first, because he had just learnt that the famous guerrilla leader, Mina, had appeared in the neighbourhood; and, secondly, because the night was drawing on and by the Emperor's order escorts were directed to start only in daylight. This commandant was a Piedmontese who had long served in the French army, and was distinguished for unwonted intelligence and courage. The insurgents were extremely afraid of him, and, except for a few ambuscades, which it was impossible to foresee, he had, by employing address and vigour in turn, got the whole district in hand. I will instance each quality, which will give you some idea of kind of war which we had to wage in Spain, though plenty of the educated class were on our side.

The parson of Montdragon was one of the fiercest opponents of the French. When, however, Napoleon passed through the town on his way back to Paris, in January 1809, the reverend gentleman, like all the rest of the inhabitants went in front of the post-house to have a look at the Emperor. The commandant caught sight of him, went straight up to him, took him by the hand, and, leading him to the Emperor, said, loud enough for everyone to hear, 'I have the honour to present to your Majesty the curate of this town, one of the most devoted servants of your brother King Joseph.' Napoleon, taking what the wily Piedmontese said as sound currency, received the clergyman most kindly, and thus he found himself against his will compromised in presence of his whole flock. That very evening, as he was going home, he was shot in the arm. He knew his compatriots too well not to understand that if the French were not victorious in the struggle his fate was sealed. From that moment he declared openly for them, and, at the head of the partisans on King Joseph's side, known as Joséphins, he rendered us useful service.

Not long before I passed through Montdragon the same commandant had shown great courage. He had had to send the greater part of his garrison away to guard an expected convoy of provisions, and when he had a few hours later to furnish escorts to some officers bearing despatches he had but a score of soldiers left. It was market-day, and the market-place was full of country folks. The postmaster, one of our bitterest foes, harangued them, bidding them profit the weakness of the French garrison to cut their throats. At last the crowd made for the house, whither the commandant had retired with his small reserve. An impetuous attack was met by a vigorous defence, but our men would have given way in the end. Then the commandant ordered the door to be opened, sallied out with his little force, went straight up to the postmaster and ran him through the heart, then had the body dragged into the house and placed on the balcony. This vigorous action was followed by a well-delivered volley, whereupon the crowd fled in terror. That evening the garrison returned, and the commandant had the postmaster's body hung on the public gibbet as an example; nor, though he had many friends and relations in the town, did anyone lift a finger.

Next morning I started at daybreak. To my disgust, the Spanish postilion who was leading stopped under the gallows and lashed with his whip the corpse which was hanging there. I reproved the scoundrel sharply, but he answered, laughing: 'It is my postmaster; when he was alive he gave me many a cut with a whip, and I don't mind giving him back a few' —a very characteristic instance of the vindictive disposition of the lower class of Spaniards.

I got to Vittoria drenched through, and so feverish that I had to stop with General Séras, for whom I brought despatches. You will remember that he was the general who had made me sergeant ten years before, after the affair between the Bercheny detachment and the Barco Hussars. He welcomed me warmly, and wished me to rest there for a time; but my errand would not bear delay, and I rode on next day in spite of my fever, which was not improved by the frightful weather. That day I crossed the Ebro at Miranda, where the spurs of the Pyrenees end, and where ended then the power of the famous partisan leaders named Mina.

The first of these guerrilleros was the son of a rich farmer near Montdragon, and was studying for holy orders when the War of Independence broke out in 1808. It is a fact, not generally known, that at that time many Spaniards, with some of the secular clergy at their head, wishing to shake off the yoke of the Inquisition and the monks, not only longed for the continuance of Joseph on the throne, but even joined our troops in trying to beat off the insurgents. Young Mina was of this number; he levied a company of 'friends of order,' and made war on the bandits. By a curious reaction, however, Mina, captivated by the adventurous life, became an insurgent himself, and fought us desperately in Biscay and Navarre, at the head of a band which at this time amounted to near 10,000 men. The commandant of Montdragon managed at last to seize him at a wedding festivity in the house of a relation; and Napoleon put him into prison at Vincennes. Mina was an able and straightforward guerrilla chief. When he returned in 1814 he opposed Ferdinand VII., for whom he had fought so well; and when about to be arrested he escaped to America, where he got mixed up in Mexican revolutions, and was shot. During his confinement at Vincennes the insurgents took for their chief an uncle of his. This man, a rough blacksmith, of bloodthirsty disposition, and no ability, gained great influence solely through his name. The Seville Junta sent some educated officers to direct this new chief, who did us a great deal of damage.

I entered now upon the vast and dreary plains of Old Castile. At first sight an ambush seems quite impossible in this treeless and mountainless country; but it is so undulating that this apparent security was deceptive. The hollows between the frequent hillocks allowed bands of insurgents to hide, and pour forth unawares upon French detachments, marching with confidence through a country where they could apparently see four or five leagues all round them and discover no enemy. A few disasters had made our men more cautious, and they no longer crossed the plains without searching the hollows with skirmishers. This precaution, however, was not available in the case of such escorts—five or a six gendarmes—as were allowed to officers bearing despatches; so that many of them lost their lives on the plains of Castile. Still, I liked better to travel in this open country than in the mountains of Biscay and Navarre, where rocks command the roads; and the inhabitants are likewise far more enterprising than the Castilians.

I went on my way without accident as far as the little town of Briviesca; but between that place and Burgos we saw twenty mounted Spaniards appear suddenly round a low hill. They fired several shots at us without effect; then my escort, my servant, and

I drew our swords, and went forward without deigning to reply to the enemy, who, judging from our resolute attitude that we were the kind of people to defend ourselves vigorously, went off in another direction.

At Burgos I put up with General Dorsenne, commanding a brigade of the guard, for in the actual state of the country nearly every town and village was occupied by our troops. The roads only were insecure, and therefore those who, like me, had to travel with small escorts ran the most danger. Of this I had a fresh proof next day, when between Palencia and Dueñas I fell in with an officer and twenty-five men of the Young Guard escorting a chest of money for the garrison of Valladolid. The escort was evidently inadequate, for the guerrilleros of the neighbourhood had assembled to the number of 150, and were just attacking the detachment; on seeing my escort galloping up they took us for the advanced guard of a cavalry corps, and stopped short in their onset. But one of them, ascending a hillock, whence he got a distant view, called out that no French troops were in sight, whereupon the brigands advanced boldly towards the tempting treasure-waggon. I naturally took command of the small united forces, and bade the officer of the guard not to fire till I gave the word. Most of the enemy had dismounted, the better to get hold of the money-bags, and were poor fighters with muskets; many had only pistols. I had placed my infantry behind the wagon, and as soon as the Spaniards were within twenty paces I made them come out, and gave the order to fire. This was obeyed with terrible precision; the leader of the Spaniards and a dozen of his men dropped. The rest bolted at full speed towards their horses, which some of their friends were holding two hundred yards off; but as they were mounting I ordered the infantry and the six gendarmes to charge them, my servant Woirland joining. This little band of brave fellows, catching the bandits in disorder, killed thirty of them, and captured fifty horses, which they sold that evening at Dueñas. I had only two wounded, and those slightly. The officer and men of the Young Guard had shown much courage; if I had had only recruits we might well have suffered a disaster, especially as I was myself too weak to take part in the charge. The excitement had increased my fever, and I was forced to spend the night at Dueñas. Next day, the commandant of that place, in consequence of what had happened, sent a whole company to escort the treasure to Valladolid, and I went with them, being hardly able to sit my horse, and quite unable to gallop. The details I have given may serve further to show you the danger to which officers were exposed who were compelled by their duties to post through the insurgent provinces.

My mission being discharged, I hoped to get some rest at Valladolid; but tribulation of a new kind awaited me. Junot, the Duke of Abrantes, commanding one of the corps which was to form part of Masséna's army, had been for some months at Valladolid, quartered in the huge palace built by Charles V., an ancient house, but in perfect preservation and comfortably furnished. I made no doubt that on hearing of the immediate arrival of the marshal to take supreme command, the Duke of Abrantes would at once leave this old palace of the kings, and take up his quarters in one of the handsome houses which the town contained. To my surprise, however, Junot, whose wife, the duchess, had come to Valladolid, and held a most elegant little court there, informed me that he meant only to surrender half his palace to Masséna. He was sure, he said, that the marshal would be too polite to turn the duchess out, especially as the palace was large enough to lodge both staffs comfortably.

To understand the dilemma in which this statement placed me, you must know that Masséna was accustomed to take everywhere, and even to the wars, with him a lady named N—. So attached was he to her that he only accepted the command of the Army of Portugal on condition that the Emperor would let him take her. Being of a gloomy and misanthropic turn, and preferring to live alone, secluded in his own rooms and away from his staff, Masséna needed sometimes the distraction afforded by a lively and witty companion. In this way Mme N— suited him perfectly, for she was a clever, kindly, and amiable woman, who, besides, quite understood the awkwardness of her position. It was impossible that she could lodge under the same roof with the Duchess of Abrantes, a descendant of the Comneni, and full of family pride. On the other hand, it was not fitting that the marshal should be quartered in a private house, while his subordinate was in the palace. So I was obliged to explain the state of things to Junot, who, however, would only laugh, and say that he and Masséna had often lodged in one cottage in Italy, and that the ladies might settle it among themselves.

In despair I spoke to the duchess herself. She was a woman of quick wit, and decided to go and establish herself in the down. Junot opposed this obstinately, much to my annoyance; but what could I do against a commander-in-chief? Things were still in this position when, after being several days in bed with fever, I got a message by express to say that the marshal was coming in a few hours. I had at the venture taken a house for him in the town, and, weak as I was, would have mounted my horse to meet him and let him know what had happened, but his mules had gone so quickly that on going downstairs I found the marshal himself, leading in Mme N——. I was beginning to explain my difficulties, when in rushed Junot, bringing the duchess with him. He fell into Masséna's arms; then before all the staff he kissed Mme N——'s hand, and introduced his wife. Imagine the ladies' confusion! They stood like stones, without a word. The marshal had the wit to restrain himself; but he was deeply hurt when the Duchess of Abrantes, pleading indisposition, left the dining-room just as Junot was leading in Mme N——.

These details, which at first sight may seem superfluous, are here related because the scene had serious results. The marshal never quite forgave Junot for refusing to give up the old palace to him, and for putting him in a false position before a number of general officers. Junot, on his side, made common cause with Marshal Ney and General Reynier, the commanders of the two other corps forming with his the Grand Army of Portugal. This gave rise to mischievous differences, which had a great deal to do with the unlucky result of the campaign in 1810 and 1811, and the unhappy effects which flowed from that, and weighed so heavy on the destiny of the French Empire. So true is it that causes apparently trivial or ridiculous often lead to great calamities. General Kellerman, commanding in Valladolid, reported to Masséna all the trouble which I had taken to spare him a part of this unpleasantness; but he bore me a grudge for it all the same.

In due course the marshal's staff arrived at Valladolid. It was pretty numerous, since, peace appearing to be settled for some time in Germany, officers desirous of promotion had asked as a favour to be allowed to fight in Portugal; and those who had the most interest got on to the staff of the general-in-chief. With his extensive command at a great distance from France, he required many officers, and his staff accordingly consisted of fourteen aides-de-camp and four orderly officers.

The promotion of Sainte-Croix to the rank of general had been a misfortune for Masséna. In him he lost a wise counsellor at a moment when, growing old, and left to his own resources, he had to oppose a foe like the Duke of Wellington, and get obeyed by lieutenants, one of whom was a marshal as well as himself, while the other two, with the title of commander-in-chief, had long been used to take their orders directly from the Emperor. Although Sainte-Croix was with the Army of Portugal in command of a brigade of dragoons, his new duties did not allow him to be constantly by Masséna's side. The marshal's character, once so firm, had become in a high degree irresolute, and one soon missed the able man who during the Wagram campaign had been the life and soul of his staff. The marshal having no longer a colonel as senior aide-de-camp, the office was filled by the senior major. This was Pelet, a good comrade, a brave man, a learned mathematician, but one who had never commanded troops, for on leaving the Polytechnic School he had been placed in the corps of mapping engineers. This corps while accompanying the armies was non-combatant, and acted, to tell the truth, merely as an understudy to the engineers. It is human nature to admire what one can least do one's self, and thus Masséna, whose education was very incomplete, had an immense respect for mapping engineers who could lay nice plans before him, and had had several on his staff. Pelet had been with him in this capacity at Naples in 1806, and in Poland in 1807. He behaved with courage in the campaign of 1809, and was wounded on the bridge at Ebersberg, earning thereby his promotion to major. He was present at the battles, and often risked himself in mapping the island of Lobau and the Danube. Good service as this doubtless was, it could not give Pelet practice in the art of war, especially when it was a question of commanding 70,000 men against Wellington in a difficult country. Yet he became Masséna's chief advisor even when neither Ney, nor Reynier, nor Junot, nor any of the other generals were consulted. Sainte-Croix, no doubt, was an extraordinary genius who understood the art of war on a great scale by intuition without having every held an important command. Miracles of this kind are rare; and Masséna, after he had got into the way of yielding to the inspiration of his senior aide-de-camp, put his lieutenants out of heart and paved the way to disobedience which led us into disaster. These disasters would have been still greater if the name and fame of Masséna had not survived to act as a caution to the English leader. So afraid was Wellington of making any mistake in presence of the conqueror of Zurich, that he always acted with the utmost circumspection. The prestige of his name had influenced even the Emperor. Napoleon never considered enough that he himself had been the prime author of the success gained at Wagram, and when he set Masséna the difficult task of going five hundred leagues away from France to conquer Portugal it was through a too firm belief that he had preserved all his vigour of mind and body. This judgment may appear to you too severe, but it will be confirmed when I relate the events of the two campaigns.

Pelet, though at that time not up to Masséna's requirements, gained much in practical soldiership, especially during the Russian campaign, where he commanded a regiment of infantry. He was then serving under Marshal Ney; and though Ney had conceived a great antipathy to him, Pelet was able to recover his esteem. When Ney, cut off from the Russians by the rest of the army [should be, cut off from the rest of the army by the Russians] during the retreat from Moscow, found himself in a most dangerous position, it was Pelet who proposed to cross the half-frozen Dnieper--a perilous enterprise, but one which, being resolutely executed, saved Ney's corps. This good advice made Pelet's fortune in a military sense; he was appointed by the Emperor general to the grenadiers of the old guard, and fought valiantly at their head in Saxony in 1813, and the next year in France; also at Waterloo. Afterwards he became director of the Ordnance Office, but in his excessive attachment to scientific officers he too often took on his staff map-draughtsmen who know nothing of manœuvring. He has written several works of good repute, especially an account of the Austrian campaign of 1809, the clearness of which has unluckily been injured by theoretic discussions.

I was Masséna's second aide-de-camp; the third was Major Casabianca, a Corsican by birth, and related to the Emperor on the mother's side. Educated, able, and very brave, this officer had been attached to Masséna by Napoleon himself; so Masséna, while paying him much attention, often kept him away from the army under the pretext of honouring him. He sent him to the Emperor with the news of the capitulation of Ciudid Rodrigo, and when he came back, a month later, sent him back to Paris to announce the capture of Almeida, and, on his rejoining us as we entered Portugal, gave him the duty of reporting the position of the armies to the minister. He did not finally come back to us till the end of the campaign. In the Russian campaign he was colonel of the 11th Infantry in the same army corps with my own regiment. He was killed in a fight which he had undertaken fruitlessly and to no purpose.

The fourth aide-de-camp was Major the Count of Ligniville. He belonged to one of four distinguished families, known as the great team of Lorraine, which spring from the same house as the present sovereigns of Austria. After the battle of Wagram the Emperor Francis II. sent a flag of truce to inquire if any harm had happened to his cousin the Count of Ligniville. He had such a passion for soldiering that at fifteen he ran away and enlisted in the 13th Dragoons. He was severely wounded at Marengo, was promoted officer of the battle-field, and served brilliantly in the campaigns of Austerlitz, Jena, and Friedland. In 1809 he passed from the staff of General Becker to that of Masséna. I have told how he got into trouble with the marshal by helping me in supporting the interests of the brave servants who had driven him on the battle-fields of Wagram and Znaym. The marshal's dislike increased during the campaign in Portugal, and Ligniville went back to the 13th Dragoons, of which he soon became colonel. After the Restoration he became general, married well, and was living happily, when he ruined himself by unsound speculations. He was much depressed by this, and died soon after, much to my regret.

The fifth aide-de-camp was Major Barin, who had lost an arm at Wagram, but persisted in serving as aide-de-camp, though he could do hardly any active service; a good fellow by taciturn. My brother was the sixth. The following were captains: M. Poncher de Richebourg, a capable officer, but with no great taste for military life. He left the army when his father died, and succeeded him in the Chamber of Peers. Captain Barral, nephew of the Archbishop of Tours, had many of the qualities which make a good soldier, but they were neutralised by his extreme shyness; he retired as captain. Captain Cavalier belonged to the same corps as Pelet and acted as his secretary. Captain Desponoux came of a legal family, and had inherited from them an extremely calm temperament, only becoming animated when going into action. The fatigues of the Portuguese campaign were almost too much for him, and he succumbed to the climate of Russia. He was found in a bivouac frozen stiff. Captain Renique was in particular favour with Masséna, but, being a good comrade, he did not presume upon it. I took him into my regiment when I became colonel of the 23rd Chasseurs, and he left the army after the retreat from Moscow. Captain d'Aguesseau, a descendant of the celebrated chancellor, was one of the wealthy young men who, at the Emperor's instance, took to military life without considering their physical strength. He was a brave man but very delicate, and the incessant rain of the winter 1810-11 injured his health so far that he died on the banks of the Tagus.

Captain Prosper Masséna, whose noble conduct at Wagram I have already related, was a brave and excellent young man, and displayed the greatest friendship towards me. The marshal often associated him with me on difficult missions. After long hesitation, his father, having no command in the Russian campaign, ended by keeping him at home. When the marshal died in 1817, Prosper was so deeply affected that he was seized with violent fits. I was then in exile, and when I returned, and went to pay my respects to the marshal's widow, she sent for her son. His emotion at seeing me again was such that he again fell seriously ill; his health was hopelessly broken, and he soon departed this life, leaving his title and part of his fortune to his younger brother, Victor.

The youngest and the junior in rank of all the aides-de camp was Victor Oudinot, son of the marshal. He had been the Emperor's page, and had accompanied him in this capacity at the battle of Wagram. Now he had just entered Masséna's staff as lieutenant, being but twenty years old. Later he became lieutenant-general. We shall hear of him again in the course of my story; I will now merely say that he gained the reputation of being one of the best horsemen of his time.

Besides the fourteen aides-de-camp, the marshal had four orderly officers: Captain Beaufort d'Hautpoal, of the Engineers, Lieutenant Perron, a Piedmontese, ugly, but witty and jovial—he kept us all merry during the winter of 1810, by a theatre of marionettes which he got up, and which the marshal and generals sometimes attended for their amusement. He died at the battle of Montmirail, just as he was leaping astride on to a Russian gun. The next was Lieutenant de Briqueville, a man distinguished by bravery, carried to the point of imprudence, as he showed when fighting in 1815, at the head of his regiment, between Versailles and Rocquencourt, when he got entangled between two park walls, losing many men, and receiving three sabre-cuts on the head. He entered the Chamber as deputy for Caen, and went into violent opposition, ultimately dying in a condition of mental excitement. Masséna's fourth orderly officer was Octave de Ségur, son of the count. Educated, exquisitely polite, of an affable disposition and calm valour, he was beloved by the whole staff. In rank, he was the junior officer, though nearly thirty years old. He left the Polytechnic School in the days of the Directory, and held the post of Sub-Prefect of Soissons under the Consulate, but resigned in disgust at the judicial murder of the Duke of Enghein, and enlisted in the 6th Hussars. He was wounded and taken prisoner in 1809 at Raab, in Hungary, and when exchanged asked leave to serve as sub-lieutenant in the Portuguese campaign, where he did brilliant service. When captain in the 8th Hussars, he was taken prisoner in Russia and, as son of our former ambassador, was treated with much consideration by Catherine II. After two years' residence at Saratoff, in the Volga, he returned to France in 1814 and was on the staff of the guard under Louis XVIII. He died, still young, in 1816.

Chapter 23
I 'Slay a Lion' in a Fever

Although the Minister of War had assured the marshal that everything was ready for the campaign, it was nothing of the kind, and the commander-in-chief had to stay a fortnight at Valladolid, looking after the departure of the troops and the transport of stores and ammunition. At last the headquarters were removed to Salamanca, where my brother and I were quartered with the Count of Montezuma, a lineal descendant of the last Emperor of Mexico. The marshal wasted three more weeks at Salamanca waiting for General Reynier's corps. These delays, while hurtful to us, were all in favour of the English.

The last Spanish town towards the Portuguese frontier is Ciudad Rodrigo, a fortress, if the strength of its works alone be considered, of the third class, but having great importance owing to its position between Spain and Portugal, in a district with few roads, and those very difficult for large guns and the apparatus of a siege train. It was, however, absolutely necessary that the French should get possession of the place. With this resolve, Masséna left Salamanca about the middle of June, and caused Rodrigo to be invested by Ney's corps, while Junot covered the operations from the attacks of an Anglo-Portuguese army, which was encamped a few leagues from us, near the Portuguese fortress of Almeida, under Lord Wellington. Ciudad Rodrigo was defended by a brave old Spanish general of Irish origin, Andrew Herrasti.

The French, unable to believe that the English would have come so near the place just to see it captured under their eyes, expected a battle. None took place; and on July 10, the Spanish guns having been silenced, a part of the town being on fire, and the counterscarp overthrown by the explosion of a powder magazine for a space of thirty-six feet, while the ditch was filled with the ruins and the breach widely opened, Masséna resolved to give the signal for the assault. To this end Marshal Ney formed a column of

1,500 volunteers, who were to mount the breach first. Assembled at the foot of the rampart, these brave men were awaiting the signal to attack, when an officer expressed his fear that the breach was not yet practicable. Thereupon three of our soldiers mounted to the top of it, looked into the town, made such examination as was useful, and fired their muskets, rejoining their comrades without being wounded, although this bold feat was performed in broad daylight. Kindled by this example, the assaulting column advanced at a run and was on the point of dashing into the town when General Herrasti capitulated. The defence of the garrison had been very fine, but the Spanish troops composing it had good reason to complain of their desertion by the English, who had merely sent reconnoitring parties towards our camp, without attempting any serious diversion. The skirmishes resulting from these nearly always turned out to our advantage. One of them was so creditable to our infantry, that the English historian Napier has been unable to refrain from doing homage to the valour of the men who took part in it. On July 11 the English General Craufurd, who was operating in the country between Ciudad Rodrigo and Villa de Puerco, at the head of six squadrons, having perceived at day-break a company of French grenadiers, about 120 strong, marching in the open, ordered two squadrons to attack them. But the French had time to form square, and were so cool that the enemy's officers could hear Captain Gouache and his sergeant exhorting their people to take good aim. The cavalry charged with ardour, but received such a terrible volley that they left the ground piled with dead, and had to retire. Seeing two English squadrons repulsed by a handful of French, Colonel Talbot advanced furiously with four squadrons of the 14th Dragoons and attacked Captain Gouache. Firmly awaiting the charge, he ordered a volley at point-blank range, which killed Colonel Talbot and some thirty of his men; after which the brave Gouache retired in good order towards the French camp without the English general venturing to attack again. This brilliant affair was much talked of in the two armies. When the Emperor heard of it he raised Captain Gouache to major, promoted the other officers, and gave eight decorations in the company.

After having mentioned a fact so glorious for the French arms, I ought to report one no less creditable to the Spaniards. The guerrillero Don Julian Sanchez, having voluntarily shut himself in Ciudad Rodrigo with his two hundred horsemen, did good service by making frequent attacks on our trenches. At length, when the want of forage caused the presence of 200 horses to be a trouble to the garrison, Sanchez left the town with his men one dark night, and, crossing the bridge over the Agreda, the approaches to which Ney had omitted to block, fell on our outposts, killed several men, pierced our lines, and went off to join the English army.

The siege of Rodrigo nearly cost me my life; not by the enemy's fire, but by reason of an illness which I contracted in the following manner. The neighbourhood of the town, being infertile, is thickly inhabited, and there had been much difficulty in finding quarters for the marshal near the trenches. Finally he was put into an isolated building situated in a spot commanding the town and suburbs. As the siege promised to last long, and there was no lodging for the staff close by, we hired, at our own cost, some planks and; beams, and erected a large room, where we were sheltered from sun and rain, and slept on boards, which, though rough, kept us clear of the damp rising from the soil. But the marshal was inconvenienced from the outset in his stone building by an intolerable stench, and on inquiry it was found that the building had been used to keep sheep in. Masséna proceeded to set his affections on our extempore house; but, not liking to use his authority to eject us, came to see us on some pretext or other, and exclaimed as he entered: 'Well, my lads, you have a nice place here! May I beg for a corner to put my bed and desk in?' This, as we saw, was sharing with the lion, and we left our excellent abode in haste, to take up our quarters in the old sheep-stall. It was paved with small stones, their interstices clogged with filth, and highly uncomfortable to lie on, from the want of long straw in Spain. Forced thus to lie on the bare ground and inhale the fetid exhalations rising from it, we all became more or less unwell before long. I was much the worst; for in these warm countries fever always tries most those who have already suffered from it, and my Valladolid attack returned in an aggravated form. Still I resolved to take my share in the siege, and remained on duty. Duty was often pretty laborious, especially when we had to carry orders in the night to our division on the left bank of the Agreda, which was carrying out the necessary works for the reduction of the Franciscan convent, used by the enemy as a bastion. In order to reach this point from the headquarters without coming under the fire of the place, it was necessary to make a long wind to a bridge which our troops had constructed, or else cross by a ford. One night, when all was ready for the assault and Ney only awaited Masséna's order to give the signal, it happened to be my turn for duty, and I had to take the order. It was a dark, hot night; I was in a high fever, and streaming with perspiration when I reached the ford. I had only once crossed it in daylight, but the dragoon orderly who was with me had crossed it several times, and offered to guide me. This he did very well till he got to the middle, where it was not more than two or three feet deep; but then he went wrong in the darkness, and our horses, stepping on big slippery stones, fell and we were in the water. There was no fear of drowning; we scrambled on to the bank with ease; but we were wet through. In any other circumstances I should only have laughed at this involuntary bath; but, though not cold, the water checked the perspiration, and I was seized with a shivering fit. I reached the convent and passed the night in the open air beside Marshal Ney. The attacking column was commanded by a major named Lefrançois, whom I knew well. The day before he had shown me a letter from his sweetheart announcing that her father agreed to their marriage as soon as Lefrançois was lieutenant-colonel. It was with this object that he had asked permission to lead the storming party. The attack was brisk, the defence stubborn. After three hours' fighting our troops remained in possession of the convent, but poor Lefrançois was slain. His loss was much felt in the army, and grieved me deeply.

In hot countries sunrise is usually preceded by piercing cold. I was the more sensitive to it that day for having passed the night in wet clothes, so that when I returned to headquarters I was much out of sorts. Still I had to report the result of the attack to Masséna before getting into dry things. He was at that moment taking his morning walk with General Fririon, his chief of staff. In their interest in my story, or wishing to get a closer view, they gradually drew near the town, and we were not more than a cannon-shot away when the marshal let me go and rest. Hardly had I gone fifty paces from them when a gigantic shell, launched from the ramparts, fell close to them. At the fearful noise of its explosion I turned round, and, seeing nothing of the marshal and the general, who were concealed by a cloud of dust and smoke, I thought they were killed, and ran to the place. To my astonishment I found them alive and none the worse, save for some contusions from the stones which the bursting shell had thrown up. They were, however, both covered with earth, especially Masséna. He had lost an eye shooting some years before, and his remaining eye was so full of sand that he could not see his way, while the bruises he had received from the stones prevented his walking. It was necessary to get him out of range, however, and, as he was small and thin, I managed, ill as I was, to take him on my shoulders and carry him out of reach of the enemy's shot. I went on and told my comrades, and they brought the marshal in without the men finding out the danger which their commander-in-chief had run.

The fatigue and excitement of the last twenty-four hours increased my fever a good deal; still I braced myself up, and contrived to hold out till the surrender of Ciudad Rodrigo, on July 9. But as from this day forward the excitement which kept me up so far had nothing more to feed on, I must needs give in to the fever. This became so alarming that I had to be carried to the one house in the town which the French shells had left intact. It was the only time that I have been seriously ill without being wounded, but this time my life was despaired of, and I was left at Ciudad Rodrigo while the army crossed the Coa and marched on Almeida. This place not being more than four leagues as the crow flies from Ciudad Rodrigo, I could hear from my sick-bed the uproar of the cannon, and every report made me writhe with rage. Often did I try to rise, and the fruitlessness of the attempts, by showing me how utterly weak I was, increased my wretchedness. My brother and my comrades, kept by their duty at Almeida, were far away, and my solitude was only broken by the short visits of Dr. Blancheton, who, clever as he was, could only treat me very inefficiently for want of medicaments. The air of the town was tainted by the stench of many thousands of corpses which lay unburied among the rubbish of the ruined houses. A temperature of more than eighty-five degrees, aggravating these causes of unhealthiness, soon brought typhus. Both the garrison and such of the inhabitants as had remained in the place to look after what was left of their property suffered terribly. I was left to the care of my servant, and, with all his zeal, he could not get me what I required. My illness increased and I became delirious. I remember that there were in my room some large pictures representing the four quarters of the earth. Africa, which was right in front of my bed, had at her feet a huge lion, the eyes of which seemed to be fixed on me, while I could not take mine from them. At last one day I thought I saw him move, and wishing to anticipate his attack, I tottered up, took my sword, and, striking with edge and point, I hewed the lion to pieces. After this truly Quixotic feat I fell half-fainting on the floor, where the doctor found me. He had all the pictures removed from the room, after which I grew quieter. My lucid moments were not less terrible; it was painful to think of my melancholy situation and utter loneliness. Death on the battlefield seemed sweet to me compared to that which I expected, and I regretted not to have fallen like a soldier. To die in a bed of fever while there was fighting near me seemed to me a horrible, almost a shameful thing.

I had been in this dreadful position for a month, when on August 26, towards nightfall, a fearful explosion was heard. The earth trembled till I thought the house was coming down. It was the fortress of Almeida which had just blown up through the explosion of a huge powder magazine, and the disturbance was distinctly felt at Rodrigo, from which one may judge the effects which it had produced in Almeida itself. The unlucky place was destroyed from top to bottom; not six houses remained standing. Six hundred of the garrison were killed, and many wounded; some fifty French employed on the siege works were struck by splinters of stone. In pursuance of instructions from his Government, Lord Wellington, with the view of sparing English blood at the cost of that of his allies, after having entrusted the defence of Ciudad Rodrigo to the Spanish troops, who had just surrendered, had left that of Almeida to the Portuguese, Colonel Cox, the governor, being the only Englishman in the place. That brave officer, not suffering himself to be intimidated by the horrible disaster which had just destroyed almost all his means of resistance, proposed to the garrison to continue their defence behind the ruins of the city. But the Portuguese troops, terrified, and led away by their officers, especially by Bernardo Costa, the lieutenant-governor, and José Bareiros, commanding the artillery, refused, and Colonel Cox, being unsupported, was compelled to capitulate.

It has been said that the French commander had tampered with the Portuguese officers, and that the explosion was brought about by their treason; but this is a mistake. The only cause of the fire was neglect on the part of the garrison, who, instead of fetching the powder barrels one by one from the cellars and shutting the door behind each, had been imprudent enough to roll a score of them at a time into the courtyard of the castle. It seems that a French shell falling on one of the barrels exploded it, and that the others forming a train light up to the middle of the magazine, caused the explosion which wrecked the town and injured the fortifications. However that may be, the English brought the two Portuguese officers to trial, Costa being condemned and shot, while Bareiros succeeded in escaping. These two officers were certainly not guilty of treason; at most they could be reproached with not having continued a hopeless defence, the only result of which could have been to preserve the ruins of Almeida for a few days longer, while the English army was tranquilly encamped two leagues from the place without making any movement to aid them.

After having thus got possession of Almeida, Marshal Masséna, not being able to establish himself among the ruins of the town, moved his headquarters to Fort Concepcion, on the Spanish frontier. The French had destroyed part of the fortifications, but the buildings were sufficiently intact to afford lodging. There Masséna made preparations for his expedition to Lisbon. My brother and my comrades took advantage of this interval to come and see me. Their presence increased the soothing effect which the capture of Almeida had produced on my spirits. The fever disappeared, and in a few days I was convalescent. I was eager for change of air, and, with the aid of my brother and some of my friends, I contrived to ride the short distance to Fort Concepcion. My comrades, who had feared that they would never see me again, received me most affectionately; but the marshal, whom I had not seen since the day when I had carried him out of range of the guns of Rodrigo, never said a word to me about my illness. After a fortnight in the fort in good air and able to rest, I recovered my full health, and was ready for the campaign in Portugal. Before relating the events of this famous and disastrous campaign I must briefly make you acquainted with what had taken place in the Peninsula since the Emperor left it in 1809.

Chapter 24
Events in the Peninsula

While Ney was holding the Asturias and Leon, Marshal Soult, who to the conquest of Corunna had added that of the port of Ferrol, concentrated his troops at Santiago, in Galicia, and made ready to invade Portugal. Under an illusion which turned out disastrous, Napoleon never understood the enormous difference which the fact of Spain and Portugal being in insurrection produced between the nominal state of the French troops in the Peninsula and the actual number of combatants which could be arrayed against the enemy. Thus the strength of the second corps under Soult amounted on paper to 47,000; but, after deducting the garrisons at Santander, Corunna, and Ferrol, the 8,000 men employed to maintain the communications and 12,000 sick, the number of those at present under arms did not exceed 25,000, and these were tired out with fighting all through the winter in a mountain country, were short of shoes, often of provisions; and had only broken-down horses to drag the artillery over the bad roads. It was with means so feeble as these that the Emperor ordered Marshal Soult to enter Portugal. It is true he reckoned on the valour of the second corps, almost wholly composed of veterans from Austerlitz and Friedland, and proposed an attack on Portugal from another side by Marshal Victor's corps, which was to advance from Andalusia and join Soult at Lisbon; but fortune did not endorse his calculation.

On February 1, 1809, Soult, after informing Ney that he was leaving him to look after Galicia, marched towards the Minho. He tried to cross it near the fortified town of Tuy, but the strength of the current and the fire of the Portuguese militia from the opposite bank rendered the attempt abortive. Then the marshal, with wonderful activity and vigour, chose a new line of operations, and, marching up to the river, crossed it at Ribada-Via; occupied Orense; then descending again, attacked and captured Tuy, making it his place of arms. He left there part of his artillery, his heavy baggage, his sick and wounded, guarded by a strong garrison, which reduced his force to 20,000 combatants, and with these he boldly advanced to Oporto.

This great town, the second in the kingdom, was in a state of complete anarchy. The bishop, having seized the sole command, had himself traced fortifications, and had brought in the country folk in great numbers to work at them. The people were living in a state of license; the troops were insubordinate, the generals quarrelling among themselves; everything, in short, was in the utmost disorder. The Commission of Regency and the bishop were sworn foes; while the adherents of either side were assassinating the conspicuous men on the other. Such were their arrangements for opposing our army. But, though harassed by continual marching through swarms of insurgents, our army attacked the Spanish force, commanded by La Romana, and the Portuguese, under Sylveira, at Verin, defeating the former completely; while the second retreated beyond the Portuguese fortress of Chaves, which Soult captured. One of the chief inconveniences which we experienced in the Peninsula was that of guarding prisoners. A large number were taken at Chaves, and Soult, not knowing how to dispose of them, accepted their proposal to enter the French service, even though most of them had done the same thing in the time of Junot's expedition and ended by deserting.

The army next moved on to Braga, where there was a second and considerable Portuguese force, under General Freira. This unfortunate officer, seeing his advance-guard beaten by the French, was preparing to retreat, when his troops, consisting almost entirely of peasant levies, killed him with cries of treason. At the same moment the French advance-guard having appeared at the gates of Braga, the population betook themselves to the prisons, where the persons suspected of favouring the French were shut up, and slaughtered them all. Meanwhile Marshal Soult had attacked the enemy's army, which, after a short but brisk resistance, was utterly routed. In passing through Braga the fugitives killed the corregidor, and began to set the town on fire; but, being pursued by the French troops, they set-off in the direction of Oporto. The advantage gained by the capture of Braga was a good deal reduced by a loss which Soult incurred at the same time. The Portuguese general, Sylveira, having flung himself on the left flank of the French army while it was marching on Braga, had carried the town of Chaves, and captured 1,200 of our sick and 800 combatants. Ignorant of this annoying circumstance, Soult left Heudelet's division in Braga, and continued his march to Oporto. The enemy offered gallant resistance at the river Ave, but the passage was forced, the French general Jardon being killed, while the Portuguese, in a rage at their defeat, murdered their general, Vallongo. The divisions of Mermet, Merle, and Franceschi, being thus united on the left bank of the Ave, with the road to Oporto open, concentrated in front of the entrenchments which covered the town and the camp. These contained at least 40,000 men, half being regular troops, under Generals Lima and Pereiras, but the real authority was in the hands of the bishop, a hot-tempered man who swayed the multitudes as he liked. English and Portuguese historians have held him responsible for the murder of fifteen persons of high position, whom he was unwilling or unable to save from the fury of the people, exasperated by the sight of the French army.

Oporto is built on the right bank of the Douro, and commanded by lofty rocks, which at that time were garnished with 200 guns. A bridge of boats, 500 yards long, joined the town with the suburb of Villa Nova. Before attacking Marshal Soult wrote to the bishop entreating him to spare the town the horrors of the siege. The Portuguese prisoner who was sent with the message was very near being hanged. The bishop, however, entered into correspondence but without ordering the fire from the ramparts to cease. Finally, fearing, as would appear, to fall a victim to the fury of the people, which he had himself fomented by giving false hopes of success, he refused to surrender. On March 28 the marshal, in order to withdraw the enemy's attention from the centre of the entrenchments, attacked their wings. Merle's division carried several fortified enclosures on the left, while Delaborde and Franceschi threatened the works to the right. While this was going on, some battalions having cried out that they wished to surrender, General Foy advanced incautiously, followed by his aide-de-camp. The aide-de-camp was killed; the general was made prisoner, stripped naked and dragged into the town. The Portuguese detested General Loison, who had beaten them.

This general had some time back lost an arm, whence they had nicknamed him Mañeta. On seeing General Foy a prisoner, the populace of Oporto, thinking that it was Loison, began to shout: 'Kill him! kill Mañeta!' But Foy had the presence of mind to lift his two hands, and the mob, seeing its mistake, let him be taken to prison. The bishop, who had brought things to this crisis, lacked courage to face the danger, and, leaving to the generals the task of defending the town as best they could, fled across the river to the convent of La Serra, on the top of the steep hill which commands the suburb of Villa Nova, whence he was able in perfect safety to witness the horrors of the morrow's fight.

It was a fearful night for the inhabitants of Oporto. A violent storm broke out, and the soldiers and peasants fancied that in the roaring wind they heard the sound of the enemy cannon-balls. In spite of all that the officers could do, a fire of cannon and small arms was opened all along the line, and their noise mingled with that of the thunder and the incessant bells. Throughout this frightful uproar the French, sheltered in the ditches against balls and bullets, were calmly awaiting the daylight to attack the place. By the morning of the 29th the weather had cleared, and our troops marched eagerly to the fight. The marshal, as he planned on the previous day, engaged first on the wings. The stratagem succeeded perfectly; the Portuguese generals weakened their centre out of all proportion in order to strengthen their flanks; and Marshal Soult, giving the order to beat the charge, hurled the French troops on that point. The impetuous attack of our soldiers carried the entrenchments, and, pushing on, they entered the two principal forts through the embrasures. killing or dispersing all who resisted. After this success several battalions took the wings in rear, while Marshal Soult ordered another column to advance upon the town and make for the port. Driven from its entrenchments, and cut at several points, the Portuguese army fled through the town in despair. Some reached Fort Sao Joao, on the bank of the Douro, seeking to cross the river by swimming or in boats. General Loison, pointing out the danger of this course, was murdered, and as the French continued to advance, the fugitives made another attempt to cross, most of them being drowned. Meanwhile fighting went on in the town; the column sent forward by the marshal had cleared the barricades which blocked the streets and reached the bridge, where more than 4,000 persons of every age and sex were struggling to cross. The Portuguese batteries on the further shore, catching sight of the French, opened a heavy fire, which did not reach our troops, but told heavily on this heaving mass, while a cavalry detachment in flight cut its way through the terrified crowd. The boats composing the bridge soon became loaded, and several of them sank. Thus the bridge was broken; those who were nearest to the openings were pushed in by the pressure of the crowd from behind, and the river was covered with floating corpses—to such an extent that boats were capsized by them, and many trying to cross in that way were drowned. A good number of the poor creatures were rescued by the French soldiers who first came up, while the Portuguese gunners had fired on their own countrymen. By the help of planks our men crossed the gaps in the bridge, and, reaching the right bank, carried the batteries and captured the suburb of Villa Nova, securing thus the passage of the Douro. As the woes of the town seemed drawing to an end, news came that the bishop's guard, 200 in number, were holding his palace and firing through the windows. A summons to surrender being fruitless, the French broke in and put these myrmidons to the sword. So far our troops had acted according to the laws of war: the town and its inhabitants had been respected As they returned, however, excited by the capture of the bishop's palace, our soldiers saw in the public place some thirty of their comrades, captured the day before, who had been horribly mutilated by the Portuguese, and of whom most were still alive. Exasperated at this horrible sight, the soldiers thought no more of anything save vengeance, and began to take fearful reprisals which were only stopped, with much difficulty, by the efforts of the marshal, the officers, and many of the cooler heads among the men themselves. Ten thousand; Portuguese are said to have been slain that day, including those killed in the entrenchments. Our own loss was not more than five hundred. To the universal satisfaction, General Foy was set free. As for the bishop, having seen the ruin of his ambitious projects—it was said that he wished, for his own benefit, to sever the northern provinces from the rest of the kingdom—he fled to Lisbon, where he not only became reconciled to the Commission of Regency and was received into that body, but was soon appointed Patriarch of Portugal.

The fall of Oporto gave Soult a solid base of operations, and replenished his supplies. As at Braga, he adopted a policy of conciliation, endeavoured to heal the misfortunes of war, and recalled the inhabitants who had fled. A curious result, which historians have not explained, and of which naturally the newspapers said little, followed from this course of action. The Portuguese could not forgive the House Braganza for its flight to America; nor did they wish to become a dependency of Brazil or an English colony, which seemed the most likely alternatives. Accordingly they preposed to choose a king; and Soult's orderly rule after the previous anarchy had made him so popular that the leading men went to him suggesting that an independent government should he formed, with himself at its head. Soult, regarding their plan with favour, began to appoint civil officials, raised a Portuguese legion, and managed so well that in a fortnight addesses came in from the captured towns, signed by thirty thousand persons of all classes, and expressing consent to the new order of things. The Duke of Rovigo states in his memoirs that Soult refused these proposals; but several of the generals who were then at Oporto have assured me that they were present at receptions where the Portuguese addressed him as 'your Majesty,' and that he accepted the title with much dignity. Finally, when I put a question on the subject to my old colonel and excellent friend General Peter Soult, the marshal's brother, he answered me frankly that the Emperor on sending his brother to Portugal had authorised him to employ every means to detach the country from the English alliance, and that when the crown was offered to him he considered this not merely the best but the only means of making the interests of Portugal identical with those of France, and therefore that, subject to the Emperor's approval, he made use of it. A further proof is, that instead of expressing any discontent with the marshal's action Napoleon extended his powers considerably, herein yielding only to the exigencies of the situation which made Marshal Soult indispensable. Is it true that Napoleon wrote to him, 'I remember nothing but your conduct at Austerlitz'? This point has never been cleared up. Marshal Bertrand told me that while talking with Napoleon at St. Helena he often tried to turn the conversation towards Soult's short-lived royalty, but that the Emperor would say nothing, from which Bertrand inferred that he had neither incited nor restrained him.

Originally, no doubt, the Emperor's idea was to unite the whole Peninsula into a single state under his brother Joseph; but when he realised that the mutual hatred of the Spanish and Portuguese made this impossible, he would, in his desire to detach Portugal from English influence at any cost, have consented to allow one of his lieutenants to wear the crown, and Soult being, the choice of the majority of the nation, Bertrand thought that Napoleon would have made up his mind to endorse that choice. However that may be, as soon as the offer of the Portuguese to Soult was known in the army there was great excitement, the junior officers and the men who were very fond of the marshal having no fault to find with the plan except its supposed antagonism to the Emperor's wishes. As soon as it was known that the marshal would do nothing without the Emperor's consent, the great majority took his side and was ready to support his projects. Still a large number of senior officers were afraid that Soult's accession to the Portuguese throne would bind the emperor to maintain him there, and that the second corps would be left in the country to settle there after the Roman fashion, whereby they would be engaged in an endless war. Their scheme, therefore, was to make a truce with the English, and, after choosing a leader and appealing to the French troops in Spain, to return altogether to France and force the Emperor to conclude a peace.

This plan, which was inspired by the English Government, was easier to form than to execute. It may be doubted whether all the armies and the mass of the French nation would have agreed to it. Steps were, however, taken to carry it out. The English General Beresford, marshal in the Portuguese army, was the soul of the plot, and carried on through an Oporto merchant named Viana a correspondence with the French malcontents, who were mean enough to suggest the arrest of Marshal Soult. As may be supposed, the discovery of this conspiracy put Marshal Soult into much perplexity.

Chapter 25
The Second Invasion of Portugal

While Soult was attending to the administration of the conquered country, the English and Portuguese troops which Sir Arthur Wellesley and Marshal Beresford were bringing up from Lisbon and Coimbra were every day drawing nearer the Douro. General Sylveira, after retaking Chaves from the French, descended the Tamega to Amarante, and, capturing that village with its bridge, brought his army in rear of Soult. Generals Heudelet and Loison were despatched to this point, and drove Sylveira from Amarante; but Wellesley, with the intention of turning the French left, sent a strong Anglo-Portuguese force across the Douro in front of Lamego. These marched upon Amarante, and General Loison in spite of his orders to defend that town to the uttermost abandoned the only passage by which the French army could escape from its perilous situation. Seeing that part of the enemy's force was making its way to his rear, while the remainder were marching on Oporto and threatening an attack in front, Marshal Soult resolved to abandon the town and retreat upon the Spanish frontier. His march had been fixed for April 12, but was delayed twenty-four hours by the necessity of collecting the artillery and starting the baggage trains. This delay was fatal to him; the conspirators were busy, the marshal's orders were disobeyed or misunderstood, and their execution falsely reported to him. Things were therefore as bad they could be when the English columns reached Villa Nova on the morning of the 12th. Soult had withdrawn his troops from the suburbs on the previous day, destroying the bridge which connected with the town, and carrying off every boat from the left bank. Thus secured against any attempt at crossing the Douro in front of Oporto, the marshal's only fear was that the English fleet might land troops on the right bank at the river's mouth, and he had a careful watch kept on the banks below the town. But Sir Arthur Wellesley, hovering like an eagle over Oporto and the surrounding country from the heights of the Serra, became aware that above the town the French pickets were few and far between, and so confident in the protection afforded by the broad river that they neglected to patrol.

It may well happen in war that a battalion, a regiment, even a brigade, should be surprised; but history affords very few examples of an army being attacked unawares in broad daylight without being warned by its outposts. This, however, befell the French at Oporto in the following manner. Above the town the Douro flows in a sharp bend round the foot of the Serra. This part of the river the French might conceivably neglect when it was covered by the troops at Villa Nova and on the hill; but as soon as they abandoned these positions and concentrated on the right bank, they ought to have placed outposts above the town. However, whether through negligence or treason not only was this precaution omitted but a large number of boats were left unguarded outside the town close to an unfinished building called the New Seminary, the enclosure of which going down on each side to the bank might hold four battalions. Seeing so important a position deserted, Sir Arthur Wellesley conceived the bold plan of making this point the base of his attack, and, if he could procure a boat, of crossing the river under the eyes of a seasoned army and one of its most renowned generals.

A barber, eluding the French patrols, had come over from the city during the previous night in a small boat. This an English colonel seized, and with a few men crossed the river and brought back three large barges, by means of which a battalion was conveyed to the Seminary. Taking possession of this, they sent over a great many boats, and in less than an hour and a half 6,000 English were in a strong position in the heart of the French army, and protected by guns placed on the Serra hill. The French outposts had seen nothing and the army was at its ease in Oporto, when suddenly the town resounded with the noise of the drums and the call to arms. Then one might judge of the stuff of which French soldiers are made, and of their valour. Undiscouraged by the surprise, they rushed furiously to the Seminary, and had torn down the main gate and slain many of the English before overpowered by the cannonade from the left bank and threatened in rear by an English force which had landed in the town. They were ordered by the marshal to quit the place and retire on Vallonga, a small town two leagues away in the direction of Amarante. The English did not venture to pursue that day, having lost heavily in the encounter. Lord Edward Paget, one of their best generals, was severely wounded; and on our side, General Foy. Otherwise our loss was not great. Our veterans were so experienced, so hardened to war, that they recovered from a surprise more readily than any other troops. The English writers admit that order was restored in the French ranks before they reached Vallonga. The marshal might well blame himself for letting himself be surprised in this fashion; but it is only justice to say that when the disaster came he showed that his personal courage and steadiness did not fail him in the most difficult circumstances.

The marshal's one chance of safety on leaving Oporto was by the bridge of Amarante, which he believed to be held by Loison; but on the morning of the 13th he heard at Peñafiel that that general had abandoned it and withdrawn to Guimaraens. With unabated energy, seeing that his retreat by road was cut off, he resolved, silencing all timid and treacherous counsels, to retire by cross-country paths, difficult as the country was. He at once destroyed his artillery and baggage, placed his sick and his infantry ammunition in the teams, and under a pelting rain crossed the Sierra de Catalina by a narrow rocky path, and thus reached Guimaraens. There he found the divisions of Loison at Lorge, who had come by road from Amarante.

Thus the French forces were concentrated at Guimaraens without having been attacked; from which Soult sagaciously inferred that the English had marched straight to cut off the retreat of the French at Braga, there being no longer any road practicable for their artillery. The malcontents, Loison among them, said that the only course left was to capitulate as at Cintra; but, with admirable decision, Soult ordered all the guns of Loison's and Lorge's divisions to be destroyed, and, having the Braga road on the left, took again to the mountain paths, thus gaining a day on the enemy, and reaching Salamonde in two marches. There, still resolved to avoid the beaten tracks, he crossed at right angles the road from Chaves to Braga, and pushed on through the mountains towards Montalegre. After marching some way the scouts brought word that the bridge over the Cavado at Ponte Novo was broken, and that

1,200 armed peasants with artillery were posted there to prevent its reconstruction. If this obstacle could not be removed, retreat was impossible, and the troops worn out, short of food and boots, and with cartridges mostly spoilt by the wet, must surrender as soon as the English army came up with their rear.

Even in this extremity Soult's courage did not fail. Summoning Lieutenant-Colonel Dulong, who was justly reputed one of the bravest officers in his army, he bade him take a hundred picked grenadiers and try to surprise the enemy in the night. The only part of the bridge not destroyed was a course of masonry about six inches wide, and along this Dulong and twelve men crawled on their stomachs towards the enemy's outposts. One grenadier lost his balance and fell into the swollen river; his cries were drowned by the storm and the roar of the torrent. Dulong with the remaining eleven reached the further bank, found the outpost asleep, and killed or dispersed them. The Portuguese soldiers, encamped not far off, thinking that the French army had crossed the Cavado, fled likewise. The bridge was at once repaired, and the army saved. The brave Dulong was severely wounded the next day in an attack on an entrenchment thrown up by the Portuguese in a difficult defile. This was the last bit of fighting which the French had in their painful retreat. On the 17th they reached Montalegre, where they crossed the frontier into Spain, and concentrated at Orense, being again in communication with Ney's troops. Dulong was promoted to colonel. He died a lieutenant-general in 1828.

Thus ended the second invasion of Portugal. Marshal Soult had lost from all causes 6,000 men; and of the fifty-eight guns with which he started he brought back one only. Yet his reputation as a valiant soldier and capable general was unshaken, for people took into consideration both the steadiness which he had displayed and the great difficulties which he had to sustain, no less from the intrigues of conspirators than from the Emperor's omission to have him properly supported by Marshal Victor. Napoleon, having been used to receive punctual obedience from his lieutenants in former campaigns, expected to find the same in the Peninsula; but distance and the title of marshal rendered them more independent. Thus Victor, who should have marched on Lisbon by the Tagus valley, waited so long at Talavera, that the Spanish general Cuesta had time to collect a large army in the mountains of Guadalupe. Then Victor, rousing himself from his apathy, beat him in several battles, notably at Medellin on the Guadiana, and reached Merida on March 19, a month after the date fixed by the Emperor. But when reminded by King Joseph of Napoleon's order to enter Portugal and join Soult, Victor, being the junior, and not wishing to take a subordinate position, not only refused, but stayed the advance of Lapisse's division, which was already in possession of the bridge of Alcantara over the Tagus, and might have caused a diversion in favour of Soult before the English could reach Oporto. Finally, after a month's delay, learning that Soult had left Portugal, Victor retired, first blowing up the bridge of Alcantara, the fine monument of Trajan's genius.

Soult, after providing himself with artillery from Corunna, held an interview with Ney, and proposed to unite their available forces and re-invade Portugal. But, as they could not agree, he brought his troops to recruit themselves at Zamora. Of the officers compromised in the plot at Oporto, Captain Argenton, adjutant of the 18th Dragoons, who was the soul of the conspiracy, was tried by court-martial and sentenced to death, but succeeded in escaping. His colonel, M. Lafitte, was retired. General Loison and Colonel Donnadieu, who were accused, but without evidence, were not punished; but Loison's being allowed to remain with the Army of Portugal could not fail to be mischievous.

At this time Soult sent General Franceschi to Madrid to explain his views to Joseph. This excellent officer fell into an ambush laid by the guerrilla chief, called the Capuchin, and, being taken to Seville and Granada, was treated by the central junta as a criminal and thrown into prison. Afterwards he was removed to Cartagena, where he died of yellow fever. This was a great loss to the army, for Franceschi possessed all the qualities of a consummate general.

Chapter 26
The Road to Busaco

Towards the end of 1809 the Emperor had placed all the army corps in Spain under the orders of his brother Joseph; but as he was no soldier, Napoleon only allowed him a nominal anthority, and, by making Soult chief of the staff, gave him the real command of all the French troops in the south of Spain. While these were successful in capturing Seville and Cordova, and even investing Cadiz, the seat of the governing junta, General Suchet was administering Aragon and Valentia, most of the fortified towns in which he had taken by siege. Saint-Cyr and Augereau were active in Catalonia, where the warlike population was defending itself with vigour. The troops of the Young Guard were steadily keeping up an irregular warfare against the guerrillas of Navarre and the northern provinces. Generals Bonnet and Drouet occupied Biscay in the Asturias; Ney held the province of Salamanca, and Junot that of Valladolid. The French had evacuated Galicia, the country being too poor to maintain our troops. Such was, in brief, the position of our armies in Spain when Masséna entered Portugal after taking Ciudad Rodrigo and Almeida. His troops were composed as follows. The second corps of veterans from Austerlitz, who had been under Soult the previous year at Oporto, and whom General Reynier now commanded with Merle and Heudelet as generals of division; the sixth corps, also veterans, commanded by Ney, the divisions being under Marchand, Loison, and Mermet; the eighth corps, composed of moderately good troops, commanded in chief by Junot, with Solignac and Clausel, the future marshal, as generals of division; two divisions of cavalry under Montbrun, and a powerful field artillery directed by General Eblé. General Lasouski commanded the engineers.

Deducting the garrisons left at Rodrigo, Almeida, and Salamanca, with the sick, the total number of combatants amounted to 50,000, with sixty guns and a great quantity of ammunition chests.

This was far too large a train for a rough country like Portugal, where there were scarcely any high roads. Almost the only communications are narrow, rocky paths, often very steep, and everything is transported on mule-back. There are even districts where roads are absolutely unknown. Lastly, except in certain valleys, the soil is mostly arid, and offers insufficient resources for maintaining an army. Masséna had therefore every reason to go through the least difficult and most productive country. He did, however, just the contrary.

Having left the neighbourhood of Almeida on September 14, 1810, the army assembled next day at Celorico, where it saw the rich valley of the Mondego opening before it and might march on Coimbra by Sampayo and Ponte de Murcelha, over roads which, if not good, were at least tolerable. But under the influence of Major Pelet, his adviser, the marshal left the practicable country where the troops might have lived in comfort, and went off to the right into the mountains of Viseu, where the roads are the worst in Portugal. One need only look at the map to see how unreasonable it was to go by Viseu on the way from Celorico to Coimbra; a mistake all the greater from the fact that Viseu is separated from the Sierra d'Alcoba by high hills, which the army might have avoided by marching down the valley of the Mondego. The neighbourhood of Viseu produces no corn or vegetables, and the troops found nothing there but lemons and grapes--not very sustaining food.

Masséna's expedition very nearly came to an end at Viseu through lack of foresight on the marshal's part. He made his artillery park march on the extreme right of the column outside the masses of infantry, its only escort being an Irish battalion in the French service and a company of French grenadiers. Marching in single file more than a league in length, the park was proceeding slowly and laboriously by difficult roads, when suddenly on its right flank appeared the English colonel Trant, with 4,000 or 5,000 Portuguese militia. If the enemy, profiting by his superior strength, had surrounded the convoy and made a resolute attack, all the ammunition and provisions of the army would have been captured or destroyed. But Colonel Trant, as he himself said afterwards, could not suppose that a general of Masséna's experience could have left unsupported a convoy so essential to the safety of his army, and, supposing that a powerful escort must be close at hand, he dared to advance only with extreme caution. He confined himself, therefore, to attacking only the leading company of grenadiers, who answered by a heavy fire, killing some fifty men. The militia men recoiled in alarm, and Trant, doing what he should have done at first, overlapped a portion of the convoy. As he went forward he discovered the weakness of the escort, and sent a flag of truce to the commander, summoning him to surrender or he would attack him all along the line. The French officer adroitly consented to negotiate, in order to give the Irish time to come up from the rear of the convoy. They appered at length, coming up at the double. As soon as the French officer saw them he broke off the conference, saying: 'I cannot treat any further; here is my general coming to my support with 8,000 men.' Each resumed his position, but Trant shortly left his and made off, thinking he had to with the advanced guard of a strong column. Thus the artillery was saved, but the army soon learnt the danger in which it had been and the excitement was great. Ney, Junot, Reynier, and Montbrun went straight off to Viseu and addressed strong remonstrances to General Fririon, chief of the staff. He, however, asserted that, in spite of his demands, no information of the march of the columns had been given him, everything being settled by Masséna and Pelet. Horrified and indignant at this state of things, the commanders of the four corps called on Masséna with a view of making well-deserved remarks on it. Ney was the speaker, and from the aide-de-camps room we could hear him protesting; but Masséna, foreseeing that the conversation would become animated, took the generals into a more distant apartment. I do not know what was decided, but it appears that the commander-in-chief promised to change his mode of action, for in a quarter of an hour we saw Masséna walking quietly in the garden, taking the arm of each of his lieutenants in turn. Unanimity seemed to be restored, but it was not for long.

As I have already said, childish reasons sometimes produce great and mischievous results. We had a striking example of it, which influenced the result of a campaign which was to have driven the English out of Portugal, but which by its failure increased their confidence in Wellington, while it seasoned the troops who did most to bring about our defeat in the following years. All the army knew that Masséna had brought Mme N— to Portugal with him. This lady, having crossed the whole of Spain in a carriage, and having remained at Salamanca during the sieges of Rodrigo and Almeida, thought fit to follow Masséna on horse-back as soon as he set out to march through a country impracticable for carriages, which produced a very bad effect. The marshal, who generally took his meals alone with her, had had his table laid that day under a clump of lemon-trees, the aide-de-camp's table being a hundred yards away in the same garden. Dinner was about to be served, when the commander-in-chief, wishing probably to cement the good relations which had just been established between himself his lieutenants, remarked that as each of them had several leagues to go in order to reach his headquarters it would best for them to dine with him before starting. All four accepted, and Masséna, in order to prevent any further remarks on the incident of the convoy, ordered that for once the aide-de-camp's table should be set by his.

So far all went well; but just before sitting down Masséna sent for Mme N—. On seeing the generals she drew back, but he said to Ney, 'My dear marshal, kindly take Madame.' Ney turned pale, and nearly burst out; but, restraining himself, he led the lady by the finger-tips, to the table, and placed her, by Masséna's direction, on his right. During the whole meal, however, Ney said not a word to her, but talked to Montbrun, his neighbour on the left. Mme N— , who was too quick-witted not to see how false a position she was in, was seized with a nervous attack, and fell in a faint. Then Ney, Reynier, Montbrun and Junot left the garden, not without a vigorous and audible expression of his views on the part of Ney. Reynier and Montbrun also said plainly what they thought; Junot spoke so bitterly, that I took the liberty of reminding him of the way in which he had met Mme N— at Valladolid. He answered, laughing, 'Because an old hussar like me has his games sometimes, that is no reason for Masséna to imitate them. Besides, I must stand by my colleagues.' From that day forward the four generals were on the worst of terms with Masséna, who, on his side, bore them no goodwill.

This quarrel among the chiefs could not fail to aggravate the causes making for the ill-success of the campaign. There arose mainly from our utter want of topographical knowledge of the districts in which we were fighting; arising from the omission of the Portuguese Government—either as a defensive measure, or through indolence—to have good maps made of the kingdom. The only one in existence was as bad as could be; so that we had, as it were, to feel our way along. There were officers in plenty who had campaigned in Portugal with Soult and Junot, but they had not been in the provinces where we were, and could be of no use as guides. On the staff we had some thirty Portuguese officers, among them two generals—the Marquis of Alorna and Count Pamplona who had come to France in 1808 with the contingent furnished to Napoleon by the court of Lisbon. Though they had only obeyed the orders of the former Government, they were proscribed by the Commission of Regency, and thus had returned to seek possession of their confiscated goods in the train of our army. Masséna had hoped to get some useful information from these exiles; but except in the neighbourhood of Lisbon they knew nothing of their own country; while the English, who had been going all about it for two years knew its configuration perfectly, gaining thereby a great advantage over us.

Another cause told no less powerfully against us. Lord Wellington, being allowed a perfectly free hand by the Government, used it to compel all the people to leave their houses, destroy all provisions and mills, and retire with their cattle to Lisbon on the approach of the French, who thus were unable to obtain any information, and had to beat the country to a great distance in order to get provisions. The Spaniards had constantly refused to adopt this terrible means of resistance at the instance of the English; but the Portuguese were more docile. We thus crossed vast districts without seeing a single inhabitant; such an exodus had not been seen within human memory. The city of Viseu was totally deserted when we entered it, yet Masséna halted the army there for six days. This was a second mistake added to that which he had committed in leaving the valley of the Mondego. If on the morrow of his arrival at Viseu the French general had made a rapid march and attacked the Alcoba, on which Lord Wellington had then very few troops, the fault might have been repaired. But our delay of six days allowed the English to ford the Mondego above Ponte de Murcelha, and to unite their army on the ridges of the Alcoba at Busaco. No military writer of any country has been able to account for Masséna's inactivity of nearly a week at Viseu, but the marshal's staff can testify that Mme N——'s fatigue had much to do with delaying Masséna and keeping him at that place. The country was in arms, and it would have been impossible to leave her behind without exposing her to the danger of her being captured. Moreover, when he had made up his mind to start, Masséna made only very short marches, halting first at Tondella. The next day, September 26, after establishing his headquarters at Mortagoa, on the right bank of the Criz, he lost precious time in securing the lady's quarters; and it was not till two in the afternoon that he set out with his staff for the outposts—five good leagues off, at the foot of the Alcoba.

This mountain ridge, about three leagues in length, abuts upon the Mondego to the east, and to the west is connected with detached hills of great steepness, impassable for an army. At the highest point is a convent, named Saceo. The central part of the summit forms a sort of plateau, on which the English artillery was posted. It had freedom of action along the whole front of the position, and its range extended to beyond the Criz. A road passing round the ridge of Busaco afforded easy conumunication between the various portions of the enemy's army, while the slope facing towards the direction from which the French approached was, from its sharpness, well adapted for defence. The enemy's left rested on the hills above Barria; his centre and reserves on the convent; his right on the heights, a little in rear of San Antonio de Cantara. So formidable was the position that the English had some fear that the French commander-in-chief might not venture to attack.

When Masséna came up on the evening of the 26th he found that the army had in his absence been posted by Ney as follows: the 6th corps on the right, at the village of Moira; the centre facing the convent; Reynier's corps on the left, at San Antonio; and the 8th corps, under Junot, with the artillery, marching to take up a position in reserve in rear of the centre. The cavalry, under Montbrun, was at Bienfaita.

When an army has undergone a check it is but too common to find the generals throwing the blame on each other. This happened after Busaco, and thus it is necessary to mention here the opinion expressed before the battle by Masséna's lieutenants, who, having first urged him on to the commission of his greatest blunder, after the unfortunate event criticised his conduct. I have said that on the day but one before the battle the corps under Ney and Reynier were at the foot of the Alcoba, and in presence of the enemy. While impatiently waiting for the commander-in-chief, these two generals exchanged in writing their respective views on the position of the Anglo-Portuguese army. There exists a letter, dated on the morning of September 26, in which Marshal Ney says to General Reynier, 'If I were in command I would attack without a moment's hesitation.' Both expressed the same feeling in their correspondence with Masséna:—'The position is far less formidable than it looks and if I had not been in so subordinate a position I would have carried it without awaiting your orders.' Relying on the assurance of Generals Reynier and Junot that nothing could be easier, Masséna made (although the contrary has since been affirmed) not the smallest attempt to reconnoitre and, merely replying, 'Very well, I will be back at daybreak, and we will attack,' he turned and rode back to Mortagoa. Great was the astonishment at this abrupt departure, for, seeing Masséna join his troops, who were encamped within cannon-shot of the enemy, everyone supposed that he would use the remaining daylight to study the position which he had to carry, and would stay with the army. In going off thus, without seeing anything for himself, he no doubt made a great mistake; but I do not think that, after lulling to sleep his usual vigilance and urging him to attack, his lieutenants had any right to blame him as they afterwards did. On the contrary, they might well have found fault with themselves; for, after spending two days at the foot of the Alcoba, they advised a front attack, in spite of the steepness, and made no inquiries as to the possibility of turning it—a course, as you will presently see, offering no difficulty.

It was a misfortune for the army that General Sainte-Croix was not then with Masséna. His instinct for war would certainly have led him, taking advantage of the marshal's confidence in him, to induce him to abandon the idea of attacking directly so formidable a position before making sure that it could not be turned. But he was with his brigade some leagues to the rear, escorting a convoy.

Hardly had the commander-in-chief with his staff left the army than night came on—and Masséna having only one eye was not a good horseman. Our road was strewn with large stones and pieces of rock, so we had, in the darkness, to go for more than two hours at a walk to accomplish the five leagues to Mortagoa. As we went along I meditated sadly on the probable results of the battle which we were going to fight on the morrow at such a disadvantage, and imparted my reflections in a low voice to my friend Ligniville and to General Fririon. We were all most anxious that Masséna should alter his dispositions; but no officer save Pelet was allowed to submit any suggestions to him directly. Yet the matter appeared urgent, and we decided to employ an artifice, which we had sometimes used with success, for bringing the truth indirectly to his notice. Agreeing upon our parts, we got near the marshal, feigning not to see him in the darkness; then we began to talk about the coming battle, and I said that I was sorry the commander-in-chief intended to assault the position in front without being certain that it could not be turned. Then General Fririon playing his part as arranged, answered that Ney and Reynier had stated positively that there was no other way to get past, to which Ligniville and I replied that we could not believe that, for it was impossible that the people of Mortagoa should have lived for centuries devoid of direct communication with Boialva, and with no other way to the Oporto road than by Busaco, over the steepest part of the mountains. I added that when I had made the same remark to the aides-de-camp of Ney and Reynier, and asked which of them had reconnoitred the extreme left of the enemy's position, not one answered, from which I concluded that no one had vlsited that part. If Masséna saw badly his hearing was extremely keen, and, as we hoped, he had not missed one word of our talk. So much struck was he, that he came up to our group, and, joining in the conversation, admitted—cautious as he was—that he had assented too easily to the plan of assaulting in front. He said that he would counter-order this, and that if a way could be found of turning the position he would let the army rest next day, and on the following night would concentrate it opposite the vulnerable point and attack unawares. No doubt there would be a day's delay, but the chances of success would be better and the probable loss lighter.

So determined did the marshal appear, that when we reached Mortagoa he bade Ligniville and me try to find some inhabitant who could show us a road to Boialva without passing Busaco. At length, we found an old gardener who had stayed to take care of a sick monk. He brought us to this monk, who answered our questions freely; he had often been from Mortagoa and Boialva by a good road which branched off a short league from the place where we were. He was all the more surprised at our not knowing this, that part of our army in going from Viseu to Mortagoa had passed the turning. Guided by the old gardener, we went to verify the monk's statement, and found that an excellent road actually went in the direction of the mountains and appeared to pass round the enemy's left. Yet Marshal Ney had stayed two days at Mortagoa without exploring this road, a knowledge of which would have saved us many disasters.

Ligniville and I, delighted at our discovery, hastened to report it to the marshal; but we had been away more than an hour, and we found him with Major Pelet, surrounded by maps and plans. Pelet said that he had examined the mountains with a telescope by daylight and had seen in their configuration no sign of a pass to our right; moreover, he could not believe that Marshal Ney had not explored the neighbourhood while he was at Mortagoa, and as he had not found a pass it was clear that none existed, nor could we convince him of the contrary. In vain did we offer to go round and ascend the hill which the monk assured us was less steep than that of Busaco, or even to go as far as Boialva if they would give us three battalions of the headquarters guard. In vain did General Fririon beg the marshal accept this offer: all was useless. Masséna was very tired, he said that it was near midnight and that we must be off at four o'clock to reach the camp by daybreak, and with that he went to bed. Never did I pass a more melancholy night; and my comrades were as sad as I. At last the hour came for our start, and we reached the outposts with the first morning light of September 27, an ill-omened day which was to hold one of the most terrible reverses which the French army ever suffered.

Chapter 27
The Battle of Busaco

On finding himself in front of the position which he had scarcely examined on the previous day Masséna appeared to hesitate, and, coming up to the place where I was chatting with General Fririon, he said sadly, 'Your suggestion of yesterday was worth considering.' Our hopes rekindled by these few words, we doubled our efforts to induce the commander-in-chief to turn the mountain by Boialva, and he was already coming over to our way of thinking, when Ney, Reynier, and Pelet came up and interrupted our talk with the remark that all was ready for the attack. Masséna made a few more remarks, but at length, overborne by his lieutenants, and fearing, no doubt, that he might be blamed for letting slip a victory which they declared to be certain, he gave orders towards seven o'clock to open fire.

The 2nd corps, under Reynier, attacked the enemy's right: Ney their left and centre. The French troops were drawn up on stony ground, sloping steeply down to a great ravine which separated us from the Alcoba, which was lofty, steep, and occupied by the enemy. From their commanding position they could see all our movements, while we saw only their outposts half-way up the hill between the convent of Busaco and the ravine, which at this point was so deep that the naked eye could hardly make out the movements of troops; who were marching through it, and so narrow that the English bullets carried right across it. It might be regarded as an immense natural ditch, serving as the first line of defence to the natural fortifications formed by great rocks; cut almost into a vertical wall. Besides this, our artillery, engaged in very bad roads and obliged to fire upwards, could render very little service; while the infantry had to contend not only against a mass of obstacles and the roughest possible ascent, but also against the best marksmen in Europe. Up to this time the English were the only troops who were perfectly practised in the use of small arms, whence their firing was far more accurate than that of any other infantry.

Although you might expect that the rules of war would be alike among civilized nations, they do, as a fact, vary immensely even in identical circumstances. Thus, when the French have to defend a position they first garnish the front and flanks with skirmishers, and then crown the heights conspicuously with their main body and reserves, which has the serious inconvenience of letting the enemy know the vulnerable point of the line. The method employed in similar cases by the English seems to me far preferable, as was often demonstrated in the Peninsular War. After having, as we do, garnished their front with skirmishers, they post their principal forces in such a way as to keep them out of sight, holding them all the time sufficiently near to the key of the position to be able to attack the enemy at once if they come near to reaching it; and this attack, made unexpectedly upon assailants who have lost heavily and think the victory ready theirs, succeeds almost invariably. We had a melancholy experience of this at Busaco. In spite of the numerous obstacles which favoured the defence, the brave men of the 2nd corps had just succeeded, after an hour of desperate work, performed with really heroic courage, in scaling the mountain, when, as they arrived panting at the summit of the ridge, they found themselves in front of a hitherto unperceived line of English infantry. After receiving them at fifteen paces with an admirably aimed and sustained fire which stretched more than five hundred men on the ground, this line dashed at the survivors with the bayonet. The unexpected attack, accompanied by a storm of grape on their flank, shook some of our battalions; but they quickly rallied, and, in spite of their heavy losses, our troops, astonished but not disconcerted, charged the English line, broke it at several points, and carried six guns. But Wellington had brought up strong reserves, while ours were at the foot of the mountain, and the French, pressed on all sides, and compelled to give up the narrow ground which they occupied on the plateau found themselves, after a long and brisk resistance, driven in a heap down the steep descent up which they had climbed. The English lines followed them halfway down, firing volleys to which our men could not reply—and murderous they were. All resistance being useless in so unfavourable a position, the officers ordered the men to take skirmishing order about the broken ground, and under a hail of bullets they reached the foot of the mountain. At this point we lost General Graindorge, two colonels, eighty officers, and seven or eight hundred men.

After such a check prudence would have forbidden to send any troops weakened by heavy losses a second time against a triumphant enemy with his position unaltered; yet General Reynier ordered Foy's and Sarrut's brigades to return to the charge; and Masséna, who witnessed this madness, allowed the second attack. It met with the same fate as the first. While this was taking place on our left, fortune was not more favourable to the 6th corps on our right. Although it had been arranged to attack simultaneously at all points, and Masséna had repeated the order about seven o'clock at the moment of engaging, it was half-past eight before Ney set his troops in motion. He asserted afterwards that he had been delayed by the difficulty of the position on that side, and it certainly was greater than on the left. Our people had just made one great mistake in sending the 2nd corps into action before the 6th was ready; Ney made one similar when he engaged Loison's, Marchand's and Mermet's divisions without any cohesion. The troops attacked vigorously, and although entire files were swept away by cannon and musketry, the brigades of Ferey and Simon, with the 26th of the line, clambering up the steep rocks, flung themselves on the enemy's guns and captured three of them. The English, being reinforced, returned to the attack; General Simon, with his jaw smashed, fell, and was taken prisoner on one of the guns which he had just captured. Almost every field officer was killed or wounded, and three volleys at close quarters completed the rout of the French masses, who returned in disorder to their starting-point. Thus ended the principal fight. The losses of the 2nd and 6th corps were immense. They amounted to more than 5,000 men, including 250 officers killed, wounded, or prisoners. General Graindorge, Colonels Monier, Amy, and Berliet killed; two others wounded; General Simon wounded and taken prisoner; Generals Merle, Mancune, and Foy severely wounded, besides two colonels and thirteen majors. The enemy in their sheltered position lost far less heavily; but they admitted 2,300 men disabled. We learnt afterwards that if we had attacked the day before the English would have withdrawn without fighting, because 2,500 of their best troops were then on the other side of the Mondego, and only arrived at Busaco the night before the battle. Such was the result of the six days lost by Masséna at Viseu, and his hurry to return on the 26th to Mortagoa instead of reconnoitring the position.

Our efforts having thus utterly failed in face of a hillside so steep that an unburdened man would have climbed it with difficulty, it surely behoved our leaders to put a stop to firing which had now become useless. Yet a brisk file-firing went on all along the lines at the foot of the position, which our soldiers, in their excitement, were to assault anew. These small encounters with an enemy hidden by lofty rocks were very costly to us, and there was a general feeling that they should cease, though no one gave the formal order. Just then the two armies witnessed a touching incident, forming a contrast to the scenes of slaughter all round. General Simon's valet, hearing that his master had been left badly wounded on the summit of the Alcoba, tried to make his way to him; but the enemy, not understanding his motive for approaching their lines, fired on him repeatedly, and the faithful servant was compelled to return to the French outposts. As he was lamenting his inability to aid his master, the cantinière of the 26th, belonging to the brigade, took the things from the valet's hands, loaded them on her donkey, and went forward, saying, 'We will see if the English will kill a woman'; listening to no objections, she went up the hill, and, passed coolly between the lines of skirmishers, who, savage as they were, ceased firing till she was out of range. Presently she saw the English colonel, and explained what she had brought. He received her kindly, and had her taken to General Simon with whom she stayed several days, tending him to the best of her power, and only leaving him when the valet arrived. Then, getting on her donkey, she went through the enemy's army, by that time in retreat on Lisbon, and rejoined her regiment, without having received an insult of any kind, though she was young and very pretty. On the contrary, the English made a point of treating her with great respect.

The two armies maintained their respective positions; it was a sad night for us; the future appeared gloomy enough. At daybreak on the 28th, the Alcoba echoed with mighty cheering and the strains of the English military bands. Wellington was reviewing his troops, who were saluting him with their hurrahs; while the French at the foot of the mountain were in gloomy silence. Masséna should have mounted his horse then, reviewed his army, harangued his soldiers, until they replied by their cheers to the defiant enthusiasm of the enemy. The Emperor and Marshal Lannes would certainly have acted thus. But Masséna held aloof walking about all alone, and making no arrangements; while his lieutenants, especially Ney and Reynier, the very men who the day before had urged him to engage, saying that they would answer for victory, were loudly accusing him of imprudence in attacking a strong position like Busaco. When, finally, they joined the commander-in-chief, it was to propose that he should advertise our failure to the army, and all the world by abandoning Portugal and take the army back into Spain. Then old Masséna, recovering a little of the energy of Rivoli, Zurich, and Genoa, and many another memorable occasion, rejected their proposal as unworthy of the army and of himself.

The English have called the affair of Busaco a political battle, because the British Parliament, alarmed at the enormous cost of the war, appeared resolved to withdraw the troops from the Peninsula and content itself in future with supplying arms and ammunition to the guerrillas. As this plan tended to destroy Wellington's influence, he had resolved to prevent it from being carried out by replying with a victory to the fears of the English Parliament, and this determined him to await the French at Busaco. His plan succeeded, and Parliament voted further supplies for the war which was to be so disastrous to us.

While the marshal was discussing with his lieutenants, General Sainte-Croix came up. On seeing him everyone expressed regret that he had not been present the day before to act as the marshal's good genius. Masséna now understood the mistake he had made in not turning the enemy's left as we had advised him, and, on hearing the state of things from Masséna himself, Sainte-Croix advised him to revert to that plan. With the general's assent, he galloped off, accompanied by Ligniville and me, to Mortagoa, whither he sent for his brigade of dragoons. As we passed through the village we picked up the convent gardener, who, at sight of a piece of gold, consented to act as our guide, laughing when he was asked if there really existed a road to Boialva.

While Sainte-Croix's brigade, and a regiment of infantry led the way in this new direction, the 8th corps and Montbrun's cavalry followed close behind, and the rest of the army prepared to do the same. Urged by Sainte-Croix, Masséna had at last spoken with authority, and imposed silence on his lieutenants when they persisted in denying the existence of a pass on the right.

In order to conceal from the English the movement of such of our troops as were at the foot of the Alcoba, they did not march until night, and then in dead silence. But information was soon given by the despairing cries of the French wounded, whom we were under the sad necessity of abandoning. A great number of horses, and all the beasts of burden, were employed to carry the men whom there was hope of curing; but those who had lost their legs, or were otherwise severely wounded, were left lying on the dry heath, and as the poor fellows expected to have their throats cut by the peasants as soon as the armies were out of the way, their despair was terrible.

The French army had reason to fear that Wellington, seeing them execute a flank march so near him, would attack them vigorously. This might have led to the capture of Reynier's entire corps, which would be the last to leave its position, and would remain for some hours unsupported in presence of the enemy. But the English general had no time to think of turning the French rear-guard, for he had just learnt that he was being himself turned by the pass of which the French commander-in-chief had so long denied the existence. What actually happened was this. After we had marched all the night of the 28th, the gardener, going with the head of Sainte-Croix's column, brought us by a road practicable for artillery as far as Boialva, that is to say, to the extreme left flank of the English army, so that all the positions on the Alcoba had been outflanked without a blow, and Wellington, under pain of exposing his army to be taken in rear, had to abandon Busaco in haste, to regain Coimbra, and cross the Mondego there, with a view of retreating upon Lisbon, which he did with all speed. Our advanced guard only met with a small detachment of Hanoverian hussars posted at Boialva, a pretty village situated at the southern issue from the mountains. The fertility of the country gave hopes that the army might find abundant subsistence there. A shout of joy went up from our ranks, and the soldiers very soon forgot the fatigues and dangers of the previous days, perhaps also the unhappy comrades whom they had left dying before Busaco.

To complete the success of our movement, a good road joined Boialva with the village of Avelans on the road from Oporto to Coimbra. Sainte-Croix occupied this, and by a further piece of luck we discovered a second road from Boialva to Sardao, another village on the high road. At last, then, we had the proof of the existence of this pass, so obstinately denied by Ney, Reynier, and Pelet. Masséna must have reproached himself for having omitted to reconnoitre the strong position before which he had lost several thousand men, and which his army had now turned without meeting the least resistance. But Wellington was still more to blame for not having guarded that point, and surveyed the road leading to it from Mortagoa. It was of no use for him to say afterwards that he did not believe the road had been practicable for artillery, and that he had besides ordered Trant to cover Boialva with 2,000 militia. Such an excuse is not permissible for experienced fighting men. It might perfectly well be answered that as to the state of the road the English commander should have reconnoitred it before the battle, and that, in the second place, it is not enough for the chief of an army to give orders, but that he should make sure that they have been executed. Boialva is only a few leagues from Busaco, and yet Wellington never ascertained that this pass, so important to the safety of his army, had been guarded according to his orders; so that if Masséna had been better inspired, and had, during the night of the 26th, sent an army corps to Boialva to attack the left flank of the enemy while threatening him in front with the rest of his force, the English would certainly have suffered a sanguinary defeat. From all this we conclude that in the circumstances neither Wellington nor Masséna showed himself equal to his high reputation; and that they deserved the blame which their contemporaries addressed to them, and which history will confirm.

Chapter 28
The Lines at Torres Vedras

As soon as the army was clear of the defile of Boialva, Massey marched on Coimbra by way of Milheada and Tornos. At the latter point there was a cavalry engagement, in which Sainte-Croix overthrew the English rear-guard, forcing them back on Coimbra. On October 1 the French entered the place. Deceived by the result of the battle of Busaco, and the assertion of English officers that the French army was retiring into Spain, the unhappy inhabitants of that city had abandoned themselves to a display of rejoicing. The festivities were not at an end, when suddenly came the news that the French had turned the mountains and were marching straight on Coimbra—that indeed they were not a day's journey distant. Indescribable panic prevailed; the population of 120,000 souls simultaneously with the news of the enemy's approach received orders to leave their home forthwith. Their departure was, by the admission of English officers, a most terrible sight; I refrain from relating the heart-breaking incidents.

Wellington's army, hampered by the mass of fugitives of every age, sex, and class, men and beasts of burden in inextricable confusion, retired in the greatest disorder toward Coimbra and Pombal, many perishing in the passage of the Mondego. This was good for Masséna. He should have sent Junot's corps, which, not having fought at Busaco, was fully available, in pursuit, and by a sudden attack he might have caused heavy loss to the English army, which, by the testimony of some of our men who had been captured at Busaco and had escaped, was in disorder beyond words to our great surprise, and as if he wished to allow the time to restore order to get away, the commander-in-chief billeted his army in Coimbra and the adjacent villages, and waited three clear days. His excuse for this delay was the necessity of reorganizing the 2nd and 6th corps which had suffered at Busaco, and of establishing hospitals at Coimbra; all which he might have done while the 8th corps was in pursuit of the enemy. But the real notion for the stay at Coimbra was, in the first place, the increasing want of confidence between Masséna and his lieutenants; and, further, his difficulty in deciding whether to leave a division in the place to cover his rear and protect the sick and wounded, or to take all his available forces from the battle which was expected to be fought outside Lisbon. Either course had its advantages and disadvantages; but he need not have taken three days to make up his mind. Finally he decided to leave a half-company to guard the convent of Santa Clara and protect the wounded who were assembled there from the first fury of an attacking force, with orders to capitulate as soon as an officer appeared.

But no definite instructions were given; and, under the impression that a division would remain, the colonels put all their infirm men, most of whom could perfectly well have marched, and desired nothing better, in the vast convent. More than three thousand were thus left behind, with two lieutenants and eighty men of the naval brigade as their sole guard.

I was surprised that Masséna, who was sure to require sailors when he reached the Tagus, should have sacrificed a number of these valuable men, who could not easily be replaced, when he might have left some infantry of inferior value. It was clear that in less than twenty-four hours the enemy's irregular troops would occupy the town; and indeed in the evening of the very day, October 3, on which the French had left it, the Portuguese militia entered.

Our poor wounded had barricaded themselves in the convent, having no longer any doubt that Masséna had abandoned them, and were preparing to sell their lives dearly. The naval lieutenants behaved admirably. With the help of some infantry officers who were among the wounded, they collected all the men who still had muskets and could use them, and succeeded in holding the Portuguese in check all the night. On the morning of the 6th Brigadier Trant, the commander of the militia, arrived; and the naval officers capitulated to him in writing. Hardly, however, had the wounded French surrendered the few arms which they had than the militia fell on the poor wretches, many of whom could not stand, and butchered over a thousand. The rest, sent without mercy to Oporto, perished on the road; as soon as anyone fell out from fatigue the Portuguese killed him. Yet this militia was organized and led by English officers, commanded by an English general; and in not checking these atrocities Trant dishonoured his country and his uniform. In vain does Napier allege in his excuse that only ten French prisoners were sacrificed; the fact is, that nearly all were murdered either in the hospital at Coimbra or on the road. Even in England the name of Trant has become infamous.

From Coimbra Masséna had written to the Emperor; but the difficulty was to transmit the despatch through the insurgent population. A Frenchman must have failed, and it was necessary to find someone who knew the country and could speak the language. A Portuguese officer named Mascareguas, who had entered the French service with General d'Alorna, offered to be the bearer. I saw him start disguised as a mountain-shepherd, with a little dog in his basket, in which costume he hoped to reach Almeida, where the French commandant would put him in the way of proceeding to Paris. But it was of no use for Mascareguas, who belonged to the first nobility of Portugal, to attempt to conceal his distinguished bearing and manner and his refined speech. The peasants were not taken in; he was arrested, brought to Lisbon, and condemned to death; and in spite of his appeal for the noble's privilege of decapitation, he was hanged as a spy in the public square.

The three further days wasted by the French at Coimbra allowed the English to get away, and it took us three days more to come up with their rear-guard at Pombal. Before our coming the body of the celebrated marquis of that name had lain in a magnificent tomb, erected in an immense mausoleum of wonderful architecture. This had been wrecked by the stragglers from the English army. They had broken the tomb and thrown the bones under the feet of their horses, which they had stabled in the vast building. A strange instance of the vanity of human things! There, lying in the filth, when Masséna and his staff visited the place, were the scanty remains of the great minister who put down the Jesuits!

From Pombal we went on to Leyria, and at 9 A.M. our advance-guard was on the banks of the Tagus, at Santarem. There we found immense stores of provisions; but this advantage was almost neutralized by autumnal rains such as are not seen out of the tropics except in the southern shores of the Peninsula, and which assailed us after unbroken fine weather. Both armies suffered much from this cause; but ours reached Alemquer, a market town at the foot of the hills of Cintra, which gird Lisbon at a few leagues' distance. We quite expected to have to fight a battle before entering Lisbon, but, as we knew that the town was open on the landside, we had no doubt of success. Meantime, however, all the neighbourhood of Lisbon had been covered with fortifications. For a year and a half the English had been working at them; but neither Ney, who had just spent a year at Salamanca, nor Masséna, who for six months had been making ready to invade Portugal, had the least inkling of these gigantic works. Reynier and Junot were equally ignorant; most surprising of all—incredible, indeed, if the fact were not absolutely certain—the French Government itself did not know that the hills of Cintra had been fortified. It is inconceivable how the Emperor, who had agents in every country, could have omitted to send some to Lisbon. At that time thousands of American, German, Swedish, and English ships were daily bringing into the Tagus stores for Wellington's army; and it would have been perfectly easy to have introduced some spies among the numerous sailors and clerks employed on these vessels. Knowledge of all kinds can be obtained by money; it was by this means that the Emperor kept himself informed of all that went on in England and among the great Powers of Europe. Nevertheless, he never gave Masséna any information as to the defences of Lisbon; and it was only on reaching Alemquer that the French general discovered that the hills were fortified and connected by lines of which the right touched the sea in rear of Torres Vedras, the centre was at Sobral, and the right rested on the Tagus, near Alhandra.

The day before our troops appeared at this point the English army had entered the lines, driving before it the population of the surrounding districts, to the number of 300,000 souls. Utter disorder prevailed; and those among the French officers who guessed what was taking place among the enemy regretted afresh and very keenly that Masséna had resolved a fortnight before to attack the position of Busaco in front. If that position had been turned, the enemy would have been taken in flank and have retired upon Lisbon, and our army, in full strength and ardour, would have attacked the lines on its arrival, and certainly have carried them. With the capture of the capital the English must have retreated precipitately, and the reverse would have been irreparable. But our heavy losses at Busaco had chilled the ardour of Masséna's lieutenants, and bred ill-will between them and him; so that now all were trying to paralyse his operations, and representing every little hillock to be a new height of Busaco the capture of which would cost copious bloodshed. In spite, however, of this want of loyalty, Masséna despatched the 8th corps towards the enemy centre, and Clausel's division carried the village of Sobral—a very important point for us. Just when a simultaneous attack along the whole line was expected, General Sainte-Croix, who had urged this course, was killed by a cannon-shot in front of Villa-Franca. That excellent officer was with General Montbrun making a reconnaissance toward Alhandra, and as they passed along the Tagus, on which several Portuguese sloops were cruising, and firing out our outposts, poor Sainte-Croix was cut in two by a chain-shot. It was a grievous loss for the army, for Masséna, and above all for me who loved him like a brother.

After the death of the only man capable of giving him good advice the commander-in-chief fell back into his state of perpetual indecision, wavering under the clamour of his lieutenants, who, in their present faint-heartedness, represented all the hills of Cintra as bristling with cannon ready to make mince-meat of us. In order to know what he was really to think about it, Masséna, who since the advice which Ligniville and I had offered at the battle of Busaco, had evinced some kindness towards us, directed us to examine the front of the enemy's lines. They were undoubtedly of imposing strength, but very far from what people were pleased to say. The English entrenchments formed an immense arc round Lisbon at least twenty French leagues in length. Every officer of the least experience knows well that a position of this extent cannot present the same difficulties everywhere and must have its weak spots. We became aware of several such by seeing officers, and even cavalry pickets, ride up quite easily; and we also became convinced that our engineer officers who had mapped the hills had figured an armed redoubt wherever they saw a little earth recently disturbed. The English, to lead us into a mistake, had on every small elevation traced works of which most had not yet got beyond the stage of planning. But even if they had been completed it seemed to us that the ground was sufficiently irregular to conceal the movements of a portion of our army, and that by employing one corps to make a feint on the front while the other two pushed real attacks on the weakest points of this long line, they would find the English troops too widely scattered, or at any rate with their reserves at a considerable distance from the points attacked.

The age of Louis XIV. was a period when great use was made of lines, and history shows that the greater part of those which were attacked were carried for want of the power of mutual support among the defenders. We thought that at some point of their vast extent it would be easy to pierce the English lines, and an opening once made, the enemy's troops who would be in some cases a day's journey from the opening would recognize that they had not time to come up, except in very inferior strength, and would retire, not to Lisbon, whence vessels cannot get out in all winds, but to Cascaes, where their military fleet and transports were assembled. Their retreat would have been very difficult, and might perhaps have become a rout. In any case their embarkation in presence of our army would have been a second edition of Sir John Moore's at Corunna. We have since seen English officers, among others General Hill, admit that if the French had attacked within the first ten days after their arrival they would have easily penetrated together with the confused multitude of peasants in the midst of whom the English armies could never have disentangled themselves nor made any regular dispositions for defence.

When my comrade and I reported in this sense to Masséna, the old soldier's eyes sparkled with martial ardour, and he at once issued marching orders to prepare for the attack which he reckoned on making the next day. However, on receiving the orders, his four lieutenants hastened to his quarters and a stormy discussion took place. Junot, who had commanded in Lisbon, and knew it well, declared that it seemed impossible to him to maintain so large a town, and expressed himself strongly for the attack. General Montbrun shared his opinion; but Ney and Reynier hotly opposed it adding that the loss at Busaco, together with that of the wounded who had been abandoned at Coimbra, and the numerous sick who had been for the moment disabled by the rains, had so largely diminished the number of combatants that it was not possible to attack a strong position, and further, that the men were demoralized—an inaccurate statement, for the troops were showing great ardour in demanding to march upon Lisbon. Losing his patience, Masséna repeated vivâ voce orders he had already given in writing, and Ney declared in so many words that he would not carry them out. The commander-in-chief was minded then to remove Ney from the command of the 6th corps, as some months later he was obliged to do. But he considered that Ney was beloved by his men, whom he had commanded for seven years; that his removal would involve that of Reynier which would complete the discord in the army at a moment when unanimity was so eminently needed. The energetic advice of Sainte-Croix was no longer at hand to sustain him, and Masséna quailed before the disobedience of his two chief lieutenants. They could not indeed decide him to leave Portugal, but they extorted from him a promise to move away from the enemy's lines, and to retire ten leagues back behind Santarem and Rio Mayor and there await fresh orders from the Emperor. I saw with regret this little retreat, which seemed to me to auger one more general and definitive, nor, as you will soon see, did my presentiment deceive me. I turned my back therefore with sorrow on the hills of Cintra, fully persuaded that if we had profited by the confusion into which the fugitives had thrown the English camp we might have forced the unfinished lines. But what was then easy was no longer so a fortnight later. Compelled to feed the vast population, which at his bidding had streamed in upon Lisbon, Wellington used the arms of 40,000 stout peasants by making them work at the completion of the fortifications with which he proposed to cover Lisbon, and thus the place became of immense strength.

Chapter 29
Steeplechasers & Deserters

During our stay at Sobral I saw another artifice employed by the English, and one of sufficient importance to be worth noting. It is often said that thoroughbred horses are of no use in war, because their price is so high and they require so much care that it would be almost impossible to provide a squadron, much more a regiment, with them. Nor indeed do the English use them on campaign; but they have a habit of sending single officers, mounted on fast thoroughbreds, to watch the movements of a hostile army. These officers get within the enemy's cantonments, cross his line of march, keep for days on the flanks of his columns, always just out of range, till they can form a clear idea of his number and the direction of his march. After our entry into Portugal, we frequently saw observers of this kind flitting round us. It was vain to give chase to them, even with the best-mounted horsemen. The moment the English officer saw any such approach he would set spurs to his steed, and nimbly clearing ditches, hedges, even brooks, he would make off at such speed that our men soon lost sight of him, and perhaps saw him soon after a league further on, note-book in hand, at the top of some hillock, continuing his observations. This practice, which I never saw anyone employ like the English, and which I tried to imitate during the Russian campaign, might perhaps have saved Napoleon at Waterloo by affording him a warning of the arrival of the Prussians. Anyhow, these English 'runners,' who were the despair of the French general from the moment we left Spain, increased in boldness and cunning as soon as we were in front of Sobral. One could see them come out of the lines and race with the sped of stags through the vines and over the rocks to inspect the positions occupied by our troops.

One day, however, when there had been a little skirmish of outposts, in which we had remained in possession of the ground, a light-infantryman, who had for some time had his eye on the best mounted and boldest of the enemy's 'runners,' and knew his ways, shammed dead, quite sure that as soon as his company was out of the way the Englishman would come back to look at the little battlefield. He did come and was unpleasantly surprised to see the supposed dead man jump up, kill his horse with a musket-shot, and then charge him with the bayonet, summoning him to surrender, which he had no choice but to do. The prisoner, on being presented to Masséna by his captor, turned out to be a member of the highest English nobility, a Percy, descended from one of the most illustrious Norman chiefs, to whom William the Conqueror gave the Duchy of Northumberland, which his offspring still hold. Sir Percy was honourably received by the French commander and taken to Sobral. Being curious to mount the clock tower, in order to observe how our army was posted, he was allowed to do so; and from this lofty point, telescope in hand, he witnessed an amusing sight, at which, in spite of his own bad luck, he could not help laughing: the capture of another English officer. This gentleman, having returned from India after twenty years' absence, and hearing in London that his brother was serving in Portugal, had sailed for Lisbon, and hurried up on foot to the front to greet his brother, whose regiment was on duty. It was a lovely day, and the new comer diverted himself by admiring the beautiful country and studying the fortifications and the troops which occupied them. So intent was he on this, that he walked past the outposts without knowing it, and was between the two armies. Just then he caught sight of some fine figs, and not having tasted European fruit for a long time, took a fancy to climb the tree. While he was quietly regaling himself, the soldiers of a neighbouring French picket, surprised to see a red coat among the branches, came up, and seeing what it was, captured the English officer, amid the laughter of all those who witnessed the incident from afar. This Englishman, however, better advised than Mr. Percy, begged his captors to keep him on the outskirts of the French army hoping, that if he saw nothing of its internal arrangements he might be exchanged. His foresight proved successful; for Masséna, having no fear of his being able to give any information as to the disposition of our troops, sent him back on parole, begging Lord Wellington to exchange against him Captain Letermillier, who had been taken at Coimbra, and afterwards became one of our best colonels. Mr. Percy, who had laughed much at his comrade, on learning that he had been exchanged, requested the same favour; but this was refused, as he had seen too much, and might report it. The unlucky young man followed the French army as a prisoner, and shared its sufferings for six months. On our return to Spain he was transferred to France, where he passed several years.

Unable to obtain any backing from his lieutenants in his proposed attack on the lines, and being short of provisions, Masséna was compelled, on November 14, to retire ten leagues back from the hills and establish his army in a corn-growing district, where positions could be found suitable for defence. He selected the country between the Rio Mayor, the Tagus, and the Zezere, establishing the 2nd corps at Santarem, the 8th at Torres Novas (where also he fixed his headquarters), the 6th at Thomar, the artillery park at Tancos, while the cavalry were at Ourem with their outposts pushed as far as Leiria. Inferring from this movement that the French were in full retreat for Spain, the English followed, but cautiously and at a distance, fearing a trick to draw them out of their lines. When they found that we were halted behind the Rio Mayor they gave us some trouble, but were vigorously met, and judging that want of provisions would soon drive us to leave this district, well adapted for the defensive, they contented themselves with watching us. Lord Wellington's headquarters were fixed at Cartaxo, opposite Santarem, from November 1810 till March 1811 the armies faced each other, separated only by the Rio Mayor. The English, having their food supplies brought by the Tagus from Lisbon, lived in comfort; but the provisioning of our army, having no stores, and being in a contracted space, was a serious problem. Our troops, however, worked with admirable patience and industry, each contributing, like bees in a hive, his share to the common welfare. Workshops were started in every battalion; and each regiment, organising a system of raids on a large scale, sent out detachments, armed and well led who returned driving thousands of donkeys laden with provisions of all kinds, and immense herds of sheep, pigs, and goats, the booty being proportionately divided on its arrival. As the nearer districts became exhausted, the raids had to be pushed further afield, even to the gates of Abrantes and

Coimbra; and the attacks of the infuriated peasantry, though always beaten off, caused some loss. Besides these, the foraging parties had a new form of enemy to contend with, resembling in its organization the robber bands of the middle ages.

A French sergeant, wearied of the misery in which the army was living, resolved to decamp and live in comfort. To this end he persuaded about a hundred of the worst characters in the army, and going with them to the rear, took up his quarters in a vast convent, deserted by the monks, but still full of furniture and provisions. He increased his store largely by carrying off everything in the neighbourhood that suited him; well-furnished spits and stewpans were always at the fire, and each man helped himself as he would; and the leader received the expressive if contemptuous name of 'Marshal Stockpot.' The scoundrel had also carried off numbers of women; and being joined before long by the scum of the three armies, attracted by the prospect of unrestrained debauchery, he formed a band of some three hundred British, French, and Portuguese deserters, who lived as a happy family in one unbroken orgy. This brigandage had been going on for some months, when one day, a foraging detachment having gone off in pursuit of a flock as far as the convent which sheltered the so-called 'Marshal Stockpot,' our soldiers were much surprised to see him coming to meet them at the head of the bandits, with orders to respect his grounds and restore the flock which they had just taken there. On the refusal of our officers to comply with this demand, he ordered his men to fire on the detachment. The greater part of the French deserters did not venture to fire on their compatriots and former comrades, but the English and Portuguese obeyed and our people had several men killed or wounded. Not being in sufficient numbers to resist, they were compelled to retreat, accompanied by all the French deserters, who came back with them to offer their submission. Masséna pardoned them on condition that they should march at the head of the three battalions who were told off to attack the convent. That den having been carried after a brief resistance, Masséna had 'Marshal Stockpot' shot, as well as the few French who had remained with him. A good many English and Portuguese shared their fate, the rest were sent off to Wellington, who did prompt justice on them.

Early in November, Masséna had sent General Foy to report his position to the Emperor: three battalions being required to escort him in safety to the Spanish frontier. Meanwhile, not knowing when the expected reinforcements might arrive he feared that the English army might cross the Rio Mayor, and make an unexpected attack on our divisions at a time when every regiment had detached at least a third of its men to search for provisions. If the enemy had arrived in the middle of our cantonments while so many soldiers were away, a catastrophe would certainly have followed; and the dispersed troops would have been liable to be beaten in detail before they could reassemble. Luckily for us, however, Lord Wellington based all his plans on lapse of time, and did not venture upon any enterprise.

Meanwhile the Emperor, whose only news of Masséna's army had so far been obtained from the London newspapers, having at length received the despatches brought by Genera Foy, ordered the Count of Erlon, commanding the 9th corps,' cantoned near Salamanca, to march upon Portugal, and to send Gardanne's brigade forward at once with instructions to find the French army, and take it the ammunition and the draught horses of which it presumably stood in need. With all the Emperor's perspicacity it was impossible for him at Paris to judge of the numerous difficulties which would hamper Gardanne in carrying out his orders. Napoleon could never believe that the flight of Portuguese occupants at the approach of a French corps had been so universal that it was impossible to come across an inhabitant from whom one could receive the slightest information. This, however, was what befell Gardanne. A former page of Louis XVI., whom the Emperor had made governor to his pages, he was lacking in initiative, and only did well under the direction of an able general. Now he completely lost his bearings. Not knowing where to find Masséna's army, he wandered in all directions, and when he at length reached Cardigos, a day's march, as his maps showed, from the Zezere, he did not realise that in war a flying column in search of a friendly force should always steer itself by rivers, forests, large towns, and mountain chains, for if the troops whom he has to reach are anywhere near, they will certainly have pickets at these important points. It is hard to understand why Gardanne forgot this rule of the craft, but he actually lost a good many men by a precipitate retreat without having seen the enemy. If he had but pushed on three leagues to the Zezere he would have seen our outposts, as it was he returned to Spain taking back reinforcements, ammunition, and horses.

Masséna began to fear lest provisions might run short on the right bank of the Tagus, and resolved to tap a new country by throwing a portion of his army across the river into the fertile province of the Alemtejo. To this end he ordered a division to cross the Zezere and occupy Punhete, a small town at the point where that river flows into the Tagus. This seemed a good point to establish a bridge, but materials were lacking. Everything was, however, supplied by the zeal and activity of General Eblé, well supported by his subordinate artillery officers. Forges and saw-mills were built; tools, planks, beams, anchors and ropes manufactured, numerous boats were constructed, and the work progressing as it were by magic, we conceived the hope of being able to cast a solid bridge over the Tagus. Lord Wellington prepared to oppose the crossing of the river, bringing troops up from Lisbon to form a camp on the left bank opposite Punhete: whence we augured that before we could establish ourselves on the further side of the great river we should have to sustain a hot engagement. All this while the French army was occupying the positions which it had taken up in November. Several English divisions were encamped on the right bank of the Rio Mayor, Lord Wellington's headquarters being at Cartaxo. There died the celebrated General La Romana.

The weather was fearful; the roads had become torrents, and the difficulty of seeking provisions, and especially forage, was much increased. Yet our French gaiety did not desert us. In every camp societies were got up for theatricals, and the houses deserted by the inhabitants supplied us with plenty of costumes in the wardrobes which the Portuguese ladies had left behind. We found also plenty of French books; our quarters were comfortable, and we continued to pass the winter pretty well. Our reflections were, however, often sad, both as to the situation of the army, and our own position. For three months we had had no news from our families, from France, even from Spain. Would the Emperor send us reinforcements sufficient to take Lisbon, or should we be compelled to retreat before the English? Our minds were full of these thoughts, when on December 27 it was suddenly reported that General Drouet, Count of Erlon, had just joined the army with the 9th corps, 25,000 to 30,000 strong. But our satisfaction was much reduced on finding that the Count of Erlon's army had never contained more than 12,000 men: half of whom he had left on the Spanish frontier under General Claparède, bringing with him only Cornoux's division, 6,000 strong, a reinforcement quite inadequate to meet the English and take Lisbon. Instead of going at once to the commander-in-chief at Torres Novas, the Count of Erlon stopped ten leagues short of it at Thomar, Ney's headquarters. This was a great blow to Masséna, and he sent me to the commander of the 9th corps to ask for an explanation of a course as much opposed to politeness as to military regulations. When he gave me this commission he had no doubt that the Count of Erlon had been placed by the Emperor under his orders, but there he was wrong. The instructions given by the chief of the staff to the commander of the 9th corps were only to enter Portugal, find Masséna's army, hand over to him some hundreds of draught horses with ammunition, and then to return to Spain with his troops. It is hard to understand how, after the reports which the Emperor had received from Foy and Casabianca as to the bad plight of the army, he could have limited himself to sending such weak support.

I found that the Count of Erlon had been lodging with Ney twenty-four hours. The marshal, who was anxious to get away from Portugal, had detained his guest in order that the influence of the commander-in-chief might not induce him to put their 6,000 men at his disposal, and thus enable him to resist the proposal to retreat. The Count was therefore making ready to depart next day, without visiting Masséna; to whom he begged me to make his excuses on the plea that important business called him back to the frontier.

An aide-de-camp's duties are pretty difficult, since in performing them he often has to convey instructions to his superiors which may wound their self-esteem. Sometimes in the interests of the service he has on his own responsibility to act as interpreter of his general's wishes by giving in his name orders which he has not dictated. This is a serious—even a dangerous matter; but the tact of the aide-de-camp must enable him to judge of the circumstances. My position was as delicate as it well could be, for Masséna, not having foreseen that the commander of the 9th corps might wish to leave Portugal, had put nothing in writing on the subject. Still, if he did take away his troops the operations of the army would be paralyzed, and the commander-in-chief would blame the caution which had made me shrink from speaking in his name. I took, therefore, a bold resolve; and although I had never met the Count of Erlon (Ney being present the while, and strongly opposing my arguments), I took the liberty of saying that at least he ought to give Marshal Masséna time to consider the orders which he had brought from the chief of the staff, as well as time to reply to them. Finally, when the count had repeated that he could not wait, I struck my great stroke by saying: 'Since your Excellency forces me to fulfil my errand to the last word, I have to inform you that Marshal Masséna, Commander-in-Chief of the French forces in Portugal, has directed me to convey to you both in his own name and that of the Emperor, a formal order not to move your troops, but to report yourself to him to-day at Torres Novas.' The count made no reply but ordered his horses. While they were being got ready, I wrote to Masséna telling him what I had been obliged to do in his name; and I learnt later on that he approved. The Count of Erlon was a gentle and reasonable man. As soon as he had left Ney's camp he admitted that it would not have been proper for him to leave the Army of Portugal without calling on the commander-in-chief; and all the way from Thomar to Torres Novas he treated me with much kindness, in spite of the vigour with which I had thought myself bound to appeal to him. No doubt his interview with Masséna finally convinced him, for he agreed to remain in Portugal and his troops were sent into quarters at Leyria. Masséna's gratitude for the firmness and readiness which I had shown was increased a few days later when he learnt that Lord Wellington had formed a plan of attacking our camp, and had been checked by the arrival of the Count of Erlon; while, if the reinforcement had been withdrawn, the English would have marched on us, and profited by our extended line to crush us with superior numbers.

Chapter 30
My Cavalry Duel With the English

We began the year 1811 at Torres Novas, and its early days were marked by an event which saddened all the staff, the death of our comrade d'Aguesseau. This excellent young man, the heir of an illustrious name and possessor of a large fortune, had been drawn by the desire of acquiring fame into the career of arms which might have been supposed to be closed to him by his delicate health. He had borne the fatigues of the Austrian campaign pretty well, but those which we had to undergo in Portugal were beyond his powers, and he died in the prime of life. We erected a monument to him in the principal church of Torres Novas.

Colonel Casabianca, whom Masséna had sent with despatches to the Emperor, had returned with the Count of Erlon, bringing information that Marshal Soult, who was in command of a powerful army in Andalusia, had received orders to enter Portugal and join the commander-in-chief.

Disquieted by our preparations, and wishing to know in what condition our works were, Wellington employed a strong measure which he had often found successful. One very dark night an Englishman, dressed in officer's uniform, got into a small boat on the left bank a little above Punhete, landed in silence, passed through the French outposts, and at daybreak walked boldly towards our workshops examining everything at his ease as if he had belonged to the staff of our army. Our artillerymen and engineers coming to their work in the morning perceived the stranger, arrested him, and brought him to General Eblé, to whom this scoundrel impudently declared that he was an English officer, and that, in disgust at a piece of favouritism which had been committed to his injury, he had deserted in order to take service in our Irish legion. On being taken before the commander-in-chief he not only repeated his story, but offered to give detailed information as to the positions of the English troops, and point out the places where we might with most advantage cross the Tagus. You will hardly believe that Masséna and Pelet, much as they despised the fellow, put faith in his tale, and wishing to profit by his advice, spent whole days over the maps with him, taking notes of what he said. We of the staff were not so much taken in, for nothing could persuade us that an English officer would have deserted, and we declared plainly that in our opinion the pretended captain was nothing but a clever spy sent by Wellington; but nothing that we could say shook Masséna's and Pelet's belief. Yet our conjectures were well founded, as it was soon proved, when General Junot came to headquarters, and his aide-de-camp recognized the so-called English officer as having acted the deserter once before in 1808, when the French army was occupying Lisbon. Junot also remembered him perfectly, although he was now wearing an infantry uniform instead of the hussar uniform which he wore at Lisbon, and advised Masséna to shoot him. But the stranger protested that he had never served in the cavalry, and to prove his identity showed a captain's commission with which Wellington had probably supplied him in order to enable him to pass for what he professed to be. Masséna therefore did not like to order his arrest, but his suspicions were aroused, and he ordered the commanding gendarme to have him closely watched. The spy got an inkling of this, and the following night got down very cleverly from a third-floor window and reached the neighbourhood of Tancos, whence he probably swam across the Tagus, for some of his clothes were found on the bank. Thus it was clearly shown that he was an agent of the English general, and that Masséna had been tricked. His wrath fell upon Pelet, and rose to fury when he discovered that the sham deserter, who had been so imprudently admitted into his study, had walked off with a small note-book in which the effective strength of each regiment was entered. Later on we learnt that this clever scamp was no officer in the English army, but a captain of Dover smugglers, who, to abundant resource and audacity, added the power of speaking several languages and of wearing every kind of disguise.

Meanwhile time passed and brought no change in our position, for although the Emperor had thrice bidden him to reinforce Masséna, Soult, imitating the attitude of Marshal Victor towards himself in 1809, had stopped on the way about the end of January to besiege Badajos. We could hear the firing distinctly, and Masséna regretted much that his colleague should be wasting precious time on a siege instead of marching towards him just when we were about to be compelled by scarcity of provisions to abandon Portugal. Even after the capture of Badajos, the Emperor blamed Marshal Soult's disobedience and said, 'He captured me a town, and lost me a kingdom.'

On February 5 Foy rejoined the army, bringing up a reinforcement of 2,000 men. He came from Paris, where he had held long conferences with the Emperor, and announced afresh that Soult was soon coming to join us. But as the whole of February went by and he did not appear, the Count of Erlon, whom by an inexplicable blunder the Emperor had not placed under Masséna's orders, declared that his troops could not live any longer at Leyria, and that he was going to march back to Spain. Marshal Ney and General Reynier seized this opportunity to set forth again the misery of their cause in a country which was completely ruined, and the commander-in-chief was obliged at last, after several months of obstinate resistance, to consent to a retreat towards the frontier, hoping to find there the means of supporting his army without entirely abandoning Portugal, and to invade again as soon as the reinforcements arrived. Our retreat began on March 6th. General Eblé had with much regret employed the previous days in destroying the barges which he had taken so much trouble to build, but in the hope that part of his preparations might one day be of use to a French army he had all the iron-work secretly buried in the presence of twelve artillery officers, and drew up a report which must be in the Ministry of War, showing the place where this precious depository is to be found. Its position will probably remain unknown for many centuries. The preparations were kept so secret and executed during the night of March 5 in such good order, that the English, whose outposts were only separated from ours by the little stream of the Rio Mayor, did not discover our movement till the morning of the next day, by which time General Reynier's troops were five leagues away. Lord Wellington, in his uncertainty whether the object of our movement was to cross the Tagus at Punhete or really to retire towards Spain, lost twelve hours in hesitation; and by the time he resolved to follow, which he did without energy and at some distance, the French army had gained a march upon him. Meanwhile, General Junot, having gone prancing imprudently in front of the English hussars, was struck on the nose by a bullet; but the wound did not hinder him from retaining the command of the 8th corps during the rest of the campaign. The army moved in several columns on Pombal, Marshal Ney with the 6th corps forming the rear-guard, and valiantly defending his ground foot by foot. As for Masséna, roused at length from his torpor, he gained between the 5th and 9th of March three days on the enemy, and completely organized his retreat—one of the most difficult operations of war. Contrary to his usual custom, also, he was so cheerful as to surprise us all.

The French army, continuing its retreat with regularity and in compact order, was leaving Pombal when the rear-guard was briskly attacked by the advanced guard of the enemy. Marshal Ney drove them back; and in order to bar their passage completely and save our baggage wagons, he set fire to the Town. The English historians have cried out against this as a cruel action—as if a general's first consideration should not be the safety of his army. Pombal and its neighbourhood forming a long and narrow defile through which the enemy must pass, the best way to stop them was to burn the town. It was an extreme measure, but one which in similar cases the most civilised nations have been compelled to take, and the English themselves have often acted in the same manner.

On March 12 there was a smart engagement before Redinha. Marshal Ney having found a defensible position, decided to halt there, and Lord Wellington, taking this as a challenge, sent forward a strong body. After a hot action Ney repulsed the enemy, and continued his retreat briskly, but with the loss of two or three hundred men. The enemy lost more than a thousand, our artillery having played on his masses for some time, while he had only two light guns in position. This engagement was of as little use to the English as to us. Why should Wellington, knowing that Ney had orders to retire, and that the French were in declared retreat be in such a hurry to attack merely in order to make Ney resume his march a little sooner than he would otherwise have done? I was present at this affair, and deplored the false pride of the two generals which cost so many brave men their lives with no result.

The main French army took up a position between Condeixa and Cardaxo. The critical moment of our retreat had arrived. Masséna, not wishing to leave Portugal, had resolved to cross the Mondego at Coimbra, and await orders and reinforcements from the Emperor in the fertile district between that town and Oporto; but Trant had cut the bridge of Coimbra, and the Mondego was so much swollen as to be unfordable. The only course open was, therefore, to reach Fuente de Murcelha, and there cross the rapid torrent of the Alva. Accordingly, on the 13th the headquarters started in that direction. We ought to have reached Miranda de Corvo the same day; but for some unknown reason the marshal established himself at Fuente-Cuberta, where, believing himself covered by the divisions which he had ordered Ney to post at Cardaxo and Condeixa, he had with him only a guard of thirty grenadiers and twenty-five dragoons. But Ney, under plea of an attack by superior forces, had abandoned these points; giving notice to Masséna so late that he did not get the letter till some hours after the execution of the movement, and might have been captured with all his staff. In fact, believing that he was under the safeguard of several French divisions, and finding the place agreeable and the weather fine, he had ordered his dinner to be served in the open air. We were sitting quietly at table under the trees near the entrance of the village, when suddenly there appeared a detachment of fifty English hussars, less than a hundred yards away. The grenadiers surrounded Masséna while the aides-de-camp and the dragoons mounted and rode towards the enemy. As they fled at once, we supposed they were some stragglers, seeking to rejoin their army; but we soon saw an entire regiment, and perceived that the neighbouring hillsides were covered with English troops who had almost completely surrounded Fuente-Cuberta. The imminent danger in which the headquarters were placed was due to a mistake on the part of Ney. Thinking that the commander-in-chief had had his letter, he ordered all his divisions to evacuate Cardaxo and Condeixa, thus uncovering Fuente-Cuberta. The enemy had come up in silence, and you may judge of our astonishment; but luckily night was at hand, and a thick fog rising. The English never dreaming that the French commander would be thus separated from his army, took our group for a rear-guard, which they did not venture to attack;

but it is certain that if the hussars had made a resolute charge, they would have carried off Masséna and all who were with him. Naturally when the English heard of Masséna's narrow escape they made the most of it; and Napier avers that he only escaped their hussars by taking the feathers out of his hat. Unfortunately for this story, marshals did not wear plumes.

That evening the headquarters left Fuente-Cuberta very quietly, though several regiments of the enemy were close by; one posted on some rising ground which our road crossed. To get it out of the way, the marshal employed an artifice of which the enemy, to whom French was familiar often made use against us. Knowing that my brother spoke English well, he gave him instructions; and Adolphe, advancing towards the foot of the hill and keeping in shadow, called out to the commanding officer that Lord Wellington ordered him to bear to the right, and take up a position which he indicated, in another direction than that which we were following. The colonel, unable to see my brother's uniform, took him for an English aide-de-camp, and obeyed. When he was out of the way, we passed on quickly, glad to escape a new danger, and joined the 6th corps before daylight.

During this long and toilsome march, Masséna's attention was much occupied with the danger to which Mme N—— was exposed. Several times her horse fell over fragments of rock invisible in the darkness, but although cruelly bruised, the brave woman picked herself up. After several of these falls, however, she could neither remount her horse nor walk on foot and had to be carried by grenadiers. What would have happened to her if we had been attacked, I do not know. The marshal, imploring us all the time not to abandon her, said repeatedly: 'What a mistake I made in bringing a woman to the war!' However, we got out of the critical situation into which Ney had brought us.

On the following day, March 14, after beating back a smart attack upon his rear-guard, Masséna posted the mass of his troops in a strong position in front of Miranda de Corvo, in order to give the artillery and baggage wagons time to pass the defile beyond the town. Seeing the French army halted, Lord Wellington brought up a strong force, and everything promised a serious engagement when Masséna summoned his lieutenants to receive his instructions. All but Ney came at once, and as he did not arrive the commander-in-chief ordered Major Pelet and me to go and ask him to come quickly. This errand, which seemed an easy one to discharge, nearly cost me my life.

The French army was drawn up on ground descending gently in the form of an amphitheatre towards a large crook lying between two broad hills, over the summits of which passed country roads, leading to Miranda. At the moment when Pelet and I galloped off to execute the marshals order, the English skirmishers appeared in the distance, coming up to attack the two hills. In order to be more certain of finding Marshal Ney, my companion and I separated. Pelet took the road on the left, I that on the right, passing through a wide clearing, in which were our outposts. Hearing that Marshal Ney had passed by, less than a quarter of an hour before, I felt bound to hasten to meet him, and just as I hoped to come up with him, I heard several shots, and bullets whistled past my ears. I was no great distance from the enemy's skirmishers, posted in the woods surrounding the clearing. Although I knew that Marshal Ney had a strong escort, I was uneasy on his account, fearing that the English might have cut him off, until I saw him on the other side of the brook. Pelet was with him, and both were going in the direction of Masséna. So, being sure that the orders had been conveyed, I was about to return, when a young English light infantry officer trotted up on his pony, crying, 'Stop, Mr. Frenchman; I should like to have a little fight with you!' I saw no need to reply to this bluster, and was making my way towards our outposts, 500 yards in arrear, while the Englishman followed me, heaping insults on me. At first I took no notice, but presently he called out, 'I can see by your uniform that you are on the staff of a marshal, and I will put in the London papers that the sight of me was enough to frighten away one of Masséna's or Ney's cowardly aides-de-camp!' I admit that it was a serious error on my part, but I could no longer endure this impudent challenge coolly, so, drawing my sword, I dashed furiously at my adversary. But just as I was about to meet him, I heard a rustling in the wood, and out came two English hussars, galloping to cut off my retreat. I was caught in a trap, and understood that only a most energetic defence could save me from the disgrace of being taken prisoner, through my own fault, in sight of the whole French army, which was witness to this unequal combat. So I flew upon the English officer; we met; he gave me a slash across the face, I ran my sword into his throat. His blood spurted over me, and the wretch fell from his horse to the ground, which he bit in his rage. Meanwhile, the two hussars were hitting me all over, chiefly on the head. In a few seconds my shako, my sabretache, and my pelisse were in strips, though I was not myself wounded by any of their blows. At length, however, the elder of the two hussars, a grizzled old soldier, let me have more than an inch of his point in my right side. I replied with a vigorous backhander; my blade struck his teeth and passed between his jaws, as he was in the act of shouting, slitting his mouth to the ears. He made off promptly, to my lively satisfaction for he was by far the braver and more energetic of the two. When the younger man found himself left alone with me, he hesitated for a moment, because as our horses' heads were touching, he saw that to turn his back to me was to expose himself to be hit. However, on seeing several soldiers coming to my aid, he made up his mind, but he did not escape the dreaded wound, for in my anger I pursued him for some paces and gave him a thrust in the shoulder, which quickened his speed. During this fight, which lasted less time than it has taken to tell it, our scouts had come up quickly to set me free, and on the other side the English soldiers had marched towards the place where their officer had fallen. The two groups were firing at each other, and I was very near getting in the way of the bullets from both sides. But my brother and Ligniville, who had seen me engaged with the English officer and his two men, had hastened up to me, and I was badly in want of their help, for I was losing so much blood from the wound in my side that was growing faint, and I could not have stayed on my horse if they had not held me up. As soon as I rejoined the staff, Masséna said, taking my hand, 'Well done; rather too well done! A field officer has no business to expose himself in fighting at the outposts.' He was quite right but when I told him the motives which had led me on, he blamed me less, and the more fiery Ney, remembering his own hussar days, cried, 'Upon my word, in Marbot's place I should have done the same!' All the generals and my comrades came to express their concern, while Dr. Brisset was attending to me. The wound in my cheek was not important; in a month's time it had healed over, and you can scarcely see the mark of it along my left whisker. But the thrust in my right side was dangerous, especially in the middle of a long retreat, in which I was compelled to travel on horseback, without being able to get the rest which a wounded man needs. Such, my children, was the result of my fight, or, if you like, my prank at Miranda de Corvo. You have still got the shako which I wore, and the numerous notches with which the English sabres have adorned it prove that the two hussars did not let me off. I brought away my sabretache also, the sling of which was cut in three places, but it has been mislaid. As I said, at the moment when I was sent in search of Ney, the French army was drawn up in its position, commanding Miranda de Corvo, expecting an attack. However, Wellington, deterred no doubt by his losses on the previous days, checked the march of his troops, and Masséna, seeing this determined under cover of the approaching night to pass through the town and long defile of Miranda. I was in a painful position, having been on the march for two days and a night, and now severely wounded and weakened by loss of blood, being obliged to pass another night on horseback. The roads were fearfully crowded with baggage and artillery wagons and numerous columns of troops, against which I was always running in the pitchy darkness. To crown our disasters, we came in for a heavy storm. I was soon wet through, and sat shivering on my horse, for I knew that if I got off the warm myself, I should not have the strength to mount again. Meanwhile my wound caused me acute pain; so you may judge how I suffered during the cruel night.

On the morning of the 15th the army reached the banks of the Ceira, opposite Foz de Arunce, a small town on a hill commanding the river and the level ground on the left bank. Cross the bridge, I settled myself for a moment in a house, hoping to get a little rest; but the terrible scene which was passing before my eyes prevented this. Reynier's and Junot's corps were already in Foz de Arunce, Ney's still on the other side of the river; but the commander-in-chief, knowing that the enemy was close upon us, and not wishing his rear-guard to fight with the Ceira in its rear, ordered Ney to bring all his troops across, cut the bridge, and strongly guard the neighbouring ford, so that the men might rest undisturbed. Ney, however, supposing that the enemy, tired by the labours of the two last days, were still at a distance, and deeming it pusillanimous to abandon the left bank wholly, left on that side two divisions of infantry, Lamotte's brigade of cavalry, and several guns, and did not cut the bridge; a fresh piece of disobedience which went near to cost us dear. As it happened, while Masséna was gone off to Ponte Murcelha to superintend the restoration of another bridge which was to secure the passage of the river Alva on the next day, and Ney, full of confidence, had just given General Lamotte leave to cross the Ceira by the ford, in order to forage on the right bank, Lord Wellington suddenly appeared, and instantly attacked the divisions left so imprudently on the hither bank. Ney himself, at the head of the 39th, bravely repulsed with the bayonet a charge of English dragoons, but their colonel, Lamour, having been killed by a bullet, the 39th, losing their heads, flung themselves back on the 59th and carried them away. At the same moment, one of our batteries inadvertently sent a shot in their direction, and our men, thinking they were surrounded, fled in a panic to the bridge. Lamotte, who could see all this from the other bank, tried to bring his cavalry across in support; but instead of coming by the difficult ford where he had gone over, he took the shortest way, and so blocked the bridge with his brigade just as the fugitives came up from the opposite direction. No one could pass, and a good many men, seeing the bridge thus blocked, made for the ford and threw themselves in. Most got over, but several missed their footing and were drowned. Meanwhile Ney, exhausting every effort to repair his mistake, succeeded at length in collecting a battalion of the 27th, and making his way to the divisions of Mermet and Ferey, who were holding their ground manfully, put himself at their head, and attacking on his side drove the English back to their camp. Astounded at this vigorous attack, and hearing the shouts of our men who were struggling to cross the Ceira, they imagined that the whole French army was upon them. Panic-stricken in their turn they flung down their arms, left their guns, and took to head long flight. We on the right bank then witnessed a sight unusual in war: two sides flying each from the other in complete disorder! Finally the panic on both sides was checked, and English and French returned to the abandoned ground to pick up their muskets; but both sides were so much ashamed of themselves that though they were quite close to each other not a shot was fired nor any challenges exchanged, and they retired to their positions in silence. Wellington did not even venture to oppose Ney's retreat; and he recrossed the river and cut the bridge. In this queer engagement the English had some 200 men disabled, and killed 50 of ours; but we lost 100 by drowning, and unhappily the 39th lost its eagle. The best divers failed to recover it at the time, but it was found by Portuguese peasants in the following summer, when part of the river bed was dry.

Ney visited on General Lamotte his wrath for the check he had received, and withdrew from him the command of his brigade. Lamotte was, however, a good and brave officer, and in after times the Emperor did him justice. Next, eager to have his revenge, he waited on the banks of the Ceira throughout part of the 16th in the hope of attacking Wellington when his turn came to cross, and Masséna had to send four or five aides-de-camp before he could induce him to follow the retreat. On the 17th, we crossed the Alva at Porte Murcelha, and marched for five days, reaching Celorico unmolested.

The valley between the Mondego and the Estrella is exceedingly fertile, and we lived in comfort. Thus, on finding ourselves again at Celorico, whence Masséna had had the unlucky idea of turning aside from this fertile region on our outward march, and taking to the mountain district of Busaco, the army blamed him afresh, feeling that his mistake had cost many thousands of lives, and brought the campaign to failure. The marshal now—unable to make up his mind to re-enter Spain—resolved to hold his ground at any cost in Portugal. His plan was to regain the Tagus by way of Guarda and Alfayates, and having rebuilt the bridge of Alcantara, to join the French troops under Soult before Badajos, with them to enter the Alemtejo, and at once march upon Lisbon. He hoped thus to force Wellington to march back at once for the defence of the capital, which, being unfortified on the left bank of the Tagus, would have very little means of resistance. To relieve the march, the marshal sent all sick and wounded into Spain, but I declined to go with them, preferring to remain with my brother and my comrades. Masséna having communicated his plan to his lieutenants at Celorico, Marshal Ney, who was burning with desire to recover his independence, opposed the idea of a new campaign, declaring that he was going to take his troops back to Spain because they could no longer get any bread in Portugal. This was true, but the army had been accustomed to live without bread for the last six months, each soldier receiving several pounds of meat and plenty of wine. This fresh disobedience on Ney's part roused Masséna's wrath, and he replied by a general order, removing Marshal Ney from the command of the 6th corps. This act of vigour, just and necessary as it was, had been too long delayed; he should have done it at the first sign of insubordination. Ney at first refused to go away, saying that as the Emperor had given him the command of the 6th corps he should not resign it but by his direction; but on the order being repeated, he returned to Spain, and thence went to Paris. The command of the 6th corps fell by right of seniority to General Loison. Ney's dismissal produced an impression upon the army which was all the stronger that the principal cause of it was known, and that, insisting on a return to Spain, he had expressed the general wish of the troops.

On the 24th, the army began to move back upon the Tagus, and occupied Guarda. Of all towns in the Peninsula, this is in the highest situation. Several men died from the cold, and my wound in the side became very painful. Here Masséna received several despatches from Berthier, nearly all two months old; which shows what a mistake Napoleon had made in thinking that from Paris he could direct the movements of an army in Portugal. These despatches reached the commander-in-chief in a manner which up to then had been unknown in the French army. Prince Berthier had entrusted them to his aide-de-camp, M. de Canouville, but that young officer, who was one of the beaux of the army, seeing the difficulty of reaching Masséna's army, was satisfied with depositing them at Cindad Rodrigo, and returned to Paris. Now Paris was the very place from which, on account of a notorious freak on his part, he was desired to keep away. The story is as follows: it carries us back to the time when General Bonaparte was commanding the Army of Italy, and several ladies of his family joined him at Milan. One of them married one of his most attached generals, and, as in the fashion of the time, she used, when riding, to wear a hussar pelisse over her habit, Bonaparte gave her one, handsomely furred and with diamond buttons. Some years afterwards, this lady, having lost her first husband, married a foreign prince. In the spring of 1811, the Emperor, when reviewing the guard in the Place du Carrousel, noticed among Berthier's staff Canouville, wearing the pelisse which he had formerly given to his kinswoman, the identity of which was established by the fur and the diamonds. Napoleon recognised them, and displayed much annoyance. The lady, it was said, was severely reprimanded, and one hour later the imprudent captain received an order to carry despatches to Masséna, who was enjoined in them to keep that officer with him for an unstated time. Canouville had his suspicions and, as I have just related, took advantage of the chance which prevented him from entering Portugal. But hardly had he got back to Paris, when he was packed off again to the Peninsula, where he arrived very much ashamed at his discomfiture. The conversation of this modern Lauzun amused us, as he gave us the latest news of what had been taking place in the Paris drawing-rooms during our absence, and we laughed much at the contrast between his elegant costume and the dilapidations of our uniforms after a year's campaigning. Canouville, who at first was much astonished by his rapid transition from Parisian boudoirs to a bivouac among the rocks of Portugal, soon resigned himself to the change. He was a man of good wit, and of courage, and in the following year fell bravely in the battle of the Moskowa.

Chapter 31
Fuentes d'Onoro

The despatches which Canouville had left at Ciudad Rodrigo reached Masséna, as I have said, at Guarda, just when he was making arrangements to hold the upper Tagus; and instead of going on at once with his movement, he wasted some days in replying to these letters of two months ago. This delay was injurious to us, for the enemy took advantage of it to bring up his troops, and attack us at Guarda. We repulsed him here, and so in the other partial combats which Masséna sustained while awaiting the officers whom he had sent to Alcantara. On learning from their report that it would be impossible to feed the army in a country devoid of resources, Masséna's will had at last to yield before accumulated obstacles, aggravated by the opposition of the generals and the destitution of the troops; and it was decided to return to Spain. Still, however, the commander-in-chief delayed, and Wellington profited by a false move on the part of Reynier to attack him at Sabugal. The fight was undecisive; but we lost two or three hundred more men in a glorious but useless engagement.

Next day, April 1, the army crossed the frontier and encamped on Spanish territory. It still included more than 45,000 effectives, and had sent more than 10,000 sick and wounded to Rodrigo and Salamanca. We had entered Portugal with 60,000 combatants, besides the division of the 9th corps which had joined us. During this long campaign, therefore, we had lost about 10,000 men killed, dead of illness, and prisoners.

The army took post round Almeida, Ciudad Rodrigo, and Dora. Masséna was thus in a most awkward position, for the two fortresses and the surrounding country were under the authority of Bessières, to whom the Emperor had entrusted the command of a new army, called the 'Northern,' entirely composed of troops belonging to the Young Guard. Hence arose a conflict of authority between the two marshals, Bessières wishing to keep all the supplies for his troops, while Masséna reasonably maintained that his army, which had endured so many hardships in Portugal, had a right to at least an equal share in the distribution of provisions. The Emperor, usually so farsighted, had not given any orders to meet the case of Masséna's army being forced to evacuate Spain. Great perplexity, therefore, prevailed on the frontier, especially as to the defence of Ciudad Rodrigo and Almeida. These two fortresses, though in different countries, are so near that it was unnecessary to hold both, and the Emperor had ordered the withdrawal of the garrison of Almeida and the destruction of the ramparts, already much shattered by the explosion of the previous year. But just when the governor, General Brénier, was taking steps for the destruction of the place, he had received a counter-order from the War Minister, so that Masséna, who meantime arrived from Portugal, could not decide anything. However, as the troops could not subsist in the sterile neighbourhood of Almeida, he was obliged to take them away, and abandon the place to its own resources. These consisted of a weak garrison victualled for twenty-five days. If positive orders had been received, a week during which the army was present would have sufficed to destroy the fortifications; but as soon as it was gone, the English hastened to invest the place, and next month an expedition had to be undertaken for its relief which cost many lives, and did not attain its object.

The order placing the Count of Erlon and his force under Masséna's command came at length, three months too late. After cantoning his army between Rodrigo, Zamora, and Salamanca, the marshal, on April 9, fixed his headquarters in the last-named town. While we were there an event occurred not very creditable to the English army. Colonel Waters, a member of Wellington's staff, had been taken prisoner by our troops; and as he gave his parole, Masséna allowed him to retain his sword and his horse, and to lodge each night in a private house. He thus travelled at liberty, in company with our columns, till one day when they were halted in the wood of Matilla, he seized the moment when all were reposing, and putting his excellent horse into a gallop, disappeared. Three days later he rejoined Wellington, who seemed to find the trick highly amusing. When Masséna complained that the Portuguese militia had been massacring French prisoners, and recently a colonel, the same Wellington replied, 'That he had to employ all his resources to repel a war of invasion, and could not answer for the excesses into which the peasants were led.'

Rest and good care at Salamanca soon cured me; but my satisfaction at this was alloyed by a vexatious incident which caused me much trouble. My good friend Ligniville left us in consequence of a serious difference with Masséna. The marshal had entrusted him the laborious duties of chief equerry, which he performed, I may say, quite voluntarily, and out of good-nature. Fond as he was of horses, he had much difficulty in feeding them in Spain and Portugal, but he made the best of it. It had been ascertained that in order to convey all the utensils and baggage of the headquarters, thirty mules were required, and Ligniville, before entering on the campaign, had proposed to obtain them; but Masséna, not wishing to bear the cost himself, had ordered the commissary-general to get them for him. He had these pack animals with him throughout. Now the Spaniards have a good habit of shaving their mules' backs, so that the hair may not work into lumps under the pack, and make them sore. The operation can only be done by experts, and is pretty costly. Masséna, therefore, proposed to Ligniville to make the Mayor of Salamanca pay the cost out of the local funds; but Ligniville refused to be a party to what he thought an exaction, and a scene ensued. Finally my friend told the marshal that as he showed so little gratitude for his condescension in acting as equerry he would not only vacate the post, but offer his resignation, and rejoin the 18th Dragoons, to which he belonged. In vain did Masséna try every means to make him stay; Ligniville, a calm but very determined man, was inflexible, and fixed the day for his departure. Major Pelet being away on service, I was doing the duty of senior aide-de-camp, and in that capacity I assembled all the staff officers, and proposed to them that we should show our esteem for our good comrade by riding with him a league from the town. My suggestion was accepted, and in order that Prosper Masséna should not seem to be finding fault with his father, we were careful to tell him off to remain in the ante-room while we escorted Ligniville. Our farewell was cordial, for we all liked him. Though our action was perfectly honourable, Masséna was angry at it, and accused me of instigating it; and from that time his grudge against me revived, though my behaviour during the campaign had restored his confidence and interest in me.

Meanwhile the garrison of Almeida, invested by the English, and almost out of provisions, was on the point of surrendering, and the Emperor, in order to deprive the English of this triumph, had ordered Masséna to march his whole forces to the place and blow up the ramparts. But this operation had, as I have said, now become a very delicate one, since a considerable force was blockading Almeida and we should have to fight a battle. There was another not less serious difficulty. Masséna's army, distributed through the province of Salamanca, was not exactly living in the arms of plenty. Still every cantonment could supply the small body quartered in it, while if we were to march on the English, we must concentrate our troops and provide supplies which we had no sufficient means of storing or transporting.

As governor of the province, Marshal Bessières could dispose of all its resources, but he reserved them for the regiments of the guard. He had plenty of cavalry and a formidable artillery, while Masséna, though his infantry was still respectable, was short of horses. He therefore asked Bessières to lend him some, and all the letters which he received from him abounded in the most encouraging protestations. As, however, they remained without result, and Almeida was known to be at the last gasp, Masséna no longer contented himself with writing to his colleague, whose headquarters were at Valladolid, but resolved to send an aide-de camp, who could explain the gravity of the position, and press him to send support. The commander-in-chief selected me to discharge this duty. Having been severely wounded on March 14, I was, five weeks later, not exactly in condition to ride post-haste over roads covered with guerrillas. In any other circumstances I should have remarked as much to the marshal, but as he was cross with me, and as I had, through excessive zeal, asked leave to resume my duties (not expecting to have such a severe job in the course of the next few days) I did not care to throw myself on Masséna's pity, so I started in spite of the remonstrances of my comrades and my brother, who offered to take my place. In order to perform the duty I had to gallop the whole way on post horses; the wound in my side reopened and caused me much pain, still I reached Valladolid. Marshal Bessières, to prove outright that he cherished no grudge against me in regard to the quarrel between Marshal Lannes and himself on the battlefield of Essling, in which I was so innocently involved, received me very kindly. Complying with Masséna's reiterated request, he promised to send several regiments and three batteries of field artillery as well as abundant provisions. In such haste was I to report this good news to Masséna that I started back after a few hours' rest. At one moment I thought I was going to be attacked, but at the sight of the pennons on the lances of our escort, the guerrilleros, who had a particular dread of that arm, took to their heels, and I got back to the marshal without any trouble. Satisfied as he was with the result of my mission, he did not say a single good-natured word about the zeal which I had shown. It must be admitted that the many annoyances which he had all around him did a good deal to embitter his naturally vindictive temper. He had to undergo another and crowning one. Our war in the Peninsula being directed from Paris, many strange anomalies resulted. For instance, just as the chief of the staff was directing Masséna to bring all his troops together and hasten to the relief of Almeida he was ordering the Count of Erlon, whose corps formed part of Masséna's army, to repair at once to Andalusia and join Soult. Ordered thus in two contrary directions, and knowing that his troops would be better off in fertile Andalusia than in sterile Portugal, Erlon was making ready to start for Seville. But as his departure would have deprived Masséna of two fine infantry divisions, and made it impossible for him to relieve Almeida, according to the Emperor's instructions, he declined to allow it. The other insisted, and the wretched squabbles which we had already witnessed in the past winter with regard to the corps were revived. At length, under pressure from Masséna, the Count of Erlon agreed to remain till the blockade of Almeida was raised. That a commander-in-chief should have thus to entreat his subordinate was quite unreasonable, and could only injure military discipline.

Meanwhile Bessières' promised reinforcements, not having arrived by the 21st, Masséna, reckoning only on his own resources to make his way to Almeida, concentrated his army on the 26th at Ciudad Rodrigo. But in order to feed the assembled forces, it was necessary to draw upon the supplies of Rodrigo, and thus compromise the future fate of that important place. We were only three leagues from the English who were surrounding Almeida. We could not communicate with the place, and we did not know their strength. But we knew that Wellington had gone beyond Badajos with a strong detachment, and Masséna, trusting that he would be unable to be back for eight or ten days, wished to take advantage of his absence and accomplish the re-victualling of Almeida. Wellington, however, hearing of the movements of the French, returned promptly on his tracks and was in front of us on May 1st. This was a great misfortune, for it was probable that General Spencer, who was in temporary command of the English army, would not have ventured to take the responsibility of engaging such an adversary as Masséna, and Almeida might have been re-victualled without trouble.

Great was the joy of our soldiers, who, though they had lived some days on half rations of bread and less of meat, were yet eager to fight, when, on the morning of the 2nd, they saw a weak column of Marshal Bessières' troops approaching, and took it for an advance-guard. But the reinforcement so pompously announced, and so long awaited, was confined to 1,500 cavalry, 6 guns, and 30 good teams. Bessières was bringing neither ammunition nor provisions. It was a regular hoax. Masséna was horrified, but very soon grew angry at seeing that Bessières was himself in command of this feeble succour. Indeed, the presence of that Marshal was calculated to annoy him. The Army of Portugal was, it is true, in a province subject to the jurisdiction of Bessières, but it was independent of him, and solely under Masséna's orders, nor was there any reason, because Bessières was lending a few soldiers, that he should come in person to control in some measure his colleague's actions. Masséna understood this, and said to us, 'He would have done much better to have sent me a few more thousand men with ammunition and provisions, and to have remained at the centre of his province than to come examining and criticizing what I am going to do.' Bessières was therefore very coldly received, but this did not hinder him from following Masséna during the short campaign and giving him his advice. The army started on the afternoon of May 2, and hostilities began the next day. A new series of mistakes commenced, arising from the ill-will of certain generals towards Masséna, and the want of understanding which prevailed among the rest.

We fell in with the Anglo-Portuguese army on the frontier posted in front of Almeida, and blockading the place. The troops were occupying a broad plateau between the stream of the Turones and the one which flows in the deep gorge called Dos Casas. Lord Wellington's left was near the ruined Fort Concepcion, his centre towards the village of Alameda, and his right posted at Fuentes d'Oñoro was prolonged towards the marsh of Nave de Avel, whence flows the stream which some call Dos Cases and others d'Oñoro; this brook covered his front. The French came up in three columns by the Ciudad Rodrigo road; the 6th and 9th corps, under Loison, formed the left wing, facing Fuentes; the 8th corps, under Junot, and Montbrun's cavalry, were in the centre; General Reynier, with the 2nd corps, watched Alameda and Fort Concepcion on the right. Several picked battalions, the lancers of the guard, and some batteries formed the reserve; it was commanded by General Lepic, famous for his brilliant conduct at Eylau.

Our troops were hardly in their respective positions when General Loison, without awaiting Masséna's orders for a concerted movement, charged the village of Oñoro, occupied by the Highlanders and some picked battalions. Their attack was so brisk that the enemy, although entrenched in solid stone houses, were compelled to abandon the position. But they retired into an old chapel on the top of the huge rocks which command Oñoro, and it was impossible to dislodge them. Masséna, therefore, gave orders for the moment only to occupy the village and to garnish all the houses with troops. But the order was badly executed for Ferey's division to whom the duty fell, carried away by the ardour of a first success, formed in a mass outside Oñoro, thus exposing itself to an artillery and musketry fire from the English at the chapel. Finally, to complete our disasters, our troops were thrown into disorder by a deplorable occurrence, which should have been foreseen. In Ferey's division there was a battalion of the Hanoverian legion in the French service. Their uniform was red, like the English, but they had the usual grey overcoat of the French soldier, and accordingly their commander, who had had several men killed by our people at Busaco, asked leave for his men to wear their greatcoats instead of rolling them up, as the order was. But General Loison replied that he must follow the order given to the whole corps. The result was a cruel blunder. The 66th Regiment, having been sent to support the Hanoverians, who were in the fighting line, mistook them in the smoke for an English battalion, and fired into them, while our artillery, equally misled by the red coats, played on them with grape. I must do the brave Hanoverians the justice to say that, placed as they were between two fires they endured them for a long time without recoiling a step but after losing 100 men killed and many wounded, the battalion was compelled to retire, passing along one side of the village. Another regiment, which was entering the village at that moment, seeing the red coats on their flank supposed that the position had been turned by an English column, and the enemy cleverly took advantage of the resulting confusion to recapture Fuentes d'Oñoro, which would not have happened if the generals had followed Masséna's order to line the windows with infantry. Night put an end to this first engagement, in which we had 600 men disabled; the enemy's loss was about the same, and fell chiefly upon their best troops, the Highlanders. Colonel Williams was killed.

I could never understand how Wellington consented to await the French in so unfavourable a position as that in which General Spencer's incapacity had placed the troops. The allies had in fact in their rear not only the fortress of Alameda barring their only good line of retreat, but also the Coa, a stream with steep banks and difficult approaches, which might have caused the entire loss of the army if it had been compelled to retreat. It is true that the steep and deep ravine of the Dos Casas protected the English front from Fort Concepcion to Nave de Avel, but beyond that point the sides of the ravine fall away and sink to a marsh which is easy to cross. Even so, Wellington might have used it to cover his extreme right if he had defended it with a good regiment supported by artillery, but forgetting the harm which had resulted at Busaco from assigning to Trant's irregulars the task of preventing the French from making a flank march by Boialva, he fell into the same error again when he entrusted the defence of the marsh to the irregular bands of Don

Julian, who were quite unfit to resist troops of the line. On hearing of this negligence through a cavalry patrol, Masséna ordered everything to be got ready for crossing the marsh at daybreak the next morning, in order to take the enemy's right wing in rear. Plenty of fascines were constructed during the night, and the 8th corps, with part of the 9th, marched in silence towards Nave de Avel, Ferey's division remaining before Oñoro, which was still occupied by the enemy.

At daybreak on May 5 a company of light infantry slipping through the willows and the reeds, crossed the marsh noiselessly and, passing the fascines along, filled up the bad places, which turned out to be much fewer in number than we had supposed. Don Julian and his guerrillas, deeming themselves secure behind the marsh, kept such a bad watch that our people found them asleep and killed some thirty of them. All the rest of the band, instead of keeping up a smart fire, if only to warn the English, took to its heels and fled beyond the Turones, and Don Julian, brave as he was, could not keep his undisciplined soldiers in hand. Profiting by Wellington's negligence, our troops hastened to cross the marsh, and we had on the other side four divisions of infantry, all Montbrun's cavalry with several batteries, and were in possession of Nave de Avel before the English found it out. This was one of the finest movements which Masséna ever devised, the last flicker of an expiring lamp.

By our passage of the marsh the enemy's right was completely out-flanked, and Wellington's situation became extremely difficult. Not only had he to execute a huge change of front to meet those of our divisions which were occupying Nave de Avel and Pozo Velho, but he was compelled to leave part of his troops before Fuentes d'Oñoro and Alameda to check Erlon's and Reynier's corps, which were making ready to cross the Dos Casas and attack the enemy during their evolutions. Lord Wellington had so fully believed his extreme right wing to be sheltered by the marsh, that he had only left a few cavalry scouts at that point, but seeing that wing turned he made haste to send forward towards Pozo Velho the first infantry brigade that came to hand. This advanced guard was overthrown and cut to pieces by our cavalry under Montbrun. General Mancune, following up this advance, flung himself into the wood of Pozo Velho, driving from it the Highlanders with a loss of 250 prisoners and 100 killed. Thus everything was promising a brilliant victory for the French when a discussion arose between Generals Loison and Montbrun, and the latter stayed the march of the cavalry reserve under the plea that the batteries of the Guard which had been promised him had not yet come up. In point of fact, Marshal Bessières had detained them without letting Masséna know, and he, learning of the difficulty too late, sent several guns to Montbrun. The delay, however, was doubly fatal to us, first because Loison's infantry, seeing that it was no longer supported by Montbrun's cavalry, hesitated to engage in the plain, while in the second place this disastrous halt gave Wellington time to bring up all his cavalry to support Houstoun's and Craufurd's divisions, which alone were as yet in position before us. Meantime, by Masséna's orders, General Montbrun, covering his artillery with some squadrons of hussars, advanced afresh, and, suddenly unmasking his guns, tore up Houstoun's division, and when it began to waver charged it with Wathiez' and Fournier's brigades. These cut the 51st regiment almost entirely to pieces, and completely routed the rest of Houstoun's division. The fugitives reached Villa Formosa on the left bank of the Turones, and owed their safety solely to the regiment of chasseurs Britanniques, who, ranged behind a long and stout stone wall, stayed the dash of our troopers by a fire no less well sustained than aimed.

In this part of the field Wellington had now only Craufurd's division and the cavalry, the rest of his army, which had been taken in rear, not having as yet completed the immense change of front necessary to bring them into line against the French. As the ground on which they were now fighting had been, until we crossed the marsh, the least exposed part, the English commissariat and the wounded, the servants, baggage and led horses, the soldiers who had got separated from their regiments, were crowded together there, and the vast plain as far as the Turones was covered with a disorderly multitude, in the midst of which the three squares formed by Craufurd's infantry looked like mere specks; and there we had, within cannon-shot, and all ready to charge the enemy, the corps of Loison and Junot, 5,000 cavalry, and 4 field-batteries into the bargain. The 8th corps was already clear of the wood of

Pozo Velho, the 9th was vigorously attacking the village of Fuentes d'Oñoro by the right bank of the Dos Casas, and General Reynier had orders to debouch by Alameda, and take the English in the rear. We had only to march forward. Indeed, Napier, who was present at this battle, admits that, during the whole war, there was no moment of such danger for the British army. But blind Fortune decided otherwise. General Loison, instead of marching by the left bank to take Fuentes d'Oñoro in rear, while Drouet d'Erlon attacked in front, lost much time and made false movements which allowed Wellington to reinforce that important point—the key, indeed, of the position. General Reynier, on his side, did not carry out Masséna's orders; for, under the plea that he had too strong a force in front of him, he never went beyond Alameda, and took scarcely any part in the action. In spite of all these mishaps, so great were our advantages that it was yet possible to win the battle. Montbrun's cavalry, having beaten that of the enemy, soon found itself in presence of Craufurd's infantry. It charged and broke two squares, cutting one literally to pieces. The men of the 2nd threw down their arms and fled to the plain; Colonel Hill surrendered his sword to Staff-Adjutant Dulimberg of the 13th Chasseurs, and we took 1,500 prisoners. The third English square held firm. Montbrun caused Fournier's and Wathiez' brigades to attack it, and they had pierced one of the faces when both generals had their horses killed under them and all the colonels were wounded, so that there was nobody to take charge of the victorious regiments. Montbrun hastened up, but the enemy's square had been reformed, and, in order to attack it, he would have to reform his own squadrons. While he was thus engaged, Masséna sent an aide-de-camp to General Lepic, in command of the reserve cavalry of the Guard, with orders to charge. But Lepic, biting his sword blade in desperation, replied, with much regret, that his immediate chief, Marshal Bessières, had forbidden him to take the Guard into action without his order. Ten aides-de-camp went off in every direction to look for Bessières; but he, after being for some days always at Masséna's side, had now disappeared. This was not owing to any want of courage, but of set design, or from a jealousy which made him unmindful of the interest of France and unwilling to send a single man under his command in order to secure a victory the credit of which would fall to his comrade. At last, after a quarter of an hour, Bessières was discovered at a distance from the field of battle, wandering on the further side of the marsh, and examining the construction of the fascines which had been used in the morning. He hastened up with a show of earnestness, but the decisive moment had been missed, through his fault, and did not recur. The English had recovered from the disorder caused by Montbrun's charge, and had brought up a powerful artillery which was playing our squadrons with grape, while their men were recapturing the prisoners whom we had taken. In short, Lord Wellington's change of front was completed, and his army in its new position on the plateau, with its right resting on the Turones, its left on Fuentes d'Oñoro.

At the sight of this new and solidly-constituted line, Masséna halted his troops and opened a heavy cannonade, causing much destruction in the enemy's ranks. A general charge of our cavalry might have crushed them, and Masséna hoped that Bessières would at last allow the regiment of the Guard to take part in this ' pull all together,' which would infallibly have given us the victory. But Bessières refused saying that he was responsible to the Emperor for any loss which his Guard might incur, as if all the army were not in the Emperor's service, and the essential point with him were not to hear that the English had been driven out of the Peninsula! All the soldiers, those of the Guard most of all, were indignant at Bessières' decision, wanting to know what that marshal had come before Almeida for, if he did not wish his troops to take part in the fighting which was to save the place. This unexpected mishap changed the complexion of affairs at once; every moment the English were receiving reinforcements, and one of their divisions, coming from the force blockading Almeida, had just crossed the Turones, and was forming in the plain. The position of the two armies lying thus altered, Masséna's dispositions had to be altered likewise. He resolved, therefore, to move the bulk of his troops towards Almeida, and, joining Reynier, to fall upon the right and rear of the enemy. This was the counterpart of the previous night's movement on Nave de Avel; but a new obstacle hindered its execution. General Eblé, commanding the artillery, hurried up with the news that he had, at the artillery park, not more than four cartridges per man, which, with those left in their pouches, gave not more than a score to each soldier. This was an insufficient supply with which to renew the struggle against a foe who was sure to resist desperately, and Masséna ordered every wagon to be sent instantly to Rodrigo for ammunition. But the commissary-general reported that he had made use of them to fetch from the same place the bread required for the morrow's supply. Having no other means of transport, Masséna asked Bessières to lend him the Guard's ammunition-wagons for a few hours; but he replied that his teams were already tired, and that a night march over bad roads would finish them— he could not lend them till the next day. Masséna flew into a rage, exclaiming that victory was being snatched from him a second time; but Bessiéres maintained his refusal, and a violent scene took place between the two marshals.

At daybreak on the 6th, Bessières' wagons started for Rodrigo; but they moved so slowly that the cartridges did not come till the afternoon, and Wellington had employed the twenty-four hours in entrenching his new position, especially the upper part of the village of Fuentes d'Oñoro. It could not now be taken save at the expense of torrents of French blood, and the opportunity of victory was hopelessly lost to us

Chapter 32
The Last of Spain

When it became clear that there could be no question of another battle, or of re-victualling Almeida, it became Masséna's duty to try at least to save the garrison of the place after destroying the fortifications. To this end some means must be found of communicating with the governor—a task which, as the town was strongly invested, was difficult, if not impossible. Three brave men, whose names deserve to be recorded in our annals, volunteered for the perilous duty of passing through the enemy's camp, and carrying to General Brénier instructions with regard to the evacuation. These three intrepid soldiers were Pierre Zaniboni, corporal of the 76th, Jean Noel Lami, a canteen-man in Ferey's division, and André Tillet, of the 6th Light Infantry. They had all taken part in the siege of Almeida the year before, and knew the surrounding district thoroughly. They were to take different roads, and each bore a letter in cipher to the governor. They started at nightfall on the 6th; Zaniboni disguised as a Spanish pedlar, for he spoke the language well, slipped into the English bivouacs on the plea of selling tobacco and buying dead men's clothes; Lami, as a Portuguese peasant, played much the same part at another part of the English lines. This kind of petty trade is common in all armies, and the two Frenchmen went from line to line without awaking any suspicion. Just as they were drawing near the gates of Almeida, however, the trick was discovered—in what manner has never been explained—the poor fellows were searched, and being convicted by the letters found on them, were shot as spies, according to the law of war which punishes with death every soldier who lays aside his uniform when on duty.

Tillet, with better judgment than his unhappy comrades, started in uniform, with his sword. Following at first the deep gorge of the Dos Cases stream, up to his waist in the water he crept slowly from rock to rock, hiding himself behind them at the least sound, until he was near the ruined Fort Concepcion. There, leaving the stream, he crawled on all fours through the full corn, and at length reached the outworks of Almeida, being received there at dawn on the 17th by the French outposts. The letter which he bore to General Brénier contained the order to blow up the ramparts, and retire forthwith on Barba del Puerco, whither Reynier's troops were to precede him. The arrival of his emissary was to be announced to Masséna by salvos of the heaviest guns, and on hearing these the marshal made the necessary preparations for retreating on Ciudad Rodrigo, being assured of the imminent demolition of the ramparts. These operations take some time, as the ramparts must be mined, the chambers of the mines charged, ammunition, artillery and gun-carriages destroyed, and so on. We had therefore to wait till the noise of the cannon let us know that Brénier was evacuating the place, and the two armies remained facing each other for four days without any further action. The English asked for a suspension of hostilities to bury the dead—a homage to brave warriors which all civilized nations ought to practice. In the plain the English corpses were by far the more in number; but it was quite otherwise in the village, where the enemy had fought sheltered by houses and garden walls. Many wounded were picked up on both sides; among ours was Captain Septeuil, an aide-de-camp to Berthier, who had, like Canouville, been sent from Paris to Masséna. He was still more unlucky, for his leg was smashed by a round-shot, and had to be amputated on the field. He bore the operation bravely and survived.

Seeing the French army remain stationary in front of him for several days, and doubtless hearing the salvos from Almeida, Wellington perceived that Masséna intended to facilitate the escape of the garrison. He therefore reinforced the blockading division, and gave General Campbell, who was in command of it, orders so well devised that if they had been duly carried out Brénier and his troops would have had small chance of escape. At midnight on the 10th a long, dull, explosion announced to the French army that Almeida existed no longer—at least, as a fortress. In order to puzzle the allies, General Brénier had kept them occupied for several days past on the side opposite to that by which he intended to make his escape. This was carried out without disaster, and it was the same at first with his retreat, which he led, guiding himself by the moon and the direction of the streams. He had come within a short distance of General Heudelet's division, which Masséna had sent to meet him, when he fell in with a Portuguese brigade. He attacked and dispersed it, continuing his retreat swiftly; but General Pack, warned by the sound of musketry, hastened up from Malpartida and pursued our columns, firing. Quickly, too, General Cotton's cavalry made a vigorous attack on the rear-guard, causing it some loss. Our people at length caught sight of the bridge of Barba del Puerco, and Heudelet's division advancing to meet them. Believing themselves saved, they gave vent to their joy; but it was written that the soil of Portugal was yet to be watered with French blood.

The last of our columns had to pass through a defile opening into a quarry among steep and pointed rocks. The enemy was pressing on from all sides, and several sections of our rear-guard were cut off by the English cavalry. Seeing this, the French soldiers climbed nimbly up the steep sides of the ravine, and escaped the English cavalry, only to fall into another danger. The Portuguese infantry pursued them on the heights, pouring a murderous fire into them. When at length our men, on the point of being succoured by Heudelet's division, thought that they were in sight of safety, the earth suddenly failed under their feet, engulfing part of them in a yawning chasm, at the foot of a huge rock. The head of the pursuing Portuguese column incurred the same fate, rolling pell-mell into the gulf with our people. Heudelet's division succeeded in forcing the allied troops back beyond the sight of this disaster, and when the foot of the precipice was explored, a fearful sight appeared. Three hundred French and Portuguese soldiers lay there, dead or horribly mutilated. Some sixty French and thirty Portuguese alone survived this terrible fall. Such was the last incident in the laborious and unlucky campaign of the French in Portugal. They never entered the country again. Masséna's army, leaving the battlefield of Fuentes d'Oñoro, retreated towards Ciudad Rodrigo, and went into cantonments, the English not following. We learnt, later on, that Wellington, angry with General Campbell for having, as he said, by neglect of his orders allowed the garrison of Almeida to escape, had brought that general to courtmartial, and that Campbell, in despair, had blown his brains out.

Scarcely was the French army in quarters where it could rest and recruit, than Masséna began to think of reorganising it, with a view to a fresh campaign. The work was, however, barely set on foot, when Marshal Marmont arrived from Paris. Though he held his appointment to the commander-in-chief, he presented himself at first as Ney's successor in the command of the 6th corps; then, a few days later, when he was sufficiently acquainted with the state of affairs, he produced his commission, and handed to Masséna the Emperor's order, recalling him to Paris. This unforeseen disgrace, announced in such a way indicating that the Emperor did not approve his conduct of the operations, was a crushing blow to Masséna, but he was compelled to surrender the command to Marmont; and, taking leave of the army, he retired, in the first place, to Salamanca, after a very lively altercation with General Foy, whom he accused of having made common cause with Ney to do him a disservice with the Emperor.

On learning how vigorously General Brénier had led the retreat of the garrison of Almeida, the Emperor appointed him lieutenant-general. He rewarded also Tillet's devotion and courage with the Cross of the Legion of Honour and a pension of six hundred francs. This second favour was, in later days, the subject of a discussion in the Chamber. Tillet had become a sergeant, and had obtained a retiring pension under the Restoration. It was proposed to dock him of this by applying the law but General Foy eloquently pleaded the soldier, and he kept both his pensions.

Masséna stayed a short time at Salamanca, and proceeded to Paris. On his arrival, he called upon the Emperor, who, under the plea of urgent affairs, refused for a whole month to see him. His disgrace was complete. No doubt, Masséna had committed very grave mistakes, especially in his march upon Lisbon; but it must be admitted also that the Government had done very wrong to abandon his army in a country so bare of resources as Portugal, and not to secure his communications by means of troops echelonned between his army and the Spanish frontier. At any rate Masséna rose in the opinion of his troops during the expedition undertaken to relieve Almeida. Not only was his strategy often very fine, but he showed much activity, having no more anxiety about Mme N—, whom he had left at the rear, and being able to give all his attention to the war. Still, I shall take leave to point out several faults which he committed during that expedition. In the first place, it was undertaken with insufficient means of transport, both for provisions and ammunition. It has been said that draught-horses were wanting; this is true, but there were plenty of mules in the district, which might have been requisitioned for a few days. Next was the fatal mistake occasioned by the red coats of the Hanoverians. As the same had already happened at Busaco, Masséna should have made them wear their grey overcoats before sending them into Oñoro to fight the English. By this amount of foresight, he would have retained the whole village; as it was, we lost the upper part, and could not retake it. Thirdly, when Masséna was master of a great part of the plain, and of the whole course of the Dos Casas, except the point where it passes through Fuentes d'Oñoro, he was, as I think, quite wrong to lose precious time and many men in seeking to drive the English entirely out of that strongly-intrenched village. I think that it would have been better worth while, following the example of Marlborough at Malplaquet, to have left a brigade to observe Oñoro, out of range of its fire, and to hold the garrison, and to have advanced. They would have thought themselves on the point of being surrounded, and would have been compelled to abandon the position, and rejoin Wellington, or run the risk of having to capitulate after the defeat of the English army. The important thing for us was to beat the main body of the enemy's troops in the open country. Unluckily, however, it is a principle with the French never to leave an intrenched position behind them in battle. This habit has often been fatal to us here, and, above all, at Waterloo, where we persisted in attacking the farms of La Haye-Sainte and Hougoumont, instead of masking them with a division, and marching upon the already severely-shaken English lines. We should have had time to destroy them before the Prussians came up, and to secure the victory, after which the defenders of the farms would have had to lay down their arms, as our troops had to do at Malplaquet. The fourth mistake with which Masséna may be blamed, at the battle of Fuentes d'Oñoro, was not making sure that there were a sufficient number of cartridges in his wagons. Failing this, he should have fetched them from Ciudad Rodrigo, which was not more than three leagues from the point where we were going to fight. This lack of foresight was one of the principal causes of our failure. Fifthly, if Masséna had still possessed the firmness of which he so often gave proof at Rivoli, Genoa, and Zurich, he would have put General Reynier under arrest for disobedience to orders, and the command of the second corps would have passed to General Heudelet, who would have pushed the English hard and promptly. But Masséna did not venture to take such vigorous action; the conqueror of Souvaroff had lost his energy, and let himself be defied with impunity, and the blood of his soldiers was shed to no advantage and with no glory.

It forms no part of my purpose in writing these memoirs to relate the various phases of the War of Independence in the Peninsula; but before quitting that country, I ought to point out the chief causes of the reverses sustained there by the French, in spite of the fact that our troops nowhere showed more zeal, more patience—above all, more valour.

It is needless again to go over the events of 1808 and the following year, but it may be observed that if after the expulsion of the English, under Sir John Moore, from Spain, the Emperor had himself been able to go on directing the operations, the Peninsula must have quickly succumbed. The Cabinet of London had, however, cleverly raised a new and potent enemy, and when Austria declared war, Napoleon was compelled to leave the task of repressing the insurrection in the hands of his lieutenants. King Joseph's lack of military capacity prevented any concentration of command, and complete anarchy reigned among the marshals and the various corps commanders, each confining himself to the defence of the provinces occupied by his troops, and refusing any aid to his colleagues who governed the neighbouring districts. The most peremptory orders from the Emperor were unable to produce any co-operation, there was no obedience, and each asserted that he himself needed all the resources at his disposal. Thus Saint-Cyr was nearly crushed in Catalonia without the support of a single battalion from Suchet, who was governing Aragon and Valencia; Soult, as you have seen, was left alone in Oporto, while Victor refused to obey the order to join him. Soult, in his turn, allowed Masséna to wait for him for six months in vain at the gates of Lisbon; finally, Masséna could not obtain help from Bessières to beat the British before Almeida. I could quote many more examples of selfish disobedience, but it must be admitted that the main fault lay with the Government. It was natural that, in 1809, the Emperor should have left Spain in order to meet the most pressing danger, but why, when peace was concluded in the north, did he not see the importance of returning to drive the English from the Peninsula? The most surprising thing is, that with all his genius he should have thought it possible to direct from Paris the movement of armies 500 leagues away, in a country where bearers of despatches were liable to be stopped by swarms of insurgents, and commanders-in-chief thus compelled to remain for months without news or orders. If the Emperor could not come himself, he should have entrusted the chief command of all the armies in the Peninsula to one of his best marshals, with power severely to punish disobedience. Napoleon had no doubt made Joseph his titular lieutenant, but he, a man of gentle disposition, clever and well-educated, but having no knowledge of the art of war, had become the plaything of the marshals. They did not execute his orders, and considered his very presence with the army as a hindrance. The worst mistake into which the King's good-nature led him was that of opposing the Emperor's wish with regard to Spanish soldiers captured in battle. Napoleon ordered them to be sent into France as prisoners of war, in order to diminish the numbers of our enemies in the Peninsula, while Joseph, hating to fight against men whom he called his subjects, would defend the Spaniards against us. When they were captured they were ready enough to cheer for their good King Joseph and ask to serve among his troops. He actually created a numerous army, composed exclusively of prisoners whom he had taken, well paid, well fed, and well equipped. They were loyal to Joseph as long as things went well, but at the first reverse they deserted in thousands and went off to join their insurgent compatriots until they were taken prisoners again. Then they again begged to enlist in Joseph's regiments. More than 150,000 men changed sides in this way, and as Joseph had them promptly re-clothed when they came back in rags, the Spaniards nick-named him 'the head of the army clothing department.' The French troops objected strongly to this system, and the Emperor often expressed his discontent with it, but he could never succeed in stopping it. He, on his side, contributed much to the perpetual recruiting of the enemy, for not wishing to reduce too much the French army in Germany, he called on his allies to furnish part of the contingents stipulated for in the treaties, and sent these troops to the Peninsula in order to spare French blood. His motive was doubtless laudable, but circumstances made the application of this system injurious to our cause. It is all very well to employ foreign troops in a short campaign, but it is a different thing when it is a question of fighting for several years against an enemy like the Spaniards and Portuguese who were always harassing you and could never be got at. Nothing but an ardour such as is never found in auxiliary troops can enable men to endure the fatigues of this kind of warfare. Thus not only did the troops which the Emperor obtained from his allies serve badly enough in our ranks, but they deserted daily in heaps. Italians, Swiss, Saxons, Bavarians, and other Germans were soon formed into regiments by our enemies, and the Poles passed in such numbers into the well-paid and well-fed English army, that Wellington was able to form a strong Polish legion, which fought the French without scruple.

But, in my opinion, the principal cause of our reverses, though one which has never been pointed out by any soldier who has written on the Peninsular War, was the immense superiority of the English infantry in accurate shooting, a superiority which arises from their frequent exercise at the targets, and in a great measure also from the formation in two ranks. I know that a great many French officers deny that this latter cause is a true one, but experience has shown that soldiers confined between the first and third rank nearly always fire in the air, and that the third rank cannot take aim at an enemy who is hidden from them by the two ranks in front. It is asserted that two ranks do not offer sufficient strength to resist cavalry, but the English infantry can in a moment form four deep to receive a charge, and our squadrons were never able to catch it in two ranks, though as soon as it has to fire it quickly resumes this formation.

However this may be, I am convinced that Napoleon would in the end have established his brother triumphantly on the throne of Spain if he had been content to finish this war before going to Russia. The Peninsula received no support, save from England, and England, in spite of the recent successes of her armies, was so exhausted by the incessant demands of men and money for the Peninsula, that the House of Commons was on the point of refusing the necessary subsidies for a new campaign. But at the moment of our return from Portugal rumours had got about of the design formed by Napoleon of attacking Russia at home, and the English Parliament authorized the continuance of the war. It was not fortunate for us, for the misunderstandings which I have noticed still prevailed among our commanders. Marshal Marmont got beaten by Wellington at the Arapiles, King Joseph lost the battle of Vittoria, and these reverses compelled our armies towards the end of 1813 to re-cross the Pyrenees and abandon entirely the country which had cost them so much blood. I judge that in the six years from the beginning of 1808, the French lost in the Peninsula 200,000 men killed or dead in hospital, to which one must add 60,000 lost by our various allies.

The English and the Portuguese lost also considerably, but the Spaniards most of all, by reason of the obstinacy with which they withstood the siege of many of their towns. The vigour of these famous defences, particularly that of Saragossa, has thrown such lustre over the Spaniards that the delivery of the Peninsula has generally been attributed to their courage, but this is a mistake, for without the support of English troops the Spaniards would never have resisted the French. One immense merit they have, which is that they are never discouraged. Their confidence, often deceived, cannot be destroyed. Our soldiers used to compare them to flocks of pigeons, which fly away at the least sound to return a moment later. As for the Portuguese, justice has never been done to the share which they took in the war. Less cruel, far better disciplined, and more calmly courageous than the Spaniards, they formed in Wellington's army several brigades which, when led by English officers, were in no way inferior to the British troops; but being less boastful than the Spaniards they have said less about their exploits, and have acquired less renown.

But let us return for a moment to June 1811, when Masséna resigned his command. The war in the Peninsula was so disagreeable and so toilsome that every man longed to get back to France. The Emperor, knowing this, and wishing to keep his army up to its full strength, had decided that no officer was to leave Spain without special leave, and the order recalling Masséna authorized him to bring away only two aides-de-camp, and to leave the others at Marshal Marmont's disposal. He, having his staff complete, and knowing none of us, was no more anxious to keep us than we to stay with him. He assigned us no duties, and we passed some three weeks at Salamanca drearily enough.

In consideration of my wound the minister at last sent me leave to return to France. Some others of Masséna's staff having also been permitted to leave the Peninsula, we joined a detachment of 500 grenadiers, who were on their way to reinforce the imperial guard. General Junot and his wife the duchess also took advantage of this escort. We travelled easily on horseback, with fine weather. On the journey some eccentric conduct on the part of Junot made me anxious as to his future. We reached the frontier, and I could not but smile when I thought of the evil omen which I had drawn from my encounter with the black jackass on the Bidassoa bridge when last I entered Spain. The campaign had nearly been my last, but I was in France and should see my mother and another who had become very dear to me. So forgetting past troubles, I hastened on to Paris, arriving in July, after an absence of fifteen toilsome months. Contrary to my expectation the marshal received me well, and I learnt that he had spoken very kindly of me to the Emperor. So on my first appearance at the Tuileries, the Emperor expressed his satisfaction with me, spoke with interest of Miranda de Corvo, and asked how many wounds I had now had. 'Eight, sir,' I answered. 'Well, they are eight good quarterings of nobility for you,' rejoined the Emperor.

ALSO FROM LEONAUR
AVAILABLE IN SOFTCOVER OR HARDCOVER WITH DUST JACKET

EW2 EYEWITNESS TO WAR SERIES
CAPTAIN OF THE 95th (Rifles) *by Jonathan Leach*
An officer of Wellington's Sharpshooters during the Peninsular, South of France and Waterloo Campaigns of the Napoleonic Wars.

SOFTCOVER : **ISBN 1-84677-001-7**
HARDCOVER : **ISBN 1-84677-016-5**

WF1 THE WARFARE FICTION SERIES
NAPOLEONIC WAR STORIES
by Sir Arthur Quiller-Couch
Tales of soldiers, spies, battles & Sieges from the Peninsular & Waterloo campaigns

SOFTCOVER : **ISBN 1-84677-003-3**
HARDCOVER : **ISBN 1-84677-014-9**

EW1 EYEWITNESS TO WAR SERIES
RIFLEMAN COSTELLO *by Edward Costello*
The adventures of a soldier of the 95th (Rifles) in the Peninsular & Waterloo Campaigns of the Napoleonic wars.

SOFTCOVER : **ISBN 1-84677-000-9**
HARDCOVER : **ISBN 1-84677-018-1**

MC1 THE MILITARY COMMANDERS SERIES
JOURNALS OF ROBERT ROGERS OF THE RANGERS *by Robert Rogers*
The exploits of Rogers & the Rangers in his own words during 1755-1761 in the French & Indian War.

SOFTCOVER : **ISBN 1-84677-002-5**
HARDCOVER : **ISBN 1-84677-010-6**

AVAILABLE ONLINE AT
www.leonaur.com
AND OTHER GOOD BOOK STORES

ALSO FROM LEONAUR
AVAILABLE IN SOFTCOVER OR HARDCOVER WITH DUST JACKET

RGW1 RECOLLECTIONS OF THE GREAT WAR 1914 - 18
STEEL CHARIOTS IN THE DESERT *by S. C. Rolls*

The first world war experiences of a Rolls Royce armoured car driver with the Duke of Westminster in Libya and in Arabia with T.E. Lawrence.

SOFTCOVER : **ISBN 1-84677-005-X**
HARDCOVER : **ISBN 1-84677-019-X**

RGW2 RECOLLECTIONS OF THE GREAT WAR 1914 - 18
WITH THE IMPERIAL CAMEL CORPS IN THE GREAT WAR *by Geoffrey Inchbald*

The story of a serving officer with the British 2nd battalion against the Senussi and during the Palestine campaign.

SOFTCOVER : **ISBN 1-84677-007-6**
HARDCOVER : **ISBN 1-84677-012-2**

EW3 EYEWITNESS TO WAR SERIES
THE KHAKEE RESSALAH
by Robert Henry Wallace Dunlop

Service & adventure with the Meerut Volunteer Horse During the Indian Mutiny 1857-1858.

SOFTCOVER : **ISBN 1-84677-009-2**
HARDCOVER : **ISBN 1-84677-017-3**

WF1 THE WARFARE FICTION SERIES
NAPOLEONIC WAR STORIES
by Sir Arthur Quiller-Couch

Tales of soldiers, spies, battles & Sieges from the Peninsular & Waterloo campaigns

SOFTCOVER : **ISBN 1-84677-003-3**
HARDCOVER : **ISBN 1-84677-014-9**

AVAILABLE ONLINE AT
www.leonaur.com
AND OTHER GOOD BOOK STORES